Catholic Bible Study

The Gospel of Mark

by

Most Reverend Jan Liesen, S.S.D.

and

Laurie Watson Manhardt, Ph.D.

Emmaus Road Publishing
827 North Fourth Street
Steubenville, OH 43952

Library of Congress Control Number: 2012947338
ISBN: 978-1-937155-85-8

Scripture quotations are taken from the
Revised Standard Version Bible, Ignatius Second Edition (RSVCE).
The Second Catholic Edition is published by Thomas Nelson Publishing
for Ignatius Press in 2006,
with ecclesiastical approval of the
United States Conference of Catholic Bishops.

Excerpts from the English translation of the
Catechism of the Catholic Church for the United States of America
Second Edition © 1997,
United States Catholic Conference, Inc. — Libreria Editrice Vaticana.
Cited in the text as "CCC."

Cover design and layout by
Jacinta Calcut, Image Graphics & Design www.image–gd.com

Cover artwork:
Sabine Muller, *Jesus Heals the Blind Man*

Nihil obstat: Reverend Glen J. Pothier, JCL, DTh *Censor Deputatis*
Imprimatur: Most Reverend Gerald M. Barbarito, DD, JCL, Bishop of Palm Beach
August 6, 2012

The *nihil obstat* and *imprimatur* are official declarations
that a book is free of doctrinal or moral error.

For additional information on the "Come and See~ Catholic Bible Study"
series visit www.CatholicBibleStudy.net

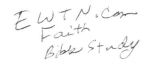

Catholic Bible Study

The Gospel of Mark

Introduction

In those days Jesus came from Nazareth of Galilee
and was baptized by John in the Jordan.
And when he came up out of the water,
immediately he saw the heavens opened
and the Spirit descending upon him like a dove;
and a voice came from heaven,
"You are my beloved Son; with you I am well pleased."
Mark 1:9–11

Somewhere between 6 BC and the year 0, an earth-shattering event occurs—Jesus Christ, the Son of God is born in Bethlehem. Thirty-three years later, the most spectacular event in human history unfolds—Jesus Christ is crucified on Calvary for the sins of the world, and rises triumphantly from the dead. The Resurrection of Jesus from the dead remains the single most fantastic event in all of human history. No one else has ever done what Jesus did. The writings of the New Testament are texts about the life and teachings of Jesus of Nazareth.

Saint Paul begins to write the first piece to become part of the New Testament around the year AD 50–52, when through the inspiration of the Holy Spirit he pens his First Letter to the Thessalonians. In his letter to the Romans (c. AD 57), Paul claims that he was set apart for the Gospel of God, which was promised beforehand by the prophets in the Scriptures, the Gospel of God's Son, descended from David, *and designated Son of God in power according to the Spirit of holiness by his resurrection from the dead, Jesus Christ our Lord* (Romans 1:4). When Paul speaks about Jesus, he always returns to the Resurrection. For him, Jesus is the Risen One, the Lord Jesus, who triumphs over sin and death.

Mark takes up his pen around the year AD 70 to write the first eyewitness Gospel account of the life and ministry of Jesus. Luke and Matthew write their accounts of the life of Jesus about ten years later, around AD 80. John writes a theological reflection on the meaning of the life, death, and Resurrection of Jesus some time later, perhaps around AD 90. But the very first and most concise Gospel account of the entire life of Jesus comes to us from Saint Mark. While Mark may not have had personal experience of the public life of Jesus, he had access to the first-hand witness of Saint Peter, whose companion he had become.

Who is Mark? *When he (Peter) realized this, he went to the house of Mary, the mother of John whose other name was Mark, where many were gathered together and were praying* (Acts 12:12). The Mark mentioned here apparently hails from a prominent Jewish Christian family in Jerusalem, with its own house and servants. He has two names: his Jewish name is "John," and his Hellenistic/Roman name is "Mark." Although he may have grown up in Jerusalem and may have seen Jesus, he never claims to be an eyewitness in the strict sense, as John does (John 21:24).

In the early forties, Paul and Barnabas took John Mark along on a trip to Antioch in Syria on Paul's first missionary journey. The early return of John Mark caused contention between Paul and Barnabas as to who should join them on the second missionary journey in the early fifties. In the end, Paul and Barnabas split up, and Mark accompanies Barnabas to Cyprus (Acts 15:36–39). The Pauline prison letters, dated around AD 61–63, indicate that Mark was with Paul, then in Ephesus, and also in Rome (Philemon 24; 2 Timothy 4:11).

Mark's close relationship with Saint Peter is confirmed in the closing of the First Letter of Peter. *She who is at Babylon, who is likewise chosen, sends you greetings; and so does my son Mark* (1 Peter 5:13). The source of the Gospel of Mark was Peter, who did not recount the words and deeds of Jesus in one big coherent testimony. Peter gave his witness to Jesus piecemeal: giving only as much as was called for by the occasion. It is Mark then who shaped the narrative framework of the Gospel of Mark, as we know it. And in doing so he was—according to Saint John the Evangelist—anxious not to omit anything of the witness of Peter, nor to add anything falsely to it. The synthesis, however, is Mark's own contribution.

Saint Clement of Alexandria (AD 150–216) provides some insight into Mark's writing of this gospel. "After Peter had openly proclaimed the Word in Rome and in spirit had announced the gospel, those present—there were many—requested Mark, since he had long followed him *[Peter]* and remembered what had been said by him *[Peter]*, to write down what had been said by him; and when he *[Mark]* had done so, he gave the gospel to those who had asked him for it; when Peter found out, he did not forbid it at all, nor encouraged it . . .

The light of godliness shone so much in the minds of the hearers of Peter, that they were not content with having heard him once, nor with the unwritten teaching of the divine preaching, but with many prayers they insisted with Mark, who wrote the gospel and who was a disciple of Peter, that he *[Mark]* would leave them also a written memory of the orally transmitted teaching and they did not give up until they had persuaded the man and thus they became the cause that the gospel named after Mark was written. The apostle learned—as it is said—about it because the Spirit revealed it to him; he rejoiced about the fervor of the people and approved that the writing was read in the churches."

Eusebius of Caesarea, *Historia Ecclesiastica*, VI, 14, 5–6.

Cardinal Vanhoye suggests a possible autobiographical note in Mark's Gospel. Recall a curious reference about a young man in the Garden of Olives who tries to follow Jesus at the time of His arrest. *And a young man followed him, with nothing but a linen cloth about his body; and they seized him, but he left the linen cloth and ran away naked* (Mark 14:51–52). This anecdotal detail is only mentioned in the Gospel of Saint Mark and may be a personal reflection. On account of the close comparison with the passage about the young man at the empty tomb (Mark 16:5–6) a symbolic reading has been proposed.

Saint Mark orders all the facts about Jesus in an account that begins with the baptism in the river Jordan by John the Baptist and ends with a lengthy Passion narrative. The Passion clearly dominates the entire Gospel. What has become clear at the death and Resurrection of Jesus is that He is the beloved Son of God, the Redeemer, the Savior of the world. Jesus is the long-awaited Messiah whose death and Resurrection accomplish salvation for all who believe in Him.

The Gospel of Saint Mark opens with a revealing title: it is a narration of the Good News *about* Jesus, who is the Christ, because He is the Son of God. In a very real sense, it is also the Good News *by* Jesus, for the Gospel is a divinely inspired narration, in which God speaks directly to the reader. The word *gospel* also has the connotation of a military victory, and thus implicitly refers to an enemy and a struggle. The name/title *Christ* will not be used again until eight chapters later. *And he asked them, "But who do you say that I am?" Peter answered him, "You are the Christ"* (Mark 8:29).

Every Gospel has to start somewhere. What is the best, most logical, most suitable beginning for a Gospel? A Gospel is not a one-directional communication. Each Gospel is the Word of God, and the reader of the Gospel finds himself or herself in the presence of the living God who requires a response. Each inspired Gospel-author has chosen a certain point to be the beginning. The choice of this starting point matches the author's strategy in bringing about the communication or dialogue between the Word of God and the reader.

Saint Mark has chosen to narrate the Good News. His Gospel does not come as a set of statements or definitions, but rather as a narration about Jesus. Recognizing Mark's choice is crucial to understanding the theological message of his Gospel. When the reader follows the fast paced narration, there is a sense of haste, a pressing urgency—Jesus has a course to complete and never stops anywhere for long. Many challenging questions heighten this urgency, and they require an answer that can only be found if the reader pays close attention and allows himself or herself to be drawn into the story. The many conflicts in the narration about Jesus and the fact that the entire Gospel is dominated by the Passion narrative determine the theological perspective—the reader is called to conversion, where suffering and conflicts will also be part of his own journey.

An immediate correlate of narrating the Good News is the involvement of the reader. When the central message—Jesus is the Son of God—unfolds, every part of the narration, whether healings, parables, teachings, exorcisms or miracles, engages the reader to better understand the identity of Jesus. Mark opens his Gospel with a prologue, Mark 1:1–13, in which a lot of essential information for the reader is packed together:

Mark 1:1–3	After the title verse, it all starts with the Word of God, quoted from the prophets.
Mark 1:4–8	John the Baptist then comes on stage both as the fulfillment of that prophecy and as one who introduces the setting and the main person, Jesus. The choice for this starting point reflects the historical reality, but as an opening strategy it also borrows from classical Greek drama in which every play would open with such a presenter, called a *prologos*. As a presenter, John gives all of the essential information about Jesus: *After me comes he who is mightier than I, the thong of whose sandals I am not worthy to stoop down untie"* (Mark 1:7), and establishes a relationship between Jesus and the readers, *but he will baptize you with the Holy Spirit* (Mark 1:7b).
Mark 1:9–13	When Jesus appears, his identity is fist explicitly stated *"You are my beloved Son; with you I am well pleased"* (Mark 1:11). God is speaking here, and the essence of His life work is summarized in His victory over Satan.

With this information, the stage is set and the reader is ready for the drama to begin to unfold. The Gospel of Saint Mark provides an opportunity for the seeker to meet Jesus and for the believer to experience deeper conversion.

What You Need

To do this Bible Study you need a Catholic Bible and the Catechism of the Catholic Church (CCC). Remember that the Catholic Bible contains seventy-three books. If you find Sirach in your Bible's table of contents, you have a complete Catholic Bible. The Council of Hippo approved these seventy-three books in AD 393, and this has remained the official canon of Sacred Scripture since the fourth century. The Council of Trent in AD 1546 authoritatively reaffirmed these divinely inspired books for inclusion in the canon of the Bible. The Douay-Rheims, one of the first English translations of the Catholic Bible, was completed in AD 1609.

Choose a word-for-word, literal translation rather than a paraphrase. Some excellent translations are the Revised Standard Version Catholic Edition (RSVCE), the Jerusalem Bible (JB), and the New American Bible (NAB). For this study, the RSVCE second edition will be quoted and will be the easiest to use for your study. The authors highly recommend that in doing the home study questions you consult the RSVCE, which is available for consultation on-line for free, if you would like to go to the EWTN web site, www.ewtn.com under "faith" and "Bible search."

How To Do This Bible Study

1. Pray to the Holy Spirit to enlighten your mind and spirit.
2. Read the Bible passages for the first chapter.
3. Read the commentary in this book.
4. Use your Bible and Catechism to write answers to the home study questions.
5. Find a small group and share your answers on those questions.
6. Watch the videotaped lecture that goes with this study.
7. End with a short wrap-up lecture and/or prayer.

Invite and Welcome Priests and Religious

Ask for the blessing of your pastor before you begin. Invite your pastor, associate pastor, deacon, visiting priests, and religious sisters to participate in Bible study. Invite priests and religious to come and pray with the Bible study members, periodically answer questions from the question box, or give a wrap-up lecture. Accept whatever they can offer to the Bible study. However, don't expect or demand anything from them. Appreciate that the clergy are very busy and don't add additional burdens. Accept with gratitude whatever is offered.

Practical Considerations

➢ Ask God for wisdom about with whom to study, where, and when to meet.
➢ Gather a small prayer group to pray for your Bible study and your specific needs. Pray to discern God's will in your particular situation.
➢ Show this book to your pastor and ask for his approval and direction.
➢ Choose a day of the week and time to meet.
➢ Invite neighbors and friends to a "Get Acquainted Coffee." Ask who will make a commitment to meet for sixty to ninety minutes each week for Bible study.

➢ Find an appropriate location. Start in someone's home or in the parish hall if the space is available and the pastor will allow it.
➢ Hire a babysitter for mothers with young children and share the cost amongst everyone, or find some volunteers to provide childcare.
➢ Consider a cooperative arrangement, in which women take turns caring for the children. All women, even grandmothers and women without children, should take turns, serving the children as an offering to God.

Pray that God will anoint people to lead your study

Faithful, practicing Catholics will be needed to fill the following positions:

➤ **Lecturers** – take responsibility to read commentaries and prepare a fifteen to twenty minute wrap-up lecture after the small group discussion and video.

➤ **Song Leaders** – lead everyone in singing a short hymn to begin Bible study.

➤ **Prayer Leaders** – open Bible study with a short prayer.

➤ **Children's Teachers** – teach the young children who come to Bible study.

➤ **Coordinators** – communicate with parish personnel about needs for rooms, microphones, and video equipment. Make sure rooms are left in good shape.

➤ **Small Group Facilitators** – will be needed for each small group. Try to enlist two mature Catholics who are good listeners to serve together as co-leaders for each small group and share the following responsibilities:

❖ Pray for each member of your small group every day.
❖ Make a nametag for each member of the group.
❖ Meet before the study to pray with other leaders.
❖ Discuss all the questions in the lesson each week.
❖ Make sure that each person in the group shares each week. Ask each person to read a question and have the first chance to answer it.

❖ In the discussion group ask each person to read a question. The reader can answer that question or pass, and others can add additional comments.
❖ Make sure that no one person dominates the discussion, including you!
❖ Keep the discussion positive and focused on the week's lesson.
❖ Speak kindly and charitably. Steer conversation away from any negative or uncharitable speech, complaining, arguing, gossip, or griping.

❖ Listen well! Keep your ears open and your eyes on the person speaking.
❖ Give your full attention to the one speaking. Be comfortable with silence. Be patient. Encourage quieter people to share first. Ask questions.
❖ If questions, misunderstandings, or disagreements arise, refer them to the question box for a teacher to research or the parish priest to answer later.
❖ Arrange for an occasional social activity.

Concerns for Small Groups

➢ Jesus chose a group of twelve apostles. So perhaps twelve or thirteen people make the best small groups. When you get too many, break into two groups.

➢ A group of teenagers or a young adult group could be facilitated by the parish priest or a young adult leader.

➢ Men share best with men and women with women. If you have a mixed Bible study, organize separate men's groups led by men and women's groups led by women. In mixed groups, some people tend to remain silent.

➢ Offer a married couples' group, if two married couples are willing to lead the group. Each person should have his or her own book.

➢ Sit next to the most talkative person in the group and across from the quietest. Use eye contact to affirm and encourage quieter people to speak up. Serve everyone and hear from everyone.

➢ Listening in Bible study is just as important as talking. Evaluate each week. Did everyone share? Am I a good listener? Did I really hear what others shared? Was I attentive or distracted? Did I affirm others? Did I talk too much?

➢ Share the overall goal aloud with all of the members of the group. We want to hear from each person in the group, sharing aloud each time the group meets.

➢ Make sure that people share answers only on those questions on which they have written answers. Don't just share off the top of your head. Really study.

➢ Consider a nursing mothers' group in which mothers can bring their infants and hold them while sharing their home study questions.

➢ Family groups can work together on a family Bible study night, reading the commentary and scriptures aloud and helping one another to find answers in the Bible and Catechism.

➢ Parents or older siblings can read to young children and help the youngsters to do the crafts in the children's Bible study book.

Class Schedule

Be a good steward of time. If Bible study starts or ends late, busy people may drop out. Late starts punish the prompt and encourage tardiness. Be a good steward of time. Begin and end Bible study with prayer at the agreed upon time. If people consistently arrive late or leave early, investigate whether you have chosen the best time for most people. You may have a conflict with the school bus schedule or the parish Mass schedule. Perhaps beginning a few minutes earlier or later could be a service to those mothers who need to pick up children from school, or those who attend daily Mass.

Possible Bible Study Class Schedules

<u>Morning Class</u>

9:30 a.m.	Welcome, song, prayer
9:40 a.m.	Video
9:55 a.m.	Small group discussion
10:40 a.m.	Wrap-up lecture and prayer

<u>Evening Class</u>

7:30 p.m.	Welcome, song, prayer
7:40 p.m.	Video
8:00 p.m.	Small group discussion
8:40 p.m.	Wrap-up lecture and prayer

The video could be shown either before or after the small group discussion, and either before, after, or instead of a wrap-up lecture. Whether or not you choose to use the videotapes, please begin and end with prayer.

Wrap-Up Lecture

Bishop Liesen provides additional information in videotaped lectures, which can be obtained from Emmaus Road Publishing, 827 North Fourth Street, Steubenville, Ohio, 43952. You can obtain DVDs of these lectures by going to www.emmausroad.org on the Internet or by calling 1-800-398-5470. Videotaped lectures may be used in addition to or in place of a wrap-up lecture.

When offering a closing lecture, the presenter should spend extra time in prayer and study to prepare a good, sound wrap-up. The lecturer should consult several Catholic Bible study commentaries and prepare a cohesive, orthodox lecture. Several members of the leaders' team could take turns giving wrap-up lectures. Also, invite priests, deacons, and religious sisters to give an occasional lecture.

The lecturer should:
➤ Be a faithful, practicing Catholic. Seek spiritual direction. Frequent the sacraments, especially the Eucharist and Reconciliation.
➤ Obtain the approval and blessing of your parish priest to teach.
➤ Use several different presenters whenever possible.
➤ Pray daily for all of the leaders and members of the study.
➤ Pray over the lesson to be studied and presented.

- Outline the Bible passages to be studied.
- Identify the main idea of the Bible study lesson.
- Find a personal application from the lesson. What practical response could one make to God's word?
- Plan a wrap-up lecture with a beginning, a middle and an end.
- Use index cards to keep focused. Don't read your lecture; talk to people.

- Proclaim, teach, and reiterate the teachings of the Catholic Church. Learn what the Catholic Church teaches, and proclaim the fullness of truth.
- Illustrate the main idea presented in the passage by using true stories from the lives of the saints or the lives of contemporary Christians.
- Use visuals—overhead transparencies or power point if possible.
- Plan a skit, act out a Bible story, and interact with the group.

- Try to make the scriptures come alive for the people in your group.
- Provide a question box. Find answers to difficult questions or ask a parish priest to come and answer questions on occasion.
- When difficult or complex personal problems arise or are shared in the group, seek out the counsel of a priest.
- Begin and end on time. When you get to the end of your talk, stop and pray.

Social Activities

God has made us social creatures, needing to relate communally. Large parishes make it difficult for people to get to know one another. Some people can belong to a parish for years without getting to know others. Newcomers may never get noticed and welcomed. Bible study offers an opportunity for spiritual nourishment as well as inclusion and hospitality. Occasional simple social activities are offered in this book. Be a good sport and try to attend the socials with your group.

- Agree on a time when most of the group can meet. This could be right before or after Bible study or a different day of the week, perhaps even Saturday morning.
- Invite people to come to your home for the social time. Jesus was comfortable visiting the homes of the rich and the poor. So whatever your circumstances, as a Christian you can offer hospitality to those God sends along your way.

"Do not neglect to show hospitality to strangers,
for thereby some have entertained angels unawares."
(Hebrews 13:2)

- Keep it simple! Just a beverage and cookies work well. Simplicity blesses others. People can squeeze together on a sofa or stand around the kitchen. Don't fuss.

> Help the group leader. If Bible study meets in someone's home, invite the group to come to your place for the social time. Don't make the group leader do it all.

Suggested Times for Socials

9:30–10:30 a.m.   Saturday coffee   12:00–1:00 p.m. Luncheon

3:00–4:00 p.m.   Afternoon tea   8:00–9:00 p.m. Dessert

Modify times to meet your specific needs. If your parish has Saturday morning Mass or a daily noon Mass, adjust the time of your social to accommodate those members of the group who would like to attend Mass and need some time to get to the social. If lunch after Bible study makes too long of a day for children who need naps, plan the social for a different day. A mother's group might meet after school when high school students are available to baby-sit.

O God, let me know You and love You so that I may find my joy in You; and if I cannot do so fully in this life, let me at least make some progress every day, until at last that knowledge, love and joy come to me in all their plentitude. While I am here on earth let me learn to know You better, so that in heaven I may know You fully; let my love for You grow deeper here, so that there I may love You fully. On earth then I shall have great joy in hope, and in heaven complete joy in the fulfillment of my hope.

Saint Anselm of Canterbury (AD 1033–1109), *Proslogion*, 16.

A Prayer to the Holy Spirit

O Holy Spirit, Beloved of my soul, I worship and adore You,
enlighten, guide, strengthen and console me.
Tell me what I ought to say and do, and command me to do it.
I promise to be submissive in everything You will ask of me,
and to accept all that You permit to happen to me,
only show me what is Your will. Amen.

CHAPTER 1

Prepare the Way of the Lord
Mark 1:1–15

As it is written in Isaiah the prophet,
"Behold, I send my messenger before your face,
who shall prepare your way;
the voice of one crying in the wilderness:
Prepare the way of the Lord,
make his paths straight—"
Mark 1:2–3

What's in a Name? The first verse of Mark's Gospel does not contain a verb. A string of nouns show relationships, which are very briefly expressed with the word *of*— *The beginning of the gospel of Jesus Christ, the Son of God* (Mark 1:1). The opening verse of this Gospel is not a sentence, in the grammatical sense of the word, but a statement that functions as a title. A good title reflects the contents of the narration. Every word in this title is chosen with care and gives meaning.

➢ The very first noun in Saint Mark's Gospel is *beginning. Beginning* simply means what it says—that this is the starting point. As a starting point, the opening verse is very abrupt. This abruptness demonstrates an awareness of something, or rather Someone totally new, who has entered human history and has also impacted the personal life of Saint Mark. Someone has ruptured the old texture of the world and of his life. The coming of Jesus equals the creation of heaven and earth: something totally new exists that was not there before.

➢ Taking into account the context of the entire Scriptures, it becomes evident that the word *beginning* is also an allusion to Genesis. *In the beginning God created the heavens and the earth* (Genesis 1:1). Mark starts his Gospel with a kind of echo of the creation account, thereby clearly suggesting that the Good News is of the same order and magnitude as the creation of the world—it is a re-creation. In a nutshell, Jesus now restores what was lost in the beginning.

➢ The expression *gospel* is not a new word invented by Saint Mark. The word *gospel* is found frequently in the Greek version of the Old Testament (the Septuagint) and in Hellenistic texts. In the Greek version of Isaiah, which was translated before the Christian era, the word *gospel* is used to announce the good news of God's reign, which is at hand (Isaiah 40:9; 41:27; 52:7; 60:6; 61:1). In pre-Christian Hellenistic texts, the word *gospel* is used as a technical expression for an official announcement. For example, a birth in the royal family, which would ensure smooth succession and political stability, or a military victory. In this specific meaning the word *gospel* is already found in the Odyssey (14,150.166), an epic Greek poem dating from at least the eighth century BC.

➤ This Gospel is very personal—it is all about **Jesus.** The victory implicitly referred to by the word *gospel* belongs to a person, whose name is Jesus. The name "Jesus" is a Hebrew name (*yesua'*), which means "God saves." *Christ* is actually not a name, but a title. *Christ*, a Greek translation of the Hebrew word, Messiah, signifies "Anointed." By the time Saint Mark writes his Gospel, around AD 70, the Church has existed for some forty years already, and what was originally a title, has become something like a second name: Jesus Christ. The name "Anointed" actually is a verb used as a noun: the acting subject of the verb is not Jesus, but God the Father. Jesus is the One who is anointed by God. And so, not only by His proper name, "Jesus," but also in what has become the second part of His name, "Christ," He already refers to God.

The Gospel is the result of a divine initiative. As is testified by the books of the Old Testament, all along God had a plan for saving His people. This plan involves someone who should go on a designated way. On this way, a messenger will be sent ahead, and the reader is invited to follow.

The Word of God—after the title verse, Saint Mark quotes Scripture. His narration begins with what was written by the prophet Isaiah. Actually, Mark's quotation is a mixture of texts taken from Exodus 23:20, Malachi 3:1, and Isaiah 40:3. The texts from Exodus 23:20 and Malachi 3:1 are molded together in Mark 1:2 and speak of a plan of God. God addresses someone confidentially about a special task, and will send a messenger ahead of this person. The purpose of the route to be taken becomes clear in the quotation from Isaiah 40:3, from a section of the book of Isaiah, often called "Deutero-Isaiah," which is concerned with the end of the Babylonian exile. A voice announces that God prepares a way for His people through the rough terrain of the wilderness, between Babylon and Israel, so that they can return home unhindered. Valleys will be filled and mountains will be leveled. In the way Saint Mark combines the quotations, it becomes clear that the person addressed by God has to embark upon this route in order to set God's people free.

The texts actually quoted by Saint Mark are not all taken from Isaiah, nor are they from prophetic books only. The point here is not textual accuracy, but the fact that this is Scripture and therefore the living Word of God. The initiative for the Gospel, the real beginning of the narration lies with God, who has a plan for the liberation of His people and who has addressed someone to carry out His plan. Saint Mark clearly expects his readers to have knowledge of the Old Testament. Careful comparison with the Old Testament texts reveals that Saint Mark even enhances the citation a little bit, adding two possessive pronouns (*your* way, *his* paths), so that the emphasis falls on this special person to whom God entrusts the important mission of freeing His people. A messenger will be sent ahead, but the reader still doesn't know who will come after that messenger.

One word that jumps out in all these quotations is *way*, or *path*, and this is no coincidence. The Gospel is all about a way. Someone will embark upon the way designated by God. If the reader wants to understand the Good News, he or she should be willing to travel down that road. In fact the oldest known appellation for Christians is: *[those] belonging to the Way* (Acts 9:2).

> John the Baptist, who is a prophet like Elijah, prepares this divinely designated way. At the same time, Saint Mark is preparing the reader to travel along this way. The One who is coming after John the Baptist will baptize with the Holy Spirit.

Preparation: John the Baptist—The location of John the Baptist "in the wilderness" allows the reader to identify him as the messenger that was spoken of by God. John the Baptist is *the voice of one crying in the wilderness* (Mark 1:3). The kind of preparation he provides involves calling people to repentance. The baptism that John administers is not a sacrament, but a one-time ritual washing in preparation for the coming of that special person whom God will send. The purpose of the baptism of John involves *repentance,* which literally means a change of mind and heart. The baptism of John therefore implies a moral conversion.

The impact of John the Baptist is enormous. The Greek text highlights it with the use of chiastic construction: **all the country of Judea, and the people of Jerusalem** (Mark 1:5). Even though, the statement should not be taken literally (or else nobody would be left in the land!), the popularity of John the Baptist should not be underestimated. When many years later, and many miles away, Saint Paul proclaims the Gospel in Asia Minor, there are several people who only know the baptism of John the Baptist (Acts 18:25; 19:3–4). For Saint Luke describing in the Acts of the Apostles the early years of the Church and *those belonging to the Way,* the baptism of John the Baptist is a fixed reference point (Acts 10:37; 13:24).

The appearance of John the Baptist is special and serves a purpose. Mark expects the reader to be acquainted with the prophet Elijah. According to 2 Kings 1:7–8, Elijah the prophet wore a hairy garment with a leather belt. *He [King Ahaziah] said to them, "What kind of man was he who came to meet you and told you these things?" They answered him, "He wore a garment of haircloth, with a belt of leather about his loins." And he said, "It is Elijah the Tishbite"* (2 Kings 1:7–8). The detailed description of John's clothing underscores the fact that he is a prophet like Elijah. The reader can now understand even better that the initiator of the words and actions of John the Baptist is God. John the Baptist fulfills the prophetic Word of God in these texts.

According to the prophet Malachi, God will send the prophet Elijah to prepare for the day of the Lord. *"Behold I will send you Elijah the prophet before the great and awesome day of the LORD comes. And he will turn the hearts of fathers to their children and the hearts of children to their fathers, lest I come and strike the land with a curse"* (Malachi 4:5–6).

Through the reference to Elijah, the reader understands that the coming of the day of the Lord coincides with the One who is to come. It becomes clear that a new era is dawning. This makes the call for repentance all the more urgent—the words and actions of John the Baptist, like the return of Elijah, are aimed at a conversion of heart as a preparation for His coming. Therefore, the reader now gets personally involved.

The "heralding" of John the Baptist is reported in direct speech, containing elements that give further information about the special person who has been called by God to carry out a mission. This person is mightier, having strength that supersedes the human strength of the Baptist. Moreover, John the Baptist will not remove His sandals. Traditionally, removing the other's sandals indicates the greater importance of the coming one, and explains why John humbles himself before this person. Here too, Saint Mark counts on the reader to be familiar with Old Testament texts and customs. In order to make his own position clear to all the people, the Baptist refers to a special law and well-known custom in Israel: the levirate law, which involves the removal of a sandal as the official confirmation.

> In ancient Israel, when a man died without offspring, his next-of-kin was bound to marry the widow and raise a family for the deceased, so that his name would not be blotted out in Israel and could be perpetuated on his piece of the Promised Land. This provision might ensure that the Promised Land would never fall into foreign hands. If the nearest of kin refused to marry the widow, *then his brother's wife shall go up to him in the presence of the elders, and pull his sandal off his foot, and spit in his face; and she shall answer and say 'So shall it be done to the man who does not build up his brother's house'* (Deuteronomy 25:9). Later, the Sadducees who do not believe in the resurrection and life after death try to snare Jesus in words by applying this law in an unbelieving way (Mark 12:18–27).

> A beautiful application of the levirate law is found in the book of Ruth. Boaz fulfills the levirate law in marrying Ruth, the widow of Machlon, son of Elimelech, of Bethlehem. Contracting this marriage poses problems, however, since Boaz is not the next-of-kin. The nearest relative is keen on getting the property that rightfully belonged to Machlon, but he is *not* keen on marrying Ruth. Boaz knows how to deal with the situation. In the course of this story, the ancient Israelite custom is explained. *Now this was the custom in former times in Israel concerning redeeming and exchanging: to confirm a transaction, the one drew off his sandal and gave it to the other, and this was the manner of attesting in Israel* (Ruth 4:7). Boaz foresaw that the other contender did not want to marry Ruth in order to raise descendants for the deceased Machlon. So, the next-of-kin conceded his right by untying the thong of his sandal and handing the sandal to Boaz.

> John the Baptist refers to this ancient Israelite custom. By saying that he is not worthy to untie the sandal of the One to come, John announces this special person as the rightful bridegroom of the bride, who is Israel.

The last element in John's proclamation is the announcement of the baptism with the Holy Spirit by the One to come. This statement is personally addressed to the people. Saint Mark speaks of the baptism with water in the past tense and about the baptism with the Holy Spirit in the future tense. This builds an expectation in the readers for the One to come. The baptism of John the Baptist has already been reported, so now attention is focused on the baptism of the Holy Spirit. Water doesn't transform a person, but the Holy Spirit does. Water affects a person superficially and calls for conversion, but the Holy Spirit penetrates the heart of a person, and enables the change of heart.

The early readers of Saint Mark would not be completely unfamiliar with such a concept as a baptism in the Holy Spirit, because the Prophet Ezekiel foretold this promise in the Old Testament. *I will sprinkle clean water upon you, and you shall be clean from all your uncleannesses, and from all your idols I will cleanse you. A new heart I will give you, and a new spirit I will put within you; and I will take out of your flesh the heart of stone and give you a heart of flesh. And I will put my spirit within you, and cause you to walk in my statutes and be careful to observe my ordinances* (Ezekiel 36:25–27).

A reference to the Holy Spirit in Mark's Gospel is rare; it occurs only here, in Mark 3:29 and again in Mark 13:11. The Holy Spirit is the presence of God working through the words and actions of the One to come. It thus becomes clear that not just the divine names are taken on by the One to come, but that he also takes on the divine functions, such as the giving of the Holy Spirit.

Jesus of Nazareth is identified and confirmed as the only Son of God. The prophecies of old are fulfilled in Jesus. A rather solemn, Old Testament phrase—*In those days Jesus came from Nazareth of Galilee* (Mark 1:9)—introduces Jesus into the Gospel. A real introduction is not necessary, since the opening verse of the Gospel already identified Jesus as the Christ, the Son of God. Here only a geographical detail is added. Jesus comes from the little-known town of Nazareth, which is further specified as being located in Galilee.

At first, the Baptist seems to remain the active person. With a passive verb, Saint Mark describes Jesus as the one who receives the baptism administered by the Baptist. John, a man of God, acting on behalf of God, now fades away from the narrative. Here, Jesus and God the Father initiate the action. The Baptist submerges Jesus into the water, but when Jesus *comes up* from the water, Mark narrates a series of events in which a divine sign *comes down* upon Jesus. It is Jesus who "sees." He has a vision and sees the heavens torn open and the Spirit descending upon Him. In the worldview in which God dwells above the firmament and human history happens below, the tearing open of the heavens indicates that a top-down communication is going to take place. At this point, the Baptist disappears and the event is described through the eyes of Jesus. The Spirit descending upon Jesus fulfills the promise of the gift of the Spirit at the new creation as announced by the prophets, especially Isaiah (Isaiah 11:1–3; 42:1–5; 61:1; 63:10–14).

Already in the title verse, Saint Mark made a reference to creation. In Genesis, the Spirit of God hovers above the waters (Genesis 1:2), and now that Spirit descends on Jesus *like a dove*. Although symbolic use of the dove was widespread in classical literature and the subsequent Christian era, the connection between the Spirit and the dove as in Mark's description of the baptism of Jesus is new. The *invisible* creative Spirit of God now comes down in the form of a dove, which Jesus can see. With the visual experience of the dove comes an auditory manifestation. Jesus hears the voice of God addressing Him in direct speech from heaven. Compared with *"You are my son"* (Psalm 2:7), the expression of the Gospel is more emphatic. An added article and adjective make it clear that Jesus is the *only* Son of God.

The divine proclamation of Jesus' dignity as Son of God is not just another piece of information. Even at this early stage of the Gospel, it becomes clear that there are two levels at work. On the horizontal level—the plane of the people of God, Jesus is the Messiah, the Christ. This is only possible because of His relationship with God as His beloved only Son—which is the vertical dimension. What remains unclear is why Jesus is well loved by God and how He acts out His Messiah-ship. The prologue ends rather abruptly and thus indicates that there will be surprises for the reader. In the end the horizontal and vertical dimensions will inevitably result in a cross.

The desert, the place of testing—Jesus emerges victoriously and restores to creation what was lost in the fall. In the Old Testament, the desert was an ambiguous place. Abraham, Elijah, and David found the desert a place of refuge and encounter with God, but also a place of temptation. At the beginning, Satan tempted Adam and Eve, and paradise was lost. Now the Spirit drives Jesus into the wilderness, where Satan tempts Jesus. But instead of falling into temptation, Jesus stays with the wild beasts, and angels serve Him. The paradise and harmony that was lost by Adam, is now restored. In this way, prophetic traditions about the restoration of the original peace in creation are fulfilled in Jesus (Isaiah 11:6–9; 35:3–5; Ezekiel 34:23–31).

John the Baptist proceeds on the way till the end. The fate of the precursor foreshadows the end of Jesus. Jesus continues the proclamation of John and brings it to a new level. Mark 1:14–15 serves as a hinge providing a transition from the prologue to the body of the Gospel. The repeated word *gospel* in Mark 1:14 refers back to the opening verse Mark 1:1 and makes a fresh start, underlining the special status of the verses in between as a prologue to the whole. Thus, the evangelist Mark makes a masterful transition from John the Baptist to Jesus of Nazareth.

John was arrested, literally "handed over." This expression has roots in the Songs of the Suffering Servant (Isaiah 52:13–53:12) and its use in the Gospel is very significant. If John is the forerunner and Jesus the one who comes after him, the fate of John implies something for Jesus and those who follow Jesus.

> John the Baptist was handed over (Mark 1:14).
> Jesus will be handed over (Mark 3:19; 14:10, 11, 18, 21, 41, 42, 44).
> Disciples will be handed over (Mark 13:9, 11, 12).

The Gospel is proclaimed when John gives witness to the truth (Mark 6:14ff), when Jesus dies on the Cross (Mark 14–15), and when the disciples give testimony before governors and kings and are persecuted and martyred (Mark 13:9–13).

The imminence of the kingdom of God is the heart of Jesus' proclamation. The kingdom is "at hand" because Jesus, the Son of the King, has come. Now the opportune time has arrived when it is possible to join God's kingdom by repentance. Repentance cannot be undertaken alone: it requires one to give and another to receive. When a sinner repents, God too comes to the repentant sinner with mercy. In Jesus, God is now near and repentance is possible. What John in his preaching could not accomplish, Jesus fulfills: "believe in the Gospel." Later, Jesus makes a strict connection between the proclamation of the Gospel and Himself: *for my sake and the gospel's* (Mark 8:35).

If Jesus said over two thousand years ago that the kingdom of God is at hand, then why has it not yet come? The question is justified . . . for historians! Historians focus on establishing as accurately as possible what was said and happened long ago. The Gospel, however, is much more than an account of events long past. An essential characteristic of the Gospel confronts the reader in whatever time he or she lives. At the time he wrote his Gospel, Mark knew very well that Jesus had died, was risen and ascended into heaven, and that Christians were "waiting" already for decades for His return. He chooses the first words of Jesus carefully: *"The time is fulfilled, and the kingdom of God is at hand; repent, and believe in the gospel"* (Mark 1:15).

No matter what is going on in your life, the time has now come for you to listen to this Good News. God has made Himself available to you, in and through this Gospel. Now, it is up to you to make yourself available to Him. When Jesus says: *"believe in the gospel,"* He does not propose some new theory, but He offers Himself. Jesus makes Himself available so that readers of all times can come in touch with Him. He began to call disciples over two thousand years ago, inviting them to come to Him, and that continues in every age through the Gospel. The proper time of the Gospel is today.

> The third Luminous mystery of the Rosary is the "Announcement of the kingdom of God and the invitation to conversion." Spend some quiet time meditating on this mystery. Jesus invites each person to conversion. Have you responded to Jesus' invitation? Would you like to respond to Him now? Just pray, "Jesus, I trust in You. Lord Jesus, draw me deeper into the mystery and plan that You have for me."

1. How does each Gospel begin?

Matthew 1:1	Geneology of Jesus
Mark 1:1–10	Title, John the Baptist, Jesus (A new beginning)
Luke 1	Birth of Jesus, Mary, Elizabeth, + Zechariah
John 1:1–5	Prologue – preexistent and incarnate Word of God who has revealed the Father to us

2. What can you learn about Saint Mark from these passages?

Acts 12:11–12	His name is John, called Mark
Acts 12:25	He traveled with Paul (Saul) and Barnabas
Acts 15:36–39	Mark deserted them at Pamphylia Barnabas took Mark with him & sailed to Cyprus
Colossians 4:10	Mark is the cousin of Barnabas. He was with Paul when Paul was in prison
1 Peter 5:13	Peter refers to him as my son

* How could you prepare a way for Jesus to come into your heart, or for God to come more deeply into your life?

Pray to the Holy Spirit
Pray to the Blessed Virgin Mary
Depend on God to help do hard things, don't worry or anger etc.

18

3. Identify the fulfillment of some Old Testament prophecies.

Exodus 23:20	I am sending an angel before you, to guard you on the way and bring you to the place I have prepared Moses John the Baptist
Isaiah 40:3	John the Baptist
Malachi 3:1–3	Jesus or John the Baptist
Mark 1:2–3	John the Baptist

* Was there a situation or person who prepared the way for you to meet the Lord?

My parents, priests
Teaching RE, going to Bible studies

4. Identify the verses in which you find the word "immediately" in Mark 1.

10. ʷᵈ he saw the heavens opened
12. The Spirit im drove him out into the desert
18. ᵐ they left their nets
20. im he called them

21. im on the sabbath he entered the synagogue + taught
23 im there was in their synagogue a man w/ an unclean spirit
29 im he left the synagogue
30 im they told ~~told~~ him of her
42 im the leprosy left him

5. Explain some things about John the Baptist.

2 Kings 1:3–8	He wore a hairy garment, a sign of prophetic calling like Elijah
Luke 1:5–25, 57–80	His father was a priest of Abijah, Zechariah, Elizabeth were both righteous. He will be great in the eyes of the Lord. He is filled w/ the Holy Spirit from the womb. He will be called prophet, go before the Lord to prepare his ways
Mark 1:2–9	lived in the desert, proclaiming a baptism of repentance for forgiveness of sins. He will prepare the way of the Lord; He pointed Jesus out + baptized him
Mark 6:14–29	He was put to death by Herod, became a martyr
Acts 13:24–25	He heralded Jesus' coming by baptizing. Humble, said I am not he, not worthy to untie his sandal
CCC 523	Surpasses all prophets, + his the last one. Goes before Jesus in the spirit + power of Elijah.

Bears Witness to Jesus by his Baptism of conversion, and through his martyrdom.

6. How could one describe Christians?

Acts 9:2
Acts 22:4
1 John 2:5–6

7. What virtue does John display?

Mark 1:7–8	*One mightier than I is coming after me. I am not worthy to stoop + loosen the thongs of his sandals.*
CCC 2546	*humility, God's poverty. The Kingdom already belongs to poor. For your sakes he became poor. 2 Cor 8:9* The joy of the poor:
CCC 2559	*humility is the foundation of prayer*

8. List three practical ways in which you could grow in this virtue. John 13:1–15

Always be happy + loving no matter what anyone says to you
The smallest chore should be done willingly.
Patience with smaller ones or repetition for adults

9. Explain the Gospel, the "Good News."

Mark 1:10–11; John 3:16
CCC 422

* How would you explain the Gospel to someone in your own words?

10. How does the Spirit of God appear? Mark 1:10

like a dove

11. How does God the Father identify Jesus?

Isaiah 42:1	*My servant, my chosen one with whom I am pleased.*
Mark 1:11	*You are my beloved son, with you I am well pleased.*

12. Identify the similarity in the following passages.

Exodus 34:28	*Moses wrote the 10 Commandments on the tablets w/ the Lord 4/o eating or drinking for forty days + 40 nights*
1 Kings 19:2–8	*Elijah walked 40 days + 40 nights to the mountain of God, Horeb, where Moses met w/ God*

Fast to be w/ God

13. Who shows up in Genesis 3:1–15 and Mark 1:13? What does he do?

The snake, the devil Satan; he tempts, he lies, he tricks

14. Who do you find in these passages?

Exodus 14:19	*the Angel of God*
Exodus 23:20	*an angel to guard you on the way + bring you to the place I have prepared (listen + obey him)*
Mark 1:13	*Jesus, Satan, angels*

15. Explain the significance of harmony with animals?

Isaiah 11:6–8
Mark 1:13

16. What was Jesus' first activity after John was arrested? Mark 1:14

17. What are Jesus' first words in Mark's Gospel? Mark 1:15

18. Identify two things that Jesus asks people to do. Mark 1:15b

19. What does "repentance" involve?

Mark 1:4, 15
CCC 1427

20. How is the heart drawn to repentance and conversion? CCC 1428

*How do you repent (turn away from sin) personally? In what ways does your life display the fruit (results) of repentance and conversion?

CHAPTER 2

Divine Authority
Mark 1:16–45

And they were astonished at his teaching,
for he taught them as one who had authority,
and not as the scribes . . .
And they were all amazed,
so that they questioned among themselves, saying,
"What is this? A new teaching!
With authority he commands even the unclean spirits,
and they obey him."
Mark 1:22, 27

Jesus calls disciples—The first disciples are called without any formal introduction. In the same way, in the Old Testament God entered the lives of Abraham and Moses and many of the prophets, like Amos. *Then Amos answered Amaziah, "I am no prophet, nor a prophet's son; but I am a herdsman, and a dresser of sycamore trees, and the LORD took me from following the flock, and the LORD said to me, 'Go, prophesy to my people Israel'"* (Amos 7:14–15). Similarly, Jesus enters the life of the first disciples. He takes the initiative and approaches them directly. Jesus "saw" Simon and Andrew, who were casting their nets. They may have seen Jesus on the shore, but took no notice of Jesus, until He addressed them personally.

It is remarkable that no conditions have to be met to become a disciple. There are no tests to be passed in order to be addressed personally and to be called to follow Jesus. No perfection or status, either socially, economically, or culturally is required. By the same token, this directness of Jesus means that there is no valid excuse to withdraw oneself from being called by Him. Apparently, Jesus is ready to call anyone, no matter what circumstance that person may be in.

> Having disciples is Jesus' idea. He wants to form a group, and calls people to become His disciples. From this point on in the Gospel, Jesus will never be alone. Discipleship is first of all to "be with" Jesus and to join Him on His route.

Come behind me—*Jesus said to them, "Follow me and I will make you become fishers of men"* (Mark 1:17). What is translated as *"Follow me"* literally means: "Come behind me." To follow Jesus means to join Him on the way, which has been marked out for Him by God (see Mark 1:2–3). To join Him may mean to walk side-by-side with Him, but can never mean to walk in front of Him. The only time that Peter obstructs Jesus, is when Jesus announces that His route is to be a path full of suffering that will lead to

His death and Resurrection (Mark 8:31). To hinder Jesus is to thwart the plan of God, which is characteristic of the devil. When Peter tries to hinder Jesus on the way, the admonition to "get behind" is repeated: *"Get behind me, Satan! For you are not on the side of God, but of men"* (Mark 8:33).

To follow behind Jesus starts with being physically present where Jesus is, but goes much further than that. The fishermen, who have no training whatsoever for the kingdom of God, are called to do the same things that Jesus is doing. With their own resources, whatever talents they may have had, they are not capable of such amazing work. But being with Jesus will change them: He will make them fit for the service of the kingdom of God. Transformation in human life comes about through the active presence of Jesus.

The call by Jesus is the most important thing that will ever happen to Peter and Andrew, and to James and John. It is bigger than anything going on in their lives, including their family ties, their livelihood and possessions. They abandon their father, the hired servants, and the nets on which they depended until now. The immediacy of their response is astonishing: it reflects the magnitude of the call and demonstrates the urgency of the kingdom of God, which is at hand, and the divine authority of Jesus who stands before them.

A typical day—Time is the organizing principle at work in Mark 1:21–39. The course of time is inconspicuously mentioned, yet it becomes very clear once attention has been drawn to it. Everything appears to happen within the span of twenty-four hours. So, the reader gets to experience what a typical day with Jesus looks like.

	Time	Activity
Mark 1:21–28	*Morning*	Jesus goes to the synagogue, and casts out an unclean spirit.
Mark 1:29–31	*Afternoon*	Jesus respects the sabbath and remains indoors. He heals Peter's mother-in-law.
Mark 1:32–34	*Evening*	Jesus heals all the sick and casts out demons.
Mark 1:35–38	*Night*	Jesus gets up early to pray. *— this is where he gets His strength - from the Father*
	Next morning	Jesus continues along the way.

Saint Mark's purpose in selecting these exemplary events and composing this "day of Jesus" is to make Jesus as present to the reader as He was to the disciples. By concatenating several historical events (threading them as precious pearls on the string of time), the Gospel depicts a vivid image of Jesus and shows the features that are characteristic for Him. What the Gospel does in words is comparable to showing a photo or perhaps a video, so that the reader gets a good first impression of Jesus. If the Gospel can do this with words, then the suggestion for the reader is to reflect on what a typical day might look like for the seeker. What does a typical day look like for you? What is characteristic of your daily life, and what place, if any, does Jesus occupy in your everyday life?

Plural—One of the most typical features of Jesus is expressed by the words: *they went* (Mark 1:21). This conveys two central aspects of Jesus: that He finds Himself on the road that the Father has marked out for Him, and that He is not alone, but is accompanied by His disciples. Previously, Jesus went out alone (singular) along the shore of the Sea of Galilee. From this point onwards, there is always a plural. The image of Jesus is not complete without His disciples. This unity is not accidental, but brings out something that is essential—there is a vital connection between Jesus and His disciples. In the words of Saint John the Evangelist: *"I am the vine, you are the branches"* (John 15:5). To have disciples is self-evident for Jesus.

The Sabbath—It is equally characteristic of Jesus that His first mentioned day is a sabbath, a day dedicated to God. This is not only evident in the morning when Jesus goes to the synagogue, but it is also seen clearly throughout the day. At noon, after the service in the synagogue, He immediately enters the nearby house of Peter and Andrew, because traveling is forbidden on a sabbath day, and Jesus respects the sabbath. Likewise, at sunset, when the sabbath officially ends, Jesus makes Himself available again, and people begin to carry their sick to the house of Peter—an activity that was fatiguing and forbidden during the sabbath—and Jesus cures them all.

Prayer—The most significant aspect of Jesus is His prayer life: He lives in relationship with the Father. When the day does not offer enough time for prayer, then Jesus will get up during the night or early in the morning to be alone and pray. It is His custom to pray in the evening and at night. *And after he had taken leave of them, he went up on the mountain to pray* (Mark 6:46). Jesus will pray throughout the night in the Garden of Gethsemane, even while the disciples are too tired to pray with Him (Mark 14:32–42). And Jesus will also teach His disciples to pray.

> The expulsion of the unclean spirit shows beyond a doubt the nearness of the kingdom of God. Jesus' teaching about the kingdom of God being at hand is proven to be true because this Teacher throws down the kingdom of the devil. In other words, the authoritative teaching cannot be separated from the Teacher. Such is the power of the proclamation of the Gospel that one cannot have the words of Jesus without having Jesus Himself, and the power of Jesus.

Jesus acts and teaches with authority—Immediately (a favorite word of Mark, used over forty times), Jesus goes to the synagogue on a sabbath to teach. The fame of the Teacher spreads immediately. The subject matter of His teaching is not expressed, but one can

God's love is like the love a mother has for her baby; a stranger in the world
LX2 — pity

infer from Mark 1:15 that the time is fulfilled, the kingdom is at hand, and it is now urgent to repent and believe in the Gospel and the preaching of Jesus.

Repetition provides a clear structure in which the authoritative teaching of Jesus is met with astonishment and amazement. This composition is typical of Mark's writing style: the repeated element serves as a frame to focus attention on the meaning of the passage in the middle. The expulsion of the unclean spirit demonstrates the newness and divine authority of Jesus' teaching.

Mark 1:21	Introduction	"Immediately"
Mark 1:22	Teaching … authority	"They were astonished."
Mark 1:23–26	Jesus' word silences and casts out the unclean spirit.	
Mark 1:27	New teaching—with authority	"They were amazed."
Mark 1:28–29	Conclusion	"At once, immediately"

The Teacher is the teaching—A dialogue ensues between Jesus and the unclean spirit. Recall the earlier encounter in which the Spirit drove Jesus into the desert for forty days and nights. In the prologue, not much of that encounter is reported except in an indirect way—Jesus is in harmony with the wild animals and is being served by the angels, which demonstrates that He has overcome Satan. In Capernaum, the unclean spirit suggests with a question that Jesus has nothing to do with evil, which is not true because Jesus proclaims that the kingdom of God is at hand and the kingdom of God cannot truly coexist with the reign of the devil. The unclean spirit knows that his suggestion is a lie and fears that Jesus has come to destroy evil. Surprisingly, the unclean spirit knows who Jesus is, knows about His coming from Nazareth, and now reveals Him to be *the Holy One of God* (Mark 1:24).

Why would the unclean spirit give away the true identity of Jesus? Is such a revelation not counter-productive to the devil's scheme? For the reader, this revelation confirms what was learned in the prologue. But, the newly called disciples and the people in the synagogue are not yet aware of the true identity of Jesus. The unclean spirit may want to draw attention away from himself and lure Jesus into fixing attention on Himself. Other encounters with unclean spirits in the Gospel will show similar tactics. Such evasive action may also be common today. If a person will not acknowledge and accept responsibility for his or her own sin, it is often a logical tactic to focus attention or blame on the weaknesses and sins of others.

The revelation of Jesus' identity, however, does not stop Jesus from casting out the demon. Here is another surprise for the reader: Why would Jesus want to silence a demon, who speaks the truth? Is it not a good thing for everyone to learn the true identity of Jesus? Apparently, there is a fruitless way of knowing Jesus. Jesus proves the authority of His teaching by casting out the unclean spirit. The kingdom of God is not only proclaimed, but also established by Jesus. He proves to be the stronger One, as foretold by John the Baptist. Ultimately the Teacher Himself is the teaching.

Mark's strategy: Questions to be asked and answered—The expulsion of the unclean spirit triggers the people to ask questions among themselves. *"What is this? A new teaching!"* (Mark 1:27). These questions are the first of many more questions about the identity of Jesus. They play an essential role in how the reader understands the Gospel. In the whole Gospel there emerges a purpose behind all the questions relating to the identity of Jesus.

There is a difference and even a tension between what we as readers know, and what the disciples and people of Palestine know about Jesus. This tension is deliberate. It is a pedagogical strategy Saint Mark chooses to grab our attention and guide our understanding. It ties in with our human condition. We may know something "by heart," but that does not mean that we really understand it. Being able to recite the profession of faith "by heart" does not make one a believer! Knowing who Jesus is does not automatically mean that one becomes a follower and disciple of Him. The many questions in the Gospel are to be read attentively and answered with an authentic knowledge that corresponds to one's life. The purpose of the Gospel is to get us to follow Jesus and to enter into a personal relationship with Him.

Divine Authority

The words Jesus addresses to the people immediately give access to the will of the Father and to the truth about themselves. This was not the case of the scribes who instead had to make an effort to interpret the Sacred Scriptures with countless reflections. Moreover Jesus united the efficacy of the word with the efficacy of the signs of deliverance from evil . . .

The divine authority is not a force of nature. It is the power of the love of God that creates the universe and, becoming incarnate in the Only-Begotten Son, descending into our humanity, heals the world corrupted by sin. Romano Guardini wrote: "Jesus' entire existence is the translation of power into humility . . . here is the sovereignty which lowers itself into the form of a servant . . ."

Authority, for human beings, often means possession, power, dominion and success. Instead for God authority means service, humility and love; it means entering into the logic of Jesus who stoops to wash his disciples' feet (John 13:5), who seeks man's true good, who heals wounds, who is capable of a love so great that he gives his life, because he is Love. In one of her letters Saint Catherine of Siena wrote: "It is necessary for us to see and know, in truth, with the light of faith, that God is supreme and eternal Love and cannot want anything but our good."

Pope Benedict XVI, *Angelus Address*, January 29, 2012.

1. What can you learn from the following passages?

Matthew 4:18–22	Jesus called 4 fisherman to be His followers, and they left what they were doing immediately and did what they were asked. He must have had quite a presence.
Mark 1:16–20	Almost the same word for word.
Luke 5:1–11	As the crowd grew, Jesus asked Simon to let him sit in his boat and put out a little way, then taught the crowd. After, he worked a miracle, showing Simon what would be possible, then called him to be a fisher of men
John 1:40–42	Andrew brought Peter to Jesus Jesus changed his name

2. Describe the activity in Genesis 12:1–3.

Called Abram to a land that God will show him. Gave him 3 promises. He had to leave father as well.
Promises: 1) make of you a great nation 2) Bless you + make your name great 3) Bless those who bless you + curse those who curse you

3. Explain the situation in Exodus 3:2–6.

The angel of the Lord appeared to Moses in as fire flaming out of a bush. This got his attention so God could call him near and tell him who He is – the God of his father and his ancestors. This shows this is the God who promised land and posterity

4. Explain Jesus' relationship with His disciples. CCC 787

Very personal, called them to him, they all did everything together. He revealed the mystery of the Kingdom to them. Gave them a share in His mission, joy & sufferings. He told them to abide in Him, and I in you, a communion between His body and ours

5. In your own words, or using a dictionary, define the word "disciple."

A believer in the thought and teaching of a leader
A follower – go where he goes, see what he sees, listen to him

6. To what does God call all people?

Mark 1:17 *in two or three words*	*Call others*
CCC 767	*To be missionary, spread the Gospel to all nations*
CCC 825	*To be perfect, holy as the Father is holy & perfect*
Matthew 28:19–20	*make disciples of all nations, teaching them all that Jesus has commanded*

7. When did Jesus go to Capernaum? Mark 1:21 *On the Sabbath*

8. Describe the activity and emotion in these verses.

Mark 1:22	*The people were astonished at His teaching. He taught with authority, different from their teachers — awe*
Mark 1:23	*There was a man with an unclean spirit — waiting and watching intently*
Mark 1:24	*He called out to Jesus "What have you to do with us? You are the Holy One of God" Have you come to destroy us? — shock*
Mark 1:25–26	*Jesus rebuked him, Be quiet! Come out of him! The unclean spirit came out of him w/ convulsion + loud shriek — scared*
Mark 1:27	*All were amazed, asked each other "what is this? A new teaching w/ authority" — shaken, don't know what to think*

9. What was the result of Jesus' curing the demoniac? Mark 1:28

His fame spread everywhere throughout Galilee

10. Outline a typical day in the life of Jesus.

Morning	Mark 1:21–28	Taught in the Synagogue Casts out unclean spirit
Afternoon	Mark 1:29–31	Went to Simon + Andrew's house, healed Peter's mother-in-law, respects the sabbath by staying indoors
Evening	Mark 1:32–34	Cured the sick, drove out demons
Night	Mark 1:35–38	Gets up early to pray in a deserted place. Then moves on to other towns

* Now, outline or describe a typical day in your life.

Morning	Pray Eat Do crosswords Bible Study or Prayer Shawl meeting
Afternoon	Get supper ready look at emails
Evening	make supper watch a little TV
Night	go to meetings wash dishes pray

* How present is Jesus in your daily schedule?

Pray in early am, before meals, as I wash dishes, and before bed. Sometimes, I am overcome with thankfulness or feeling loved by God, or me loving Him. Thurs the sunset was so beautiful, I was just thanking God for the present of joy because He made the sky my favorite color.

11. What differences can you find when you compare these accounts?

Mark 1:21–28	What is this? A new teaching! With authority He commands
Luke 4:33–37	same

12. Peter had been married. Why do priests practice celibacy today? CCC 1579

They are called to consecrate themselves with undivided heart to the Lord and to the "affairs of the Lord," they give themselves entirely to God and to people. Celibacy is a sign of this new life of service, accepted with a joyous heart.

13. What did Simon Peter's mother-in-law do, after Jesus cured her? Mark 1:29–31

Got up and waited on them

* In what special ways do you serve your family, friends, and neighbors?

Cooking, cleaning, visiting, playing games w/them, make scarves, hats mittens, watch each others' house

** What are some ways in which you could serve God? CCC 340, 852, 1653

depend on each other, serve each other, complete each other evangelize the poor, walk the way of poverty, obedience, service, self-sacrifice even unto death. "The blood of martyrs is the seed of christians" Parents are the first educators of their children. In this sense; the fundamental task of marriage and family is to be at the service of life.

14. What did Jesus do on the evening after sabbath? Mark 1:32–34

~~prayed~~ healed the sick, drove out demons

15. What did Jesus do in the early morning hours before daybreak? Mark 1:35

prayed

* Do you have a daily prayer time? When is the best time for you to pray?

before I rise from bed + immediately afterwards

16. Who went to find Jesus and why? Mark 1:36–37

Simon and those with him — the disciples to bring him back to town
probably wanted people to bask in glory

17. What was Jesus' plan and purpose? Mark 1:38–39

to go to all the villages and preach

18. What did the leper say to Jesus? Mark 1:40

19. How did Jesus respond and with what emotion? Mark 1:41–44

pity

20. What did Jesus tell the cleansed leper to do and why? What was the result?

Leviticus 13:49ff; 14:2ff
Mark 1:44
Mark 1:45

Chapter 3

Mounting Opposition
Mark 2:1–3:6

"Why does he eat with tax collectors and sinners?"
And when Jesus heard it, he said to them,
"Those who are well have no need of a physician, but those who are sick;
I came not to call the righteous, but sinners."
Mark 2:16–17

A typical day in the life of Jesus gives the reader a good idea of who Jesus is, but the picture is not complete. What is lacking in this first impression is the opposition Jesus met with from the start. Not knowing the enmity that Jesus encountered means not knowing Jesus truly. Five conflict scenarios emerge.

The Heart Grows Harder and Harder

1. Healing and forgiveness—*"in their hearts"* (Mark 2:1–12).
2. Fellowship with sinners—*Why does he eat with sinners?* (Mark 2:15–17).
3. Feasting over fasting—*Why do your disciples not fast?* (Mark 2:18–20).
4. Work on the sabbath—*Why are they doing what is not lawful?* (Mark 2:23–28).
5. Healing on the sabbath—*"their hardness of heart"* (Mark 3:1–6).

First opposition—The opponents of Jesus, some scribes and Pharisees shift from amazement: *"We never saw anything like this"* (Mark 2:12) to overt hostility and enmity: *The Pharisees went out, and immediately held counsel with the Herodians against him, how to destroy him* (Mark 3:6). Scribes were men employed to read and write. They could translate the Hebrew Scriptures, interpret the Law, and prepare documents. Pharisees were pious Jews who set themselves apart in rigorous observance of Mosaic Law. The Pharisees were precursors of modern day rabbinic Judaism. One could be a scribe, or a Pharisee, or both—the scribes of the Pharisees.

The scribes and the Pharisees disapprove of Jesus. Time and again their disapproval proves to be unfounded. It is a matter of the heart—they don't want Him. The Gospel highlights how they follow Him around. Their loaded questions indicate their desire to trip Jesus up, to ensnare Him, and to get rid of Him.

Jesus was "at home" in Capernaum (Mark 2:1). Presumably Jesus made His home with Simon Peter. Word spread that Jesus was there, and so many people gathered, that there was no more room. At this point, four men bring a paralyzed man to Jesus, but they cannot get near Him because of the crowd. They are men of faith. Names are not given, making it easier for any reader to identify with them. Faith makes them inventive. They open up the roof—*who would think of that!* And they lower the paralytic through the hole in the roof.

Jesus sees their faith and acts. He says to the paralytic, *"Child, your sins are forgiven"* (Mark 2:5). They brought the lame man to Jesus so that he might walk again, but Jesus addresses the paralysis of sin. This raises legitimate questions with some of the scribes, because they know that God alone has the power to forgive sin. Scripture is crystal clear on this matter: *I have swept away your transgressions like a cloud, and your sins like mist* (Isaiah 44:22). The scribes come to the conclusion "in their hearts" that Jesus' words are blasphemy. What someone thinks in his heart is normally hidden from others, but the Gospel reveals it to the readers. What began as a healing becomes a revelation of who Jesus truly is and of what people think of Him. Jesus perceives in His spirit what they are thinking. *"Man looks on the outward appearance, but the* LORD *looks on the heart"* (1 Samuel 16:7). Jesus voices their unspoken question, and responds with a question of His own. *"Why do you question like this in your hearts? Which is easier, to say to the paralytic, 'Your sins are forgiven,' or to say, 'Rise, take up your pallet and walk'?"* (Mark 2:8–9).

If forgiveness of sins is characteristic of God alone, so is healing a paralytic with a word characteristic of God alone. For the former there is no visible proof possible, but for the latter there is. If the lame man walks, then that proves that Jesus shares the authority of God, and therefore, He can also forgive sins. Blasphemy is the first thing some people have in mind with regard to Jesus, and even when they are proven wrong in their assumptions, it still will be the last thing they bring against Him to condemn Him to death: *"You have heard his blasphemy. What is your decision? And they all condemned him as deserving death"* (Mark 14:64).

Second opposition—In passing, Jesus sees Levi, the son of Alphaeus. Others see only the exterior, and see him as a tax collector. Jesus sees in Levi a follower, a potential disciple. Once again, Jesus calls an apostle at his workplace, just as He had previously chosen the fishermen. The Romans had introduced a devious tax collecting system in Palestine. They never personally went around exacting levies from the Jews. Instead, they sold the right to collect taxes to the highest bidder, thus ensuring that they received their tax to the full and without delay. The few wealthy tycoons who bought this right from the Romans then broke it into smaller portions and sold them with considerable gain to several local rich people, who in turn hired tax collectors to do the actual work. Both the local rich and the tax collectors increased the amount for personal benefit. Levi was one of those at the end of the chain.

Names prove challenging in the Bible. Often a person has a Hebrew name and also a Greek or Latin name. Sometimes there may also be a nickname, not unlike our own custom of calling Margaret "Peggy," or William "Bill." Jesus invites Levi, the son of Alphaeus to follow Him, and Levi does so. In Matthew's Gospel, the tax collector's name is Matthew (Matthew 9:9), and another son of Alphaeus, James also appears (Matthew 10:3) in the list of apostles. So, perhaps Matthew (Levi the son of Alphaeus), and James the son of Alphaeus could be brothers.

Table fellowship with sinners—In antiquity, and still today, dining with others implies acceptance and respect. People enjoy a good meal with family and friends. Today, it still remains difficult for Gentiles to share a meal with orthodox Jews, who use separate dishes and special preparations to keep Kosher. Jesus, dining with sinners and tax collectors, demonstrates to the scribes of the Pharisees that He is not following their rigid interpretation of the dietary restrictions given in the Torah. This time they question Jesus' behavior not just in their hearts, but go one step further and voice their question out loud. Having been proven wrong in their assumptions once, they do not, however, confront Jesus directly, but they address His disciples. The disciples were also dining with the tax collectors, but are not questioned about their own participation in the meal. On the one hand, this illogical inquiry reveals the intention of the scribes, but on the other hand it confirms what the Gospel phrases carefully: *many . . . were sitting with Jesus and his disciples* (Mark 2:15), that Jesus and His disciples indeed form a special group in the house of Levi. It is Jesus who comes to the disciples' aid and reminds the scribes of the double healing in the house of Peter. He has come to heal both the body of illness and the heart of sins. At this point, the reader is left to determine his or her own position with regard to Jesus—whether one is righteous or not, needs Jesus or not.

Third opposition—The third encounter heightens the controversy one step further. This time the disciples of Jesus are criticized for not fasting, as John's disciples and the Pharisees do. It is not clear who puts the question to Jesus, but now Jesus is questioned directly. Presumably, the scribes of the Pharisees do not approach Jesus themselves, but send their disciples instead. The only proscribed day of fasting in the old covenant was the Day of Atonement (Leviticus 16:29). By the first century, however, the waiting for the Messiah had taken a specific form in Judaism. People had taken it upon themselves to fast twice a week in order to prepare for the coming of the Anointed of God. This fast had become a visible sign of religious identity: to fast meant to be a believing Jew. And then there is Jesus, who constantly speaks of God, but is not fasting, as if not caring about the fulfillment of the promise of old.

Among those who ask the question are disciples of John the Baptist. John had already spoken of the One to come as Someone *the thong of whose sandal I am not worthy to . . . untie* (Mark 1:7). For John's disciples, who were knowledgeable about the Scripture, this should have been a clear reference to the Coming One as the Bridegroom. Jesus reminds them of this reference: *"Can the wedding guests fast while the bridegroom is with them?"* (Mark 2:19). Here is something new: in fact, this constitutes the newness of the New Covenant. God is the bridegroom of Israel. *For your Maker is your husband, the LORD of hosts is his name* (Isaiah 54:5). Hosea also spoke of the Lord as the bridegroom of Israel. *"And I will espouse you for ever; I will espouse you in righteousness and in justice, in steadfast love, and in mercy"* (Hosea 2:19). In the New Covenant, it is the Messiah who is the bridegroom of the people. In the Gospel according to Saint John, who himself was once a disciple of the Baptist, John the Baptist testified that Jesus is the bridegroom, and he, *the friend of the bridegroom* (John 3:29). The Messiah has come and therefore fasting in preparation for His coming makes no more sense; rather the presence of the Bridegroom is a reason for feasting.

At this point, the Gospel bridges the distance between the disciples and the readers, and speaks of the days to come. A new depth is revealed and the readers are addressed. Jesus announces: *"The days will come, when the bridegroom is taken away from them, and then they will fast in that day"* (Mark 2:20). The disciples do not understand it yet, but the mounting opposition will lead to Good Friday. The Christian readers of Mark's gospel recognize that Jesus' veiled reference has come to pass, and their Christian fasting is now only meaningful when done in view of their longing for the return of the Bridegroom, will come again in glory.

Attached to the controversy with those who sent disciples of John and the Pharisees, are two short parables revealing that Jesus is truly the Bridegroom. A wedding is always an occasion for wine and beautiful clothes. While the opposition is mounting and hearts are hardening against Him, the choice of these images are like a window into His heart, revealing His thoughts. Jesus thinks of the Reign of God as a wedding and demonstrates its newness: reasons for the old practices are outdated. Instead, the arrival of the Bridegroom warrants new behavior.

Fourth opposition—The next instance of hard-heartedness involves the observance of the sabbath. God instituted the sabbath as a day for rest and worship: *the seventh day is a sabbath to the* LORD *your God; in it you shall not do any work . . . therefore the* LORD *blessed the sabbath day and hallowed it* (Exodus 20:10–11). Observant Jews were expected to rest on the sabbath, and refrain from work and exertion. Traveling was considered hard word, and therefore one should go no further than *a sabbath day's journey* (Acts 1:12). As before (Mark 1:29), Jesus observes the commandment and stays close, by taking a walk through the surrounding grainfields. The disciples hunger, and pluck some grain to eat along their way. Reaping grain is prohibited (Exodus 34:21), but the disciples are hardly sowing or reaping. Nevertheless, the ever-present Pharisees are quick to criticize. This time they voice their opposition themselves directly to Jesus.

In answer, Jesus points the Pharisees to an event in the life of David, who gave his hungry men holy bread from the tabernacle (1 Samuel 21:4–6). Actually, Ahimelech the priest gave the sacred bread to David and his men to eat, but Jesus purposefully highlights how it was David who took care of his men. As David, so He, who will be recognized as the Son of David (Mark 10:47), takes care of His own and feeds them when they are hungry. In their misguided zeal, the scribes of the Pharisees have over-interpreted the Word of God and lost sight of its true meaning, which is: God takes care of man, giving him time to restore physically and spiritually. In a simple reversal, Jesus restores the purpose of the sabbath and brings His own identity into focus: the Son of man (like the "Son of David," another Messianic title derived from Daniel 7:14) is Lord, also of the sabbath.

Fifth opposition—Opposition seems to have reached a climax. The scribes and Pharisees themselves have already opposed Jesus directly. They are not asking questions any more, but are closely watching Jesus in order to accuse Him. Healing a man with a withered hand, in the synagogue, on the sabbath, seems to give them the sought-after occasion. The climax is, however, still to come. If they will not ask questions, then Jesus will reveal their hearts by asking them questions. *"Is it lawful on the sabbath to do good or to do harm, to save life or to kill?"* (Mark 3:4). This is not an ordinary question: it is a kind of rhetorical question to which everyone knows the answer. When the Pharisees, however, do not give the obvious answer, their silence is more telling and revealing than any direct accusation.

Hardness of heart angers and most of all grieves Jesus. It is not impossible to heal a withered heart, but it does not prevent Him from restoring physical health to the man with the withered hand. *The Pharisees went out, and immediately held counsel with the Herodians against him, how to destroy him* (Mark 3:6). In doing so, the Pharisees demonstrate that it is they themselves who do not observe the Law, by plotting to kill on the sabbath.

For the reader, the resemblance with the words of the demon in Capernaum is striking: *"What have you to do with us, Jesus of Nazareth? Have you come to destroy us?"* (Mark 1:24). Jesus brings about the kingdom of God by destroying evil. Those who plot to destroy Him appear dangerously aligned with evil forces. The demon said he knew who Jesus was. Do we really know Him? Without knowing the opposition in the human heart His goodness encounters, and the willingness of Jesus to go on even until His death, we do not know Him truly. Please God, may our hearts be soft. May we know You and be receptive to Your will.

The Redeemer of man, Jesus Christ is the center of the universe and of history . . .

Christ, the new Adam, in the very revelation of the mystery of the Father and of his love, *fully reveals man to himself* and brings to light his most high calling . . . By his Incarnation, he, the Son of God, *in a certain way united himself with each man* . . .

Man cannot live without love. He remains a being that is incomprehensible for himself, his life is senseless, if love is not revealed to him, if he does not encounter love, if he does not experience it and make it his own, if he does not participate intimately in it. This . . . is why Christ the Redeemer "fully reveals man to himself."

. . . How precious must man be in the eyes of the Creator, if he "gained so great a Redeemer," and if God "gave his only Son" in order that man "should not perish but have eternal life."

Blessed John Paul II, *Redemptor Hominis*, (March 4, 1979), 1.1, 8.2, 10.1.

God's Great Mercy

There is a saying of the Prophet Hosea to which Jesus refers in the Gospel: *"I desire steadfast love and not sacrifice, the knowledge of God, rather than burnt offerings"* (Hosea 6:6). It is a key word, one of those that bring us into the heart of Sacred Scripture. The context in which Jesus makes it his own is the calling of Matthew, a "publican" by profession, in other words a tax collector for the Roman imperial authority: for this reason Jews considered him a public sinner.

Having called Matthew precisely when he was sitting at his tax counter—this scene is vividly depicted in a very famous painting by Caravaggio—Jesus took his disciples to Matthew's home and sat at the table together with other publicans. To the scandalized Pharisees he answered: *"Those who are well have no need of a physician, but those who are sick. . . . For I came not to call the righteous, but sinners"* (Matthew 9:12–13; *[Mark 2:17]*). Here, the Evangelist Matthew, ever attentive to the link between the Old and New Testaments, puts Hosea's prophecy on Jesus' lips: *"Go and learn what this means, 'I desire mercy, and not sacrifice.'"*

These words of the Prophet are so important that the Lord cited them again in another context, with regard to the observance of the Sabbath (Matthew 12:1–8). In this case too he assumed responsibility for the interpretation of the precept, showing himself to be "Lord" of even the legal institutions. Addressing the Pharisees he added: *"If you had known what this means, 'I desire mercy, and not sacrifice,' you would not have condemned the guiltless"* (Matthew 12:7).

Thus in Hosea's oracle Jesus, the Word made man, fully "found himself," as it were. He wholeheartedly made these words his own and put them into practice with his behavior, even at the cost of upsetting his people's leaders. God's words have come down to us, through the Gospels, as a synthesis of the entire Christian message: true religion consists in love of God and neighbor. This is what gives value to worship and to the practice of the precepts.

Addressing the Virgin Mary, let us now ask for her intercession in order to live in the joy of the Christian experience always. Mother of Mercy, Out Lady, awaken within us sentiments of filial abandonment to God who is infinite mercy; help us to make our own the prayer that Saint Augustine expresses in a well known passage of his *Confessions:* "Lord, have pity on me. . . . I hide not my wounds; you are the physician, I the sick; you merciful, I miserable. . . . and all my hope is nowhere but in your exceeding great mercy."

Pope Benedict XVI, *Angelus,* June 8, 2008.

1. Describe the drama in Mark 2:1–12.

Lots of people at Peter's house
Friends brought a paralytic
Took tiles off roof, lowered him down
Jesus said "Your sins are forgiven." The leaders didn't like that

2. Who has the authority to forgive sins? Mark 2:7

Exodus 34:6–7	The Lord is a God gracious and merciful, slow to anger and abounding in love and fidelity
Isaiah 43:25	It is I, I who wipe out, for my own sake, your offenses; your sins I remember no more.
Micah 7:18–19	God removes guilt, delights in mercy has compassion on us, treading underfoot our iniquities
CCC 430	God alone can forgive sins, who in his son Jesus made man, will save his people from their sins
CCC 1441	The Son of man has the authority on earth to forgive sins (MK 2:10)

Mt 1:21 Jesus will save his people from their sins

3. What caused the conflict between Jesus and the Pharisees? CCC 574 Because of his acts expelling demons, forgiving sins, healing on the Sabbath, new ways of interpreting laws, eating with tax collectors + public sinners

4. What amazing faculty did Jesus reveal?

1 Samuel 16:7	He knew what the scribes were thinking God does not see the way people see. The Lord looks into the heart.
Mark 2:8	
CCC 473	Human knowledge of God's son expressed the divine life in Him. It showed itself in everything that pertains to God

* What would Jesus see if He examined your heart right now?

I'm trying to do too much, thinking highly of myself, always have to be right, quick to argue, like to be thought of highly

5. What can you learn from these parallel passages? *Those who are well do not need a physician, but the sick do*

Mark 2:13–17	*Jesus didn't worry about what his opposers thought He came for healing the sinner.*
Matthew 9:9–13	*Go and learn the meaning of the words I desire mercy, not sacrifice*
Luke 5:27–32	*I have not come to call the righteous to repentance but sinners*

6. How does Levi respond to Jesus' invitation? Mark 2:14

He got up and followed him

7. Why did Jesus come? *to heal the sick, body and soul*

Mark 2:17
John 3:16
CCC 1503

* How can a person get right with God? CCC 1484

Individual confession, personally recieving absolution "My son, your sins are forgiven" He is the physician tending each one of the sick who need him to cure him.

** What helps you to discover your sins, sinful thoughts, and sins of omission?

Prayer; asking the Holy Spirit & Jesus to reveal it to me and to catch me when I fall to my knees in sorrow for my sins. Sometimes it causes real depression. Doing a   of conscience

8. What questions/conflicts arise in Mark 2:15–16 and Mark 2:18?

Why does Jesus eat w/ tax collectors + sinners?
Why do the disciples of John fast and the disciples of the
Pharisees fast, and Jesus' disciples don't?

9. Explain Jesus' reference concerning "the bridegroom?"

Isaiah 54:5	The church's husband is your Maker
Hosea 2:19–20	You shall call me "My husband". I will espouse you forever; I will esp. you in righteousness, injustice, in steadfast love, Lord in mercy.
Mark 2:19–20	Can the wedding guests fast while the bridegroom is with them? As long as the bridegroom is with them they cannot fast.
Ephesians 5:25	Husbands, love your wives, even as Christ loved the Church and handed himself over for her
CCC 796	The unity of Christ and the Church, head and members of one body, also implies the distinction of the two within a personal relationship. Often expressed by the image of a bridegroom and bride.

10. What can you learn about "new wine"?

Isaiah 25:6	It is choice, pure
Joel 2:23–27	signifies plenty, vats spilling over, fully satisfied
Mark 2:22	new wine gets poured into new wineskins
John 2:10	Serve good wine first
Acts 2:13	People scoffed, "They have had too much new wine."

* Explain feasting in the New Covenant. What does it seem like to you?

Rejoicing
juicy, rich food + pure, choice wine

11. Compare the following passages.

Deuteronomy 23:25	When you go through your neighbor's vineyard grainfield, you may pick some of the ears w/your hand.
Mark 2:23	Jesus' disciples picked the heads of grain on the sabbath

12. What did Ahimelech do for David? 1 Samuel 21:1–6

Gave him holy bread for his men, for no other bread was on hand.

13. What happened to Abiathar (the son of Ahimelech)? 1 Kings 2:26–27

Though he deserved to die, he was saved because he carried the Ark of the covenant w/David, but dismissed him from the office of priest of the Lord

* What message did Jesus convey to the Pharisees in the above accounts?

Go and learn what this means, "I desire mercy, and not sacrifice." "If you would have known what this means, you would not have condemned the guiltless."

14. What can you learn about the sabbath?

Exodus 20:8–11	
Psalm 118:24	
Mark 2:27–28	
CCC 2173	

15. Write all of the questions asked of Jesus in Mark 2.

16. Explain the drama in Mark 3:1–5.

17. What question does Jesus ask? Mark 3:4

Is it lawful to do good on the sabbath rather than to do evil, to save life rather than destroy it?

18. What emotion does Jesus experience? Mark 3:5

grief at their hardness of heart

19. What is the cause of Jesus' emotion? Mark 3:5

20. How did the Pharisees respond to the miracles? Mark 3:6

Took counsel w/ the Herodians to put Jesus to death
So on the Sabbath, the Pharisees are trying to destroy life

* What can you do to avoid hardening your heart? Psalm 95:7–8

Hear God's voice — we are His sheep, He the Shepherd.
Follow Him.

43

Monthly Social Activity

This month, your small group will meet for coffee, tea, or a simple breakfast, lunch, or dessert in someone's home. Pray for this social event and for the host or hostess. Try, if at all possible, to attend.

After a short prayer and some time for small talk, write a few sentences about "encountering Jesus" personally. Try to explain the difference between "learning *about* Jesus" and coming to "*know* Jesus personally" in your own life.

Examples

◆ *My parents sent me to church as a child. But, they never came with me. So, I had very little opportunity to ask questions or to learn about the faith as a child. Now, I want to know Jesus more.*

◆ *My friend invited me to Bible Study. I thought I knew all about God and the Bible. Wow, was I mistaken! I am learning so much.*

◆ *I was just surfing the channels one night, and came across a movie about the Life of Jesus. All of a sudden, my faith became real for me. I learned that Jesus is not just an historical figure, but He is the living Messiah, who died for me and paid the price for my sins.*

When Jesus heals the sick, makes the blind see, drives out demons, he is actually showing himself to be the messiah. All who know scripture, should be able to know that.

Chapter 4

A New Family
Mark 3:7–35

And looking around on those who sat about him,
he said,
"Here are my mother and my brethren!
Whoever does the will of God
is my brother, and sister, and mother."
Mark 3:34–35

Jesus goes on undeterred—In the face of ever mounting opposition, others might decide to change their course and give up, but Jesus goes on following the route that the Father has set out for Him (Mark 1:2). When He retreats to the seaside, a great multitude of people from all around follows Him. Jesus' reputation as the divine healer and exorcist has spread far and wide. People suffering from physical illnesses and demonic possession press upon Jesus, hoping to touch Him and be healed. Again unclean spirits recognize Jesus, and cry out, *"You are the Son of God"* (Mark 3:11), and again, Jesus commands them to be silent.

Miracles alone did not convince the scribes and Pharisees: miracles alone cannot reveal the full truth of who Jesus is. It takes companionship with Him on His route, and openness of heart to learn who He is. Right from the start (Mark 1:16–20), it is Jesus' idea to have a special group with Him to whom He can reveal more fully who He is and who can partake in His mission. While *all* people are invited to follow Jesus, to be with Him, and to be His disciples, Jesus will choose a special group of twelve to be His apostles, *fishers of men* (Mark 1:17).

Calling whom He wants—Jesus goes to the mountaintop, a place reminiscent of the divine revelation to the Jewish people. On Mount Sinai, Moses encountered God and received the Law (Exodus 19–20). Blessings and curses were pronounced from Mount Gerizim and Mount Ebal at the end of the book of Deuteronomy (Deuteronomy 27:11ff). On Mount Horeb, the prophet Elijah encountered God and was sent on a mission (1 Kings 19).

A disciple's assignment—On the mountain, Jesus chooses *whom he desired* (Mark 3:13), and assigns them three major responsibilities. These twelve men are selected: 1) to be with Jesus, 2) to be sent out to preach, and 3) to have authority to cast out demons (Mark 3:14–15). The first two assignments seem contradictory—how can one be with Jesus and at the same time be sent out to preach? The disciples can only go out and preach if they first learn from Jesus how to do that. The instruction from Jesus involves not some words and techniques. The third assignment explains what really results from being with Jesus.

The authority to cast out unclean spirits can only come from the Holy Spirit. This Holy Spirit is with Jesus (Mark 1:10–12) and provides the impetus for His going on the route marked out by His Father (Mark 1:29). In order to cast out demons, the disciples need to receive the Holy Spirit. They have to stay with Jesus. In being with Him, the Holy Spirit will, so to speak, "rub off" on them (Mark 6:7; Luke 10:17–20). So, to be with Jesus, and to be sent out are actually two aspects of one and the same thing.

What goes on between Jesus and His disciples can be compared to what takes place in a human family. The way in which the twelve will learn what they need for their future task is the same way in which children learn from their parents. Children observe closely and copy behavior they see (rather than doing what they are told to do). Choosing twelve to be with Him is like starting a new family, not based on bloodlines, but on doing the will of God (Mark 3:35).

The Twelve—The number twelve recalls the twelve sons of Jacob, the patriarch, and the twelve tribes of Israel. Mark will only use the term "apostles" in Mark 6:30, so as to distinguish them from the disciples of John the Baptist (Mark 6:29). Normally, he refers to them simply as "the Twelve" (Mark 4:10; 6:7; 9:35; 10:32; 11:11; 14:10, 17, 20, 43).

Simon Peter always appears first in the list of apostles. Jesus gives Simon the new name "Peter," a Greek name, meaning "Rock," indicating his significant role in God's plan for the Church. Being with Jesus really changes a person and this deserves a new name. Some Christians are called by God to follow Him more closely and they become a religious and enter into a profound relationship with Jesus. They seal this bond with a profession, in which they receive a new name. Christian discipleship also involves being named by Jesus. To claim Christ's name and be called a "Christian" is a privilege, requiring spending time with Him.

Twelve patriarchs led the Jewish people. The twelve apostles shepherd the early Church. The Catholic Church enjoys a continuous, unbroken line of succession from Peter to the present day Pope in Rome. Today, the bishops, by divine institution, take the place of the original twelve apostles of Jesus in shepherding the Church of God. Whoever obeys the bishop obeys Christ, Who chose and anointed him in the power of the Holy Spirit. Whoever ignores the bishop, disobeys Christ, Who selected the bishop and ordained him (CCC 861–862).

New family ties—Going on the route that His Father marked out for Him sometimes means that there is no time to eat. *Those around Him,* that is, His relatives have a hard time understanding what Jesus is doing, and actually think that He is out of His mind (Mark 3:20–21). Later on, they approach Him, but remain outside the group of those with Him, sitting around in a circle (Mark 3:31–35). In the meantime, scribes from Jerusalem approach Jesus with false accusations (Mark 3:22–30).

The attentive reader recognizes a pattern. As with the first public miracle in Capernaum (Mark 1:21–28), repetition again provides a clear structure demonstrating what it means to be with Jesus. The typical composition of Mark involves a repeated element that serves as a frame to focus attention on the meaning of the passage in the middle. The behavior of the relatives highlights the dangerous effect of the false accusations of the scribes—they will find themselves outside the kingdom of God.

A) Jesus' relatives think that He is beside Himself (Mark 3:20–21).

B) Scribes falsely accuse Jesus of being possessed by demons (Mark 3:22).

C) With parables, Jesus unmasks the falseness (Mark 3:23–27).

B') The choice of the scribes has consequences (Mark 3:28–29).

A') Jesus defines His new family (Mark 3:31–35).

The unbeatable logic of parables—When the scribes from Jerusalem arrive on the scene, they accuse Jesus of casting out demons by the power of Beelzebul, the prince of demons. The name Beelzebul is similar to Beelzebub, "the lord of the flies" or "the lord of the dung" (2 Kings 1:2). With simple reasoning, which the gospel calls "parable," Jesus points out their flawed logic. Why would the prince of demons destroy his own stronghold? It just doesn't make sense.

Early in Mark's gospel, John the Baptist proclaimed that a mightier One would come after him (Mark 1:7). Now, by casting out unclean spirits, Jesus shows that He is the mighty and strong One. Jesus has the power to bind evil spirits. If the logic is so clear that anyone can see it, it becomes obvious that the scribes too realize this. This, in turn, means that the scribes accuse Jesus against better knowledge!

Blasphemy against the Holy Spirit—This kind of blasphemy results in an eternal sin. God is rich in mercy. His steadfast love endures forever. *The LORD is merciful and gracious, slow to anger and abounding in mercy . . . as far as the east is from the west, so far does he remove our transgressions from us* (Psalm 103:8, 12). How could someone be guilty of an eternal sin? Why would someone not receive forgiveness? The dilemma results from balancing the unfathomable mercy of God with His justice, and the gift of free will. There are no limits to the mercy God is willing to give, but mercy has to be accepted by free will. God has the power to forgive any and all sins. If a person sincerely repents and confesses his sin, the Lamb of God takes that sin to the Cross. Jesus atones for all of the sins of the world in His suffering and death.

Nevertheless, against the deliberately false accusations of the scribes comes a hard word of Jesus—it constitutes the unforgivable sin. There are indeed no limits to God's mercy, so the Catechism teaches, but "anyone who deliberately refuses to accept his mercy by repenting, rejects the forgiveness of his sins and the salvation offered by the Holy Spirit." And the Catechism adds: "Such hardness of heart can lead to final impenitence and eternal loss" (CCC 1864). The point is that the scribes are deliberate in their false accusations. It is not a matter of ignorance, but of purposely fighting against what obviously has to come from the Holy Spirit.

Not just them. The reader may think that this hardness of heart applies only to the scribes, but it should be clear that the unforgivable sin against the Holy Spirit has not so much to do with accusing Jesus falsely of being possessed, as with going deliberately against God's mercy. That is possible in many ways.

The hardness of heart of the scribes and Pharisees has something to do with their unwillingness to see into their own hearts. The biblical hardness-of-heart is for all times, and actually very modern, for in our age, the human heart (not the sentimental heart with its feelings, but the heart as the core of our being) is one of the most neglected places on earth. And the Gospel proves to be a remedy for this affliction of the heart, because it gives the reader a clear view of the heart and soul of Jesus, of the power that leads Him on, that is, of the Holy Spirit.

The false accusations of the scribes demonstrate clearly that they go against better knowledge. They do not want Jesus, and as a result will find themselves outside the kingdom of God. In Capernaum when Jesus healed the lame and forgave sins, it became evident for all to see that Jesus has the power to forgive sins. If they do not accept Him, then to whom shall they turn for forgiveness?

Jesus redefines family ties—Saint Joseph, the foster father of Jesus, has probably passed away by this time, since only Jesus' mother and brethren are mentioned. The typical pattern of the Gospel makes clear that the response of Jesus need not be interpreted as a negative slur against His family. Rather, Jesus redefines and enlarges the concept of family by drawing God into the picture. *But to all who received him, who believed in his name, he gave power to become children of God; who were born, not of blood nor of the will of the flesh nor of the will of man, but of God* (John 1:12-13).

In the Incarnation, God became man, and because of the sacrifice of Jesus on the Cross, He now invites repentant sinners to become His brothers and sisters. Thanks to Jesus, people can once again become children of God, and participate in the family of God, as brothers and sisters of Christ. The way to enter into the family of God, and the kingdom of God, is to believe in Jesus Christ, repent of one's sins, and accept baptism. The gift of salvation is freely given to all. What could prevent someone from accepting such an amazing gift? Have you opened your heart to repent of your sins, accept the mercy offered by Jesus, and come into His family—the Church?

Why is Blasphemy Against the
Holy Spirit Unforgivable?

How should this blasphemy be understood? Saint Thomas Aquinas replies that it is a question of a sin that is "unforgivable by its very nature, insofar as it excludes the elements through which the forgiveness of sin takes place."

According to such an exegesis, "blasphemy" does not properly consist in offending against the Holy Spirit in words; it consists rather *in the refusal to accept the salvation, which God offers to man through the Holy Spirit,* working through the power of the Cross. If man rejects the "convincing concerning sin" which comes from the Holy Spirit and which has the power to save, he also rejects the "coming" of the Counselor—that "coming" which was accomplished in the Paschal Mystery, in union with the redemptive power of Christ's Blood: the Blood which "purifies the conscience from dead works."

We know that the result of such a purification is the forgiveness of sins. Therefore, whoever rejects the Spirit and the Blood remains in "dead works," in sin. And the blasphemy against the Holy Spirit consists precisely in *the radical refusal to accept this forgiveness* of which he is the intimate giver and which presupposes the genuine conversion, which he brings about in the conscience. If Jesus says that blasphemy against the Holy Spirit cannot be forgiven either in this life or in the next, it is because this *"non-forgiveness"* is linked, as to its cause, to *"non-repentance,"* in other words to the radical refusal to be converted. This means the refusal to come to the sources of Redemption, which nevertheless remain "always" open in the economy of salvation in which the mission of the Holy Spirit is accomplished.

The Spirit has infinite power to draw from these sources: "he will take what is mine," Jesus said. In this way he brings to completion in human souls the work of the Redemption accomplished by Christ, and distributes its fruits. Blasphemy against the Holy Spirit, then, is the sin committed by the person who claims to have a *"right" to persist in evil* in any sin at all—and who thus rejects Redemption.

One closes oneself up in sin, thus making impossible one's conversion, and consequently the remission of sins, which one considers not essential or not important for one's life. This is a state of spiritual ruin, because blasphemy against the Holy Spirit does not allow one to escape from one's self-imposed imprisonment and open oneself to the divine sources of the purification of conscience and of the remission of sins.

Blessed John Paul II, *Dominum et Vivificantem,*
(May 18, 1986), 46.2–46.4.

1. Where did Jesus go, and who joined Him? Mark 3:7

Jesus withdrew toward the sea with his disciples

2. Who followed Jesus? Why? Mark 3:7–10

A large # of followers from Galilee & Judah
from Jerusalem, Idumea, from beyond the Jordan,
and the area of Tyre & Sidon

3. How did the unclean spirits relate to Jesus? Mark 3:11–12

They would shout "You are the Son of God,"

* Do you think unclean spirits exist today? What evidence is there?

probably

4. What can you learn about Jesus' apostles?

Mark 3:13	followed Jesus up the mountain. They wanted to be close to him, wanting to learn more about him.
Mark 3:14–15	they are a special group to whom he can reveal himself more fully and partake more fully of his mission, and send them forth to preach & have authority to send out demons
Mark 3:16–19	Jesus chose those whom he desired and assigns them responsibilities - be w/ Jesus, go out & preach, send out demons
Acts 1:13	They devoted themselves to prayer
CCC 551	Jesus chose certain men to be with him & participate in his mission. He gives them a share in his authority and sent them out to preach the kingdom of God & to heal. Through them he directs the church.

5. Which apostle has a special role and why? What is his mission?

Mark 3:16	Simon, who he named Peter
Matthew 16:15–19	Peter said "You are the Messiah, the Son of the living God." Jesus says "You are Peter, and upon this rock I will build my church, and the gates of Hell will not prevail against it."
CCC 552	Jesus entrusts a unique mission to him. Jesus builds his church upon Peter, the rock. His mission is to keep the faith, which he so boldly professed, to keep this faith from every lapse + strengthen his brothers in it — he remains the unshakeable rock

6. Who are the apostles' successors? CCC 861

The apostles consigned the duty of completing and consolidating the work they had begun to their immediate collaborators. They urged them to tend the whole flock, to shepherd the Church of God And on their death other proven men should take over their ministry

7. How should you relate to them? CCC 861–862

The office which Jesus gave to Peter is destined to be transmitted to his successors, is a permanent one. The office received by the apostles of shepherding the church, is destined to be exercised w/o interruption by the sacred order of Bishops. So whoever listens to them, listens to Jesus and whoever despises them despises Christ and him who sent Christ.

* Identify the name of your bishop and commit to praying for him every day.

Bishop John Quinn

8. What do Jesus friends think about Him? Mark 3:20–21

His relatives think he's crazy, the scribes say he is possessed by the devil.

** List three true friends, who stand by you, no matter what others may think.

Tom, Kathy, Rose Ann, Ev
my kids

51

9. How are the signs Jesus works interpreted?

| Mark 3:22–23 | He is possessed by a demon |
| CCC 548 | acting by the power of demon |

10. Who criticizes Jesus? Mark 3:22

the Scribes

11. What behaviors counteract a critical spirit? Philippians 2:1–8

Be of the same mind, w/ the same love, having the same attitude as Jesus,
Do nothing out of selfishness, or vainglory, rather humbly regard others as more important than yourselves, each looking out for the interests of others

12. How does Jesus use logic to refute the critics? Mark 3:23–24

Why would the prince of demons destroy his own stronghold?
If a kingdom were divided against itself, that kingdom cannot stand

* Recall a United States President who cited Mark 3:25 during wartime.

13. What does Mark 3:26–27 reveal about Jesus?

| Mark 1:7 | One mightier than I is coming after me |
| Mark 3:26–27 | Jesus shows that he is the mighty and strong one He has the power to bind evil spirits |

14. Explain blasphemy against the Holy Spirit.

Mark 3:28–30	The person who claims to have the right to persist in evil and thus rejects redemption; the refusal to accept forgiveness
CCC 1864	Anyone who deliberately refuses to accept God's mercy by repenting, rejects the forgiveness of his sins and the salvation offered by the Holy Spirit. Hardness of heart can lead to eternal loss.

* Find a historical or contemporary example of blasphemy. See an example below.

Newspaper headline—Even God couldn't sink the Titanic!

Those who fight for abortion

15. What can you learn about Jesus' relatives?

Mark 3:31–33	they came to see him, remained outside & called for him. Whoever does the will of God is my brother + sister + mother.
CCC 500	James and John, "brothers of Jesus" are sons of "the other Mary" Mt 13:55, 28:1. They are close relations

27:56.— There were Mary Magdalene, Mary the mother of James + Joseph, and the mother of the sons of Zebedee

** Describe your relatives and your extended family.

*** Now describe your Church family, your parish family.

16. What can you learn about the new family of God?

Mark 3:34–35
John 1:12
Romans 8:29
Hebrews 2:10–18
CCC 501

17. How do you relate to your Spiritual Mother? CCC 507

18. How do you sing and pray to her?

19. How can you enter into the family of God? John 1:12; 3:16

20. How can you relate to your Father? Why? Luke 11:2–4; John 20:17

CHAPTER 5

Parables
Mark 4:1–41

Again he began to teach beside the sea.
And a very large crowd gathered about him,
so that he got into a boat and sat in it on the sea;
and the whole crowd was beside the sea on the land.
And he taught them many things in parables,
and in his teaching he said to them:
"Listen . . . "
Mark 4:1–3

Jesus began to speak in parables to the scribes (Mark 3:23), who would not enter into the new family of the kingdom of God, and now continues to speak in parables to a crowd beside the sea. The scene at the seaside opens with: *Again he began to teach* (Mark 4:1), meaning that now we get to hear what He is saying to those who come with good intentions. A parable is an ancient literary genre, which Jesus employs with supreme mastery. Jesus uses a simple, common illustration in such a way as to confront His listeners with a spiritual truth. In this way, Jesus presents a radical choice to accept or reject His invitation to enter into the kingdom of God.

> **"Parable**—a metaphor or simile drawn from nature or common life, arresting the hearer by its vividness or strangeness, and leaving the mind in sufficient doubt about its precise application to tease it into active thought."
>
> C. H. Dodd, *The Parables of the Kingdom,*
> (New York, NY: Charles Scribner and Sons, 1961), 5.

Parables, in the strict sense of a short narrative, are used less frequently in the Old Testament. One striking example occurs after King David has committed adultery with Bathsheba and arranged for the murder of her husband Uriah the Hittite (2 Samuel 12:1ff). God sends the prophet Nathan to David. Nathan relates a report that a certain rich man and poor man lived in a city. The rich man had many flocks, but the poor man had only one little ewe lamb. When a traveler comes to visit the rich man, he takes the poor man's only lamb to cook for his guest. David's anger rises against the rich man, insisting that he deserves to die. Then, Nathan pronounces: *You are the man* (2 Samuel 12:7). The use of the parable in this case, moves David to recognize his sin and to repent.

The Synoptic Gospels record many parables of Jesus. Mark records several of them. The first of these is the parable of the sower and the seed. In a way, this parable is the mother of all parables and the most important one: *"Do you not understand this parable? How then will you understand all the parables?"* (Mark 4:13).

Jesus desires to be heard. Just as Jesus was looking intently around on those sitting with Him in a circle (Mark 3:34), so now He is looking at His audience and He not only sees them with His eyes, but also sees through them, sees the heart, and perceives what they need most. Seeing the situation of the audience (and of the readers of the Gospel), He knows how superficially people are listening, and He knows that they need help in this area to learn to pay attention and listen.

The parable begins formally with: *"Listen!"* (Mark 4:3), and ends with *"Let him hear"* (Mark 4:9), displaying the familiar pattern of repetition that serves to focus attention on the center, which is the sower and the seed.

A		*"Listen!"*	Mark 4:3a
	B	Seeds sown on the land	Mark 4:3b–8
A*		*"Let him hear"*	Mark 4:9

The image of the seed falling on different types of soil, first of all, expresses Jesus' desire to be heard by us and His desire to bring our lives to fruitfulness, which begins by being with Him, and learning how to listen and to receive what He wants to give. This not only applies to the listeners on the shore in the first century AD, but as Jesus continues to explain, also to any reader who experiences tribulation *on account of the word* (Mark 4:17), *for my sake and the gospel's* (Mark 8:35).

Teaching—For a correct understanding of the parable, pay attention to the long and careful introduction in Mark 4:1–2. Not only is "teaching" mentioned three times (*"He began to teach . . . he taught them . . . in his teaching . . ."*), but also the people stand on the shore, while Jesus sits in the boat. This is more than a convenient solution to a problem. A teacher sitting with students standing around was the typical school situation in the first century in Palestine. The introduction to the parable makes it abundantly clear that there is teaching, and that therefore especially the mind is addressed and the reader needs to understand something.

A first hint of the essence of the teaching is found in the introduction. The people stand, *beside the sea*, which in the Gospel is specified as, *on the land*. Seed repeatedly falling *on the land* is precisely the point of the parable. In other words, by being *on the land*, the listeners understand that the parable applies to them. (In the language of the Gospel, the word for *land, ground*, and *soil* is invariably the same; the variation in the English translation is a somewhat misleading embellishment). The parable is addressed *to* the listeners and is *about* them.

It is happening now—The immediate effect of the parable is that it actually happens while it is being heard or read. No one can listen to the parable without determining what to do with these words: whether to brush the words away (as seed on the road), or to engage in them for a moment (as seed in shallow rocky ground), or to let them be overruled by other concerns (as seed among choking thorns), or to really accept them and act upon them (as seed falling on good soil and bearing much fruit). When Jesus explains the parable to His disciples, He four times identifies the seed falling on the land as a group of people who are hearing the word:

Mark 4:15	*"these are the ones along the path . . . when they hear . . ."*
Mark 4:16	*"in like manner are the ones . . . when they hear . . ."*
Mark 4:18	*"others are the ones . . . they are those who hear . . ."*
Mark 4:20	*"those . . . are the ones who hear . . ."*

The parable creates its own actuality. What holds true for the entire Gospel—that it needs an answer—becomes inescapably clear in this parable, hence the need to listen carefully and respond appropriately.

Key to the Gospel—Jesus indicates that this parable is like a key to the Gospel: *"Do you not understand this parable? How then will you understand all the parables?"* (Mark 4:13). And, *He did not speak to them without a parable* (Mark 4:34). The disciples, however, do not yet understand and ask questions about the parables. The answer Jesus gives them in private is astonishing: *"To you has been given the secret of the kingdom of God, but for those outside everything is in parables; so that they may indeed see but not perceive, and may indeed hear but not understand; lest they should turn again, and be forgiven"* (Mark 4:11–12).

The word of God always encounters unwillingness—These verses have sometimes been labeled as the most difficult words of the Gospel, but in fact, they are not cryptic, once it is recognized that Jesus alludes to words from the Book of Isaiah. In his vocation account, the prophet spoke of a purposeful hardening of the people by God: as a prophet he should increase the obduracy of the people, *so that they may not see and not hear* (Isaiah 6:6–11). Like many men of God, Isaiah encountered, right from the start, defiance and unwillingness to change one's ways. In their twisted reasoning, the people accused the prophet of wanting their destruction, for—so they argued—if God had not sent the prophet and if the prophet had not spoken, they would have been (blissfully) ignorant and would not have sinned. The fact that the prophet has spoken must, therefore, mean that God does not want them to be saved and must have planned their destruction.

Isaiah's situation is very similar to what Jesus encounters. Having met with the hardness of heart of Pharisees, and the deliberately false accusations of the scribes, Jesus now alludes to the prophet Isaiah: how he mimicked the twisted reasoning of the people of his day, as if God would not want them to repent. When Jesus speaks of *those outside* (Mark 4:11), He clearly refers back to the dangerous obduracy He encountered in the Pharisees and scribes, who defiantly remained outside and would not enter into the new family of God. What Jesus wants is just the opposite. He has come to usher in the kingdom of God and calls for repentance and for faith in God's Son so that all people may enter into the kingdom of God.

An allegory—When Jesus further explains the parable He goes into detail. By this very fact, the Gospel makes clear that the parable is really an allegory in which various elements all have a meaning of their own: the sower represents Christ. The seed is God's word. The road represents an audience that does not give the word any chance. The shallow ground indicates an audience that is temporarily enthusiastic, but has no stamina. The thorny land stands for listeners for whom the word is relative and less important than other concerns. The good soil represents those who truly hear the word and respond to it. The various responses may also indicate different reactions in the same person at various times in life. Tribulation, persecution, riches, and the cares of the world are obstacles for the Christian. The disciples encounter all of these temptations as they follow Jesus. The early Christian community faced persecution in their struggles to remain faithful to Christ.

The Word is the light of the world—The lamp that is not hidden, but gives light, is Jesus. This short parable continues the same theme of openness for or defiance to the Word of God, as is clear by the same ending as in the parable of the sower. *"If any man has ears to hear, let him hear"* (Mark 4:9, 23). This second parable is also explained clearly in John's Gospel. *The light shines in the darkness, and the darkness has not overcome it* (John 1:5). *And this is the judgment, that the light has come into the world, and men loved darkness rather than light, because their deeds were evil. For every one who does evil hates the light, and does not come to the light, lest his deeds should be exposed. But he who does what is true comes to the light, that it may be clearly seen that his deeds have been wrought in God* (John 3:19–21). *Again Jesus spoke to them, saying, "I am the light of the world; he who follows me will not walk in darkness, but will have the light of life"* (John 8:12). Jesus reveals God's hidden plan of salvation to the world. He reveals God the Father's love for those who are humble and receptive. And to those who receive the truth of God's word with faith, more faith and understanding will come.

Have you listened? Jesus spoke the entire day to the people standing by the sea on the land. *On that day, when evening had come, he said to them, "Let us go across to the other side"* (Mark 4:35). The ensuing storm and miracle on the lake are connected with and are part of the teaching in parables. They demonstrate how people have been listening, and moreover, confront the reader with his or her own listening! The parables were *theory* (addressing the mind). Now, everything depends on *how* this theory is understood and put into *practice* (addressing the will).

That Jesus proposes to cross over to the other side is, at first, somewhat surprising. He is known for His compassion towards the people, never letting them go away hungry or unattended (Mark 6:34; 8:2). Why would He leave them now? The answer can only be that by leaving them He forces them to make a decision as to how they were listening. And indeed, some do follow Him immediately: *other boats were with him* (Mark 4:36), while others do not follow Him (yet).

Have you no faith? Those who follow Jesus will get more, but they also encounter what they did not expect—a storm. Storms are not unusual on the lake of Galilee. What is highly unusual, though, is that Jesus sleeps through it all! The disciples wake Him up saying, *"Teacher, do you not care if we perish?"* (Mark 4:38). Jesus does care a lot, and stills the storm with a double command, *"Peace! Be still!"* (Mark 4:39). A complete calm sets in and Jesus surprises the disciples with a double question: *"Why are you afraid? Have you no faith?"* (Mark 4:40). This question seems unwarranted. What prompts Jesus to ask these questions, since a storm can be a frightening experience? Even more surprising is the disciples' reaction to the question. They are filled with awe and do not respond to Jesus, but question among themselves, *"Who then is this, that even wind and sea obey him?"* (Mark 4:41).

What do you, reader, expect? The last question is really strange. By now, the disciples should know who Jesus is! Why do they not know this? As an attentive reader, you who are reading this book, could easily provide the correct answer, could you not? Perhaps you would answer by saying something like this: Jesus is the Son of God and Lord of all creation, and therefore He naturally has power over all the elements of creation. You are right, of course, but at the same time, your answer could not be less meaningful!

Saint Mark did not write down all these questions without a reason. He clearly expects us to answer them, as you probably just did. The point the inspired Gospel makes is, that as a really attentive reader, you should have noticed the similarity between the storm on the lake and the very first miracle, which Jesus performed and which left the people in utter amazement.

A) Earlier, Jesus has uttered the same word, with which He calms the storm. In the synagogue of Capernaum, Jesus spoke this same word to the man with an unclean spirit. Unfortunately, the RSVCE gives another translation for this word, *"Be silent"* (Mark 1:25), so that its recurrence here is less recognizable, *"Be still"* (Mark 4:39). In the language of the Gospel, however, it is an unmistakable repetition, since that word for quietness and silence is highly unusual and rather poetical, and appears in the entire Gospel of Mark only twice (Mark 1:25; 4:39).

B) Not only does this rare word for "Be still" recur, but also the words of the unclean spirit echo in the disciples waking up Jesus. The unclean spirit said, *"Have you come to destroy us?"* (Mark 1:24), and the disciples say, *"Do you not care if we are destroyed?"* (Again, the RSVCE masks the use of the same Greek word: choosing to translate the middle voice with the active meaning [*perish*] instead of the passive [*be destroyed*]). It is indeed a devilish word, as the Pharisees, who plot with the Herodians *how to destroy him* (Mark 3:6) also use it.

C) What really gives away the resemblance between the first miracle in Capernaum and the miracle on the lake, is the positive acknowledgement of the unclean spirit, who said, *"I know who you are, the Holy One of God"* (Mark 1:24). This contrasts starkly with the response of the disciples, who did not even know this, saying among themselves: *"Who then is this?"* (Mark 4:40).

But you, reader, you knew this, didn't you? Well, if you did know this correct answer, it appears . . . that you may know nothing more than what the demon knew, and that knowledge has not helped him one bit!

What the Gospel is doing here, is putting into action the theory of the parables. The inspired Word of God interacts with us, as we read it, and it teaches and guides us. In this case, it makes us aware that we have been reading with the assumption of having greater knowledge than the disciples. The Gospel clearly intends this to happen, as so much pre-knowledge was given in the prologue of which the disciples were unaware. We learned, before Peter or any disciple was called, that Jesus is the Son of God. We learned it from the most reliable source—from God Himself, speaking from the heavens at the baptism of Jesus in the Jordan. Jesus has always forbidden revelation of Himself on account of His miracles (Mark 1:25, 34, 44; 3:12; 5:43; 7:36; 8:30). His true identity is not known from miracles alone. What we need now is to read on with even greater attention to learn who Jesus truly is.

Going to the other side—If we can recognize the storm on the lake as an opportunity for the Gospel to test our listening skills and our response, perhaps we may understand the remarkable features of the miracle better. How was it possible that Jesus slept peacefully through the storm on the sea?

A tentative answer could run as follows. As should have been clear from the previously recounted twenty-four hours of Jesus (Mark 1:21–39), Jesus prays and lives in union with the Father. The disciples did not yet fully understand that bond at the time, but Jesus has complete confidence in His Father, despite all the opposition and defiance of others. Jesus may be likened to a child, sleeping in the arms of his parent, while that parent negotiates a busy crowd, trying to avoid bumping into anyone. The child can sleep peacefully and unafraid, even unaware of what goes on around him, in the complete confidence that he is in the safest place possible. Jesus is surprised that the disciples have not yet picked this up.

In the same way, the words of Jesus, *"Let us go across to the other side"* (Mark 4:35), can perhaps be understood on a more spiritual level. Ultimately, Jesus invites people to join Him in the new family of God. God is the beginning and the goal of this route. Jesus is going *to the other side,* that is, to God the Father's side, and He invites anyone who is listening to come along with Him. Are any obstacles preventing you from accepting the invitation and following along with Jesus?

1. What is a parable? Use a dictionary or the catechism to define.

2. What must you do to understand a parable? Mark 4:3, 9

3. What is the aim of the parable?

Mark 4:1–3
CCC 546

4. What must you do to understand God's will? Mark 4:3, 9, 23

5. By what means, and when can you ponder God's Word? CCC 2707

* How often, when, and where do you, personally, listen to God?

6. Outline the Parable of the Sower.

Mark 4:3–4	
Mark 4:5–6	
Mark 4:7	
Mark 4:8	

7. To whom does Jesus explain the parable? What gift do they get? Mark 4:10–11

8. How does Jesus explain this parable?

Mark 4:14	
Mark 4:15	
Mark 4:16–17	
Mark 4:18–19	
Mark 4:20	

9. What are some obstacles to responding to God's Word? CCC 29

10. Explain the lamp.

Mark 4:21–25
John 8:12
Revelation 21:23

11. What can be a lamp to enlighten? Psalm 119:105

12. Explain the parables about seeds. Mark 4:26–28

13. Explain the parable about the mustard seed. Mark 4:30–32

14. To whom did Jesus explain these parables? Mark 4:33–34

* What can you do when you lack understanding of God's ways?

15. What happens in Mark 4:35–38?

16. What does God do?

Psalm 89:9; 93:4
Psalm 107:28–29
Mark 4:39

17. What similar expression do you find in Mark 1:25 and Mark 4:39?

18. Contrast Mark 1:24 with Mark 4:38, 40.

19. What question does Jesus ask in Mark 4:40? How do you answer Jesus?

20. What emotion do the apostles show? Answer the question in Mark 4:41.

Chapter 6

What No One Could Do
Mark 5:1–43

"Your daughter is dead.
Why trouble the Teacher any further?"
But ignoring what they said,
Jesus said to the ruler of the synagogue,
"Do not fear, only believe."
Mark 5:35–36

Jesus does what no one else can do—Three miracles of healing and deliverance are recounted in Mark chapter 5. Just as Jesus showed His power over the evil forces of nature, in calming the violent sea, now Jesus demonstrates His divine power in exorcizing a man possessed by demons. Then, Jairus, an official of the synagogue, approaches Jesus to ask for healing for his daughter. Sandwiched in between Jairus' request and Jesus response, Jesus heals a woman with a bleeding disorder. Ultimately, Jesus restores the daughter of Jairus to life and health.

Miracles in Mark 5

1) Jesus exorcizes the Gerasene demoniac (Mark 5:1–20).

2) Jesus heals a hemorrhaging woman (Mark 5:25–34).

3) Jesus restores to life the daughter of Jairus (Mark 5:21–24, 35–43).

Jesus and His disciples have crossed over and have come to the Gentile territory east of the lake of Galilee and of the Jordan River. A demoniac is named after the town of Gerasa (present day Jerash in Jordan), one of the ten cities of the Decapolis, about thirty miles southeast of the Sea of Galilee.

Hopeless situation—On the inhabitable slopes of the lake, Jesus encounters a possessed man, living in torment, in a veritable hell on earth. He dwells among the tombs—the place of the dead, abandoned in loneliness and danger. The townspeople try to subdue him, by binding him with shackles and chains. However, he breaks the restraints, cries out, and bruises himself with stones. The Gospel spends many words on the situation of the man *(no one could . . . no one had the strength),* in order to stress that no one was able to capture him (Mark 5:3–4). Nevertheless, Jesus captivates him, for when this man sees Jesus, he runs up to Him and worships Him. The situation of the possessed man is truly chaotic. On the one hand, he mutilates himself; while on the other hand, he knows who Jesus is even better than the disciples do. The latter is why he is so afraid of Jesus.

The power of Jesus—No one could bind the possessed man, but Jesus has the power to bring order to this demonic chaos. Changing the life of the demoniac is, however, not some psychological process. As the healing and forgiving of the paralytic demonstrated (Mark 2:1–12), Jesus has the power to bring about a very real change. Ultimately, His power is the power of God, for whom nothing is impossible, not even resurrection from death, as the miracle in the house of Jairus will demonstrate. Recognizing this requires faith; actually, without faith in the resurrection a person will never really change his or her life. On one occasion, Jesus explains this to Sadducees, who did not believe in resurrection: *"You know neither the Scriptures nor the power of God"* (Mark 12:24).

When Jesus changes a person and brings order into his life, it is not as if that person undergoes the influence of a strong personality, but it is sharing in His life, in His power over death, in His Resurrection. Forgiveness of sins and all the sacraments bring about a very real change by participating in the life of Jesus. Since the power of Jesus is not from this world, He has the power to change the face of the earth.

As Jesus approaches the possessed man, the demon within him recognizes this power and cries out with a loud voice, *"What have you to do with me, Jesus, Son of the Most High God? I adjure you by God, do not torment me"* (Mark 5:7). Ironically, the demon, who is tormenting the man, asks Jesus not to torment him (Mark 5:7). The demon acknowledges who Jesus is, but does not make a profession of faith or an act of worship.

One against many—Jesus demands that the demon reveal his identity. *And Jesus asked him, "What is your name?" He replied, "My name is Legion; for we are many"* (Mark 5:9). In the Roman army, which occupied the Holy Land at that time, a "legion" was a military regiment consisting of six thousand foot soldiers, plus horsemen and support staff. "Legion" indicates that a vast number of demons possess this man. They realize that Jesus' announcement that the kingdom of God is at hand, means disaster for them. No force of evil, no matter how numerous or powerful, can stand against the One God. So, they try to negotiate with Jesus.

No barter with evil—Demons do not have bodies, but inhabit others; without a body they lose their grip on this world and can only go to the loathsome place from which they came. If they want to stay in the country, they need a body. Jesus understands the tactics of the demons, and on another occasion explains to the apostles: *"When the unclean spirit has gone out of a man, he passes through waterless places seeking rest; and finding none he says, 'I will return to my house from which I came'"* (Luke 11:24).

Now a great herd of swine was feeding there on the hillside; and they begged him, "Send us to the swine, let us enter them" (Mark 5:11-12). For a moment, it seems that Jesus gives in: *So he gave them leave.* The evil spirits leave the tormented man and enter into the swine. However, there can never be any barter between good and evil: *the herd, numbering about two thousand, rushed down the steep bank into the sea, and were drowned in the sea* (Mark 5:13). Jesus never meant for the demons to stay, and they are forced to leave this world.

Many have raised an issue concerning the economic value of the herd, numbering about two thousand. Did Jesus rob the townspeople of their livelihood? For the question to be legitimate a certain reading is required, or rather, it requires some reading into the Gospel. To the reader, a herd of swine may seem valuable, but it never states that the local people depended on the herd for a living. It can be inferred that they were rich and hired shepherds to look after their pigs. At first, when they have been alerted and come *to see what it was that happened,* they do not look for the herd, but are informed by the shepherds. What the Gospel makes abundantly clear is that the people were powerless against the demonic forces in the possessed man, and that Jesus did for them what they could not do themselves. The swine are lost, but they *saw the demoniac sitting there, clothed and in his right mind* (Mark 5:15). What is to be valued more—pigs or a man?

Fear of Jesus—Fear of Jesus is not uncommon. Many resist Him and His invitation to enter the new family of God. Ultimately, it might well be fear that motivates the scribes and the Pharisees: fear that their disordered choices against better knowledge will come to light, and they will have to change their ways. What do the people in Gerasa fear? The request that Jesus should leave their region recalls the futile request of the demons, who did not want to leave the region. One wonders who is really possessed, and whose life needs order.

When Jesus performs miracles or expels demons, the Gospel appears to be a success story. Keep in mind though, that He is away from His own people. People at home did not want to join Him in His new family. And now, in Gerasa too, people ask Him to leave their neighborhood (Mark 5:17). Once He is back in Palestine, they will laugh at Him (Mark 5:40). In the end, being unwelcome is such a big part of Jesus' life that He becomes an outsider in His own land. It is all the more important to know that—as the parable of the sower explained—any reader of the Gospel has the power to make Jesus welcome in his or her own heart.

The Lord has had mercy. As Jesus gets into a boat to leave, the exorcised man begs to come along. However, Jesus sends him back to witness to his neighbors all that God has done for him and how He has had mercy on him. This time, rather than insisting on silence, Jesus tells the healed person to share the good news with others.

Jesus' compassion for the Gerasene demoniac resonates throughout the region. All knew him and marvel at what Jesus had done for him. To live in a place of the dead, apart from family and friends, to cry out in anguish, to mutilate oneself, to wrench apart chains, and break shackles demonstrates an almost unimaginable level of torment. The man, exiled from normal human intercourse, is trapped in evil and isolation. The Gerasene demoniac was a man, without hope. When Jesus exorcises the man, He returns him to normalcy, and restores him to his family and friends.

The gifts of the spirit work in a holy variety of ways. Evil, on the other hand, is monotonous and repetitious in its journey to nowhere . . . One of the marks of evil is that it is always alienating. It always separates a man from his own home and his own self . . . Jesus comes to us in our inaccessible places, in those terrible solitudes in which our grip on reality and our grip on ourselves are most radically challenged. He provides us with the most basic and humanizing help. By his very presence, he assures us that we are not, after all, alone.

. . . The Savior came to save us from our sins, not to change the nature of sin. Sin always was and always will be terror-inducing. But Jesus has the power to cast our sin away, and to take the nightmare of guilt and hiding which it brings. If sin brings fear and ultimately insanity into our lives, Jesus' power is ordered to saving us from that in order to live, not in terror, but in confidence in the Father's changeless love.

. . . One of the effects of evil as well as one of its causes is alienation . . . Everyone in sin is in this situation of lost bearings, family, and friends. Being liberated from the grasp of evil involves the recovery of these important relationships.

That is why when Jesus casts out the demons his work is not yet done. The cure is not complete until the man is restored to his family. This is why Jesus tells him to "go home" and be restored to his rightful world. He tells him to go home and reclaim all that made his life worthwhile. And Jesus tells him to tell his family that this restoration is the work of the Lord's special compassion for those wanderers who even today are lost in the night.

Father John Dominic Corbett, O.P., *Praying with Saint Mark's Gospel*, (Yonkers, NY: Magnifcat, 2011), 89, 91, 97.

Healing Miracles—Following the exorcism of the Gerasene demoniac, Mark interweaves two stories of miraculous healing. The first miracle appears to be interrupted, while Jesus alleviates the misery of another suffering person. Ultimately, both a young girl and a distraught woman receive miraculous healings from God. The girl and the woman are somehow connected, and the Gospel wants to alert the attentive reader to this connection. Both for the girl and the woman, a precise number of years is mentioned: twelve, and both are addressed as "daughter." As is often the case in the Gospel of Saint Mark when this kind of repetition and interweaving occurs, there is really only one story—the framing miracle involving the daughter of Jairus explains the central miracle involving the suffering woman.

A		Mark 5:21–24a	Jairus daughter is at the point of death.
	B	Mark 5:24b–34	A woman has faith—power goes from Jesus.
A*		Mark 5:35–43	Jairus daughter dies and is brought back to life.

A well-known man—Jairus was a prominent synagogue official. Mark describes him as *one of the rulers of the synagogue* (Mark 5:22). He would have been a layman charged with the oversight of administrative and financial affairs in the synagogue, much like a parish administrator might function today. Jairus falls at Jesus' feet and begs Him to come and lay hands on his dying daughter. Saint Mark says that the little girl is *"at the point of death"* (Mark 5:23). Jairus demonstrates great faith in Jesus. He trusts that if Jesus lays hands on his daughter, she will be made well and live. Jesus immediately responds and goes with Jairus.

An unknown woman—Great crowds follow the Miracle Worker. Throngs of people press against Jesus. Many people want to see Jesus, to hear Him, and to touch Him. One of these is a woman, who suffers from hemorrhage, or some kind of chronic bleeding. She has been suffering from this malady for twelve years, just as long as Jairus' daughter has been alive (Mark 5:25, 42). If the bleeding woman is Jewish, her condition affects her and her family far beyond just the physical suffering.

Ritual Impurity from Bleeding

1) People would avoid contact with this woman, because anything she touches makes them ritually unclean. *"If a woman has a discharge of blood . . . she shall be unclean; . . . and everything on which she sits shall be unclean . . . and whoever touches these things [chairs, sofa, bed] shall be unclean"* (Leviticus 15:25–27).

2) If she is a married woman, she could not have sexual intimacy with her husband. *"If a man lies with a woman . . . and she has uncovered the fountain of her blood; both of them shall be cut off from among their people"* (Leviticus 20:18).

3) She would be excluded from worshiping in the temple. *"Thus you shall keep the sons of Israel separate from their uncleanness, lest they die in their uncleanness by defiling my tabernacle that is in their midst"* (Leviticus 15:31).

The woman has exhausted her resources, spent all her money on doctors, with no relief. In fact, she is worse off after consulting the physicians than she was before. Again, like in Gerasa on the other shore of the lake of Galilee, here is a situation where no one could do anything: all human resources had been tried to no avail.

In her heart—The anonymous woman displays great hope and faith in Jesus. *For she said, "If I touch even his garments, I shall be made well"* (Mark 5:28). As with the scribes in Capernaum (Mark 2:7), the Gospel reveals the interior of her heart, which normally cannot be known by others. She takes a big risk, because she knows that touching another person, while she is bleeding, will make the other person also ritually impure. Intentionally making someone ritually impure would be a punishable offense. She probably does not want to make anyone else unclean, but she is desperate. As soon as she touches the hem of Jesus' garment, her hemorrhaging stops, and she feels in her body that she has been healed. She experiences the miracle of healing!

Power had gone forth from Him—Immediately, Jesus feels power going forth from Him and asks, *"Who touched my garments?"* (Mark 5:30). Once again, the disciples are stunned. So many people are pushing and shoving to get close to Jesus. How could anyone possibly determine who had done this? Done exactly what? The more astonishing fact, of which the disciples are unaware, but which the Gospel has revealed, is that power has gone forth from Jesus. What kind of power would that be? And what does it mean that power *had gone forth from him*: did it take Him by surprise? What does His reaction mean? Did He not want this to happen?

Jesus doesn't just see problems, He sees people. He sees the whole person—body and soul. Throughout His ministry, Jesus will gaze intently on those people who the world overlooks. Jesus gazes into each person's eyes and sees the wounded soul and the damaged spirit. The woman approaches Jesus with fear and trembling, and falls down before Him. She tells Jesus the whole truth, which the reader already knows, because the Gospel reveals the faith she has in her heart. Jesus acknowledges the woman's faith, unexpectedly calls her "daughter," and tells her to "go in peace."

Do not fear. Only believe—Meanwhile, as Jesus has been busy healing the hemorrhaging woman, Jairus' daughter dies. People from the synagogue leader's house come to deliver the horrible news to him, and they advise him not to trouble the Teacher any further. But Jesus tells Jairus, *"Do not fear, only believe"* (Mark 5:36). This poses an incredible challenge: what is Jairus to believe when his little girl is lying dead? There can be no mistake about the little girl's death, for the climate makes immediate burial a necessity, and the mourners, usually women from the neighborhood, have already started the elegies and wailing.

Jewish mourning practices for the dead

Wailing—*"A sound of wailing is heard from Zion"* (Jeremiah 9:19);
Moaning—*There shall be moaning and lamentation* (Isaiah 29:2); and
Flute playing— *Jesus came to the ruler's house, and saw the flute players, and the crowd making a tumult* (Matthew 9:23).

At this point, Jesus wants some privacy. He allows only three of His intimate apostles—Peter, James and John—to accompany Him. These are the same three who will observe the Transfiguration (Mark 9:2), and be invited to draw near to pray with Him in Gethsemane (Mark 14:33).

Death is like sleep to Jesus—The people in Jesus' time were far more familiar with death than people in contemporary circles. They butchered their animals for food, rather than selecting plastic wrapped packages in a supermarket. Loved ones died in bed at home, rather than away in a hospital or nursing home. When someone died, they were *really* dead. When Jesus says that the child is not dead, but is sleeping, the people laugh at Him. Similarly, the Gospel of John reports Jesus saying, *"Our friend Lazarus has fallen asleep, but I go to awake him out of sleep"* (John 11:11). Jesus knew that Lazarus had been dead and in the tomb for three days, and yet He speaks of waking Lazarus from sleep. Death is not an obstacle for Jesus.

Tal'itha, Kum: little girl, get up—Jesus takes only the girl's parents and the three apostles to the place where the dead child rests. He takes her by the hand and speaks to her in Aramaic: *"Tal'itha cu'mi"; which means, "Little girl, I say to you arise"* (Mark 5:41). The words Jesus said made an indelible impression on the disciples and even many years later they can report verbatim what He said. The girl immediately gets up and walks, *for she was twelve years old*. Naturally, they are stunned, utterly amazed, overwhelmed with joy, and possibly also with some disbelief. Jesus tells them to feed the girl, proving beyond a doubt that she really is alive. When He rises from the dead, the disciples too are filled with disbelief and joy: Jesus will prove to them that He is truly alive by eating before their eyes (Luke 24:41–43).

The Message—The life of the anonymous woman was changed in an instant, although everything humanly conceivable had been tried in vain. What made this change possible is a power that went forth from Jesus, and the Gospel makes it absolutely clear that her faith released that power of Jesus. The power in Jesus corresponds to the faith in the woman. What kind of power went forth from Jesus? The account of the little girl shows that the power in Jesus is the power of life and death: the power of resurrection. What kind of person will effectively change his or her life? The interwoven miracle accounts demonstrate that only faith in the Resurrection will bring about change. If God can change death to life, He can do anything, and there is always hope for the believer. But, without faith a person will never really change.

Gospel strategy—The woman suffering from hemorrhage is not the only one in the Gospel who has direct access to the healing power of Jesus. There appear to be several persons who know unerringly how to touch the heart of Jesus, and all of them are anonymous women: the Syrophoenician woman (Mark 7), the widow with two coins in the temple (Mark 12), and the woman with the alabaster jar of precious nard balm (Mark 14). They provide a stark contrast to the disciples, who for a long time seem dumbfounded and ask among themselves who Jesus is. Behind both the anonymous women and the disciples is the strategy of the inspired author, Saint Mark, who subtly interacts with the readers through his portrayal of the people around Jesus. By the time the Gospel is written, most of these historical people are gone—the Gospel is not written for them, but for us, the readers. By accenting certain traits of the people around Jesus, the Gospel can guide the reader to faith. Ultimately, both the women and the disciples serve that same purpose. They point to what only Jesus can do.

Women Bear an Effective Witness to Faith

When speaking of the dignity and mission of woman according to the teaching and spirit of the Church, one must always look to the Gospel. The Christian sees, examines and judges everything in its light . . .

First we can recall the many cases in which women were healed, and those others in which Jesus revealed his Savior's heart, full of tenderness in his encounters with the suffering, be they men or women . . . Jesus said tenderly to the deceased daughter of Jairus: *"Little girl, I say to you, arise!"* Having raised her, he *told them to give her something to eat* (Mark 5:41, 43). He showed his sympathy for the stooped woman whom he healed. In this case, by referring to Satan he also called to mind the spiritual salvation he was bringing that woman (Luke 13:10–17).

On other pages of the Gospel we find Jesus expressing his admiration for the faith of some women. For example, in the case of the woman with a hemorrhage, he told her: *"Your faith has made you well"* (Mark 5:34). This praise has all the more value because the woman was subject to the segregation imposed by the old law. Jesus freed women from this social oppression too . . .

Again, Jesus allowed women as well as men to enter his kingdom. In opening it to women, he wanted to open it to children. When he said: *"Let the children come to me"* (Mark 10:14), he was reacting to the watchfulness of the disciples, who wanted to prevent the women from bringing their children to the Teacher. It could be said that he agreed with the women and their love for children . . .

We must add that the Gospel also shows Jesus' kindness to several women sinners. He asked for their repentance, but without acting harshly toward them because of their mistakes, all the more so because the latter involved man's co-responsibility . . . Doubtless Jesus did not acquiesce in the face of evil, of sin, regardless of who commits it. But what understanding of human weakness he had and what goodness he showed toward those who were suffering from their own spiritual misery and more or less seeking in him a Savior!

Lastly, the Gospel attests that Jesus expressly called women to collaborate in his saving work. He not only allowed them to follow him to assist him and his community of disciples, but he asked for other forms of personal commitment . . .

If Jesus Christ reunited man and woman in their equal status as children of God, he engaged both of them in his mission, not indeed by suppressing their differences, but by eliminating all unjust inequality and by reconciling all in the unity of the Church.

Blessed John Paul II, *General Audience,* July 6, 1994.

1. What differences can you identify in these accounts?

Matthew 8:28–34
Mark 5:1–20
Luke 8:26–39

2. Describe the drama in Mark 5:1–7

3. Are demons real? Where do they come from? CCC 391

Mark 5:2, 18
CCC 391
CCC 407

4. What does Jesus do? Mark 5:8–9

5. How does the demon respond to Jesus? Mark 5:9–10

* Do you think evil spirits bother people today? Explain why or why not.

6. What did Jesus do with the unclean spirits? Mark 5:11–13

7. Identify some residents of the sea from these passages.

Genesis 1:21
Job 7:12; 41:1
Psalm 148:7
Daniel 7:2–3
Revelation 13:1

8. How did the townspeople respond to the man's deliverance? Mark 5:14–17

9. What did the exorcized man ask of Jesus? Mark 5:18

10. What commission did Jesus give the man? Mark 5:19

* How would *you* explain to people, "what Jesus has done for *you*?"

11. Compare the following passages.

Matthew 9:18
Mark 5:22–23
Luke 8:40–42

12. What evidence indicates that Jesus was popular? Mark 5:21

13. Does Jesus respond to prayer and requests?

Mark 5:24
CCC 2616

14. Describe some ramifications of the hemorrhaging woman's illness.

Mark 5:25–26
Leviticus 15:19–27
Leviticus 15:31
Leviticus 20:18

15. In your own words, describe the unfolding series of events in Mark 5:28–34.

16. How do the disciples respond to Jesus' question? Mark 5:31

17. What does Jesus say to the woman? Mark 5:34

18. What happened while Jesus was healing the bleeding woman? Mark 5:35

19. What does Jesus ask of Jairus? Mark 5:36

Proverbs 3:5–6
CCC 1504

20. Explain the series of events.

Mark 5:37
Mark 5:38–40
Mark 5:41–43

* What signs and wonders of Jesus have you seen or experienced?

CHAPTER 7

Mission and Mercy
Mark 6:1–44

And Jesus said to them,
"A prophet is not without honor, except in his own country,
and among his own kin, and in his own house."
Mark 6:4

Jesus came to His own country—Jesus teaches the people at length, casts out demons, heals blindness, leprosy, paralysis, hemorrhaging, and even restores a dead girl back to life. Great crowds of people follow Him. They want to see Jesus, to hear Him, and to touch Him. While following the path His Father has chosen for Him, another reason for Jesus always being on the move becomes apparent: He never can stay for long in one place because He is not welcome. People ask Him to leave, laugh at Him, or plot against Him. When Jesus returns to His own country, and begins to teach in the synagogue, His reception is underwhelming.

Disciples followed Him—The disciples are with Jesus in Nazareth, but do not seem to take part in what goes on there. Rather, their part is to be with Jesus (Mark 3:14), and that is a great deal. They experience the exchange between the townspeople of Nazareth and Jesus, and witness rejection. This teaches them (and the reader) that a follower of Jesus should not expect being welcomed everywhere. Any person would want to be welcomed, but it is more true to the Gospel to remain in the company of Jesus, who is not always welcome, than to expect (and to become dependent on) a warm welcome. *His disciples followed him* (Mark 6:1) involves more than the reader sees—discipleship is not a one time event, but a daily concern.

As in His first public appearance in Capernaum, Jesus also goes to the synagogue in Nazareth on the sabbath and teaches. Again, people are astonished (Mark 1:22; 6:2), but this time it does not end with their amazement (Mark 1:27), but with Jesus marveling at their unbelief. Somewhere in between, there is a crack, and the expected growth from amazement to belief never takes place. What happened? In Nazareth they started by asking all the right questions. *"Where did this man get all this? What is the wisdom given to him? What mighty works!* (Mark 6:2). These questions are accurate, and it only needs a little nudge to arrive at the correct answer, because wisdom and mighty works testify to the divine attributes of God. *"It is he who made the earth by his power, who established the world by his wisdom"* (Jeremiah 51:15). The townspeople's questions already suggest that in their experience they encounter something of God; their questions are a slight acknowledgement that God could be the source of all this. They would only have to answer their own questions with "From God—by God," and they would have the correct answer. But that does not happen. Everyone gets enough to believe, but no one gets so much, that he or she has to believe.

The face of unbelief—Instead of staying with the right questions, the townspeople ask other questions. *Is not this the carpenter, the son of Mary and brother of James and Joses and Judas and Simon, and are not his sisters here with us?" And they took offense at him* (Mark 6:3). That is what unbelief looks like. Unbelief can be recognized when something that clearly pertains to God is dragged down. Often, unbelief takes the shape of some action to distract someone from the change required and the consequences that must be accepted. People do not easily acknowledge that a person, who is their equal in one area, can be their superior in another area. They become jealous and they close up.

Consider what that means for God. How could He ever send a prophet to relay His word, if it means that people will close up? Even if He came Himself, He would fare no better. There were many prophets in Israel. Some met with faith and were highly respected, while others met with unbelief and were brutally rejected and murdered. Jesus likens Himself to those prophets who were rejected: *"A prophet is not without honor, except in his own country, and among his own kin, and in his own house"* (Mark 6:4). John the Baptist was a prophet and the Gospel soon recounts his fate.

The son of Mary—Jesus is referred to as *"the" son of Mary*—singular, rather than "a" son—plural, indicating several sons. In antiquity, the term "brothers and sisters" refers to close relatives, members of an extended family, and even distant kinsmen. The Church has consistently upheld the perpetual virginity of Mary. She was a virgin before, during, and after the conception and birth of Christ. Reading into Mark 6:3 more than the verse states, can lead to wrong assumptions about the identity and relationship of these relatives to Jesus and Mary.

Mary "ever-virgin"—Against this doctrine the objection is sometimes raised that the Bible mentions brothers and sisters of Jesus [Cf. Mk. 3:31-35; 6:3; 1 Cor. 9:5; Gal. 1:19]. The Church has always understood these passages as **not** referring to other children of the Virgin Mary. In fact James and Joseph, "brothers of Jesus," are the sons of another Mary, a disciple of Christ, whom Saint Matthew significantly calls "the other Mary" [Mt. 13:55; 28:1; cf. Mt. 27:56].   CCC 500

And he went about among the villages teaching (Mark 6:6)—It should amaze the reader that Jesus does not choose another path. He has been vehemently opposed by scribes and Pharisees; relatives refused to join Him in His new family; Gerasenes begged Him to leave; in Capernaum He was laughed at, and back home in Nazareth He was not welcome. Instead of toning down, however, Jesus expands, and involves His disciples in His mission. It is understandable that He foresaw, *"if any place will not receive you and they refuse to hear you"* (Mark 6:11), for this is what He Himself experienced constantly. Jesus is not put off when things do not go His way.

Jesus commissions the apostles—The Twelve have been with Jesus, pondering His teaching, and witnessing His miracles. *Apostle* means to be "sent out." The apostles' ministry becomes an extension of Jesus' ministry of proclaiming the kingdom of God, teaching about the kingdom, casting out demons, and healing the sick. Jesus charges the apostles to travel light. They are to take nothing for their journey, except a staff. The staff is the standard implement of a shepherd. *Shepherd your people with your staff, the flock of your inheritance* (Micah 7:14).

Taking no food, money, or extra clothing, would leave the apostles totally dependent upon God. When the usual sources of security are absent, divine providence remains the only recourse. *The LORD will provide* (Genesis 22:14). The apostles will learn to trust God for all their needs. *And he said to them, "Where you enter a house, stay there until you leave the place"* (Mark 6:10). Jesus teaches the disciples to rely on local hospitality and to avoid self-concern and social climbing.

No money in their belts (Mark 6:8). Judas Iscariot is one of the Twelve who hears this commissioning, and is content to rely only on what he receives in his being with Jesus. Something will happen to him, for in the end, he wants money in his belt, and is ready to betray Jesus for money. Being a disciple, and having faith, is not a static once-for-all-time decision, but requires constant attention and perseverance.

As in Mark 3:14, there is a double direction: He called *to Him* the Twelve, and *He sent them out* (Mark 6:7). The second movement, the apostolic mission, cannot take place without the first, fellowship with Jesus. In their mission, the disciples remain in this fellowship with Jesus, and can still call upon Him by His name; nothing else is needed. Peter shows this: *"I have no silver and gold, but I give you what I have; in the name of Jesus Christ of Nazareth, rise and walk"* (Acts 3:6).

Should the apostles meet with lack of faith, or lack of hospitality, Jesus advises them to make a symbolic action, rather than taking a vengeful reprisal. In the Old Testament, David was tempted to react violently to the inhospitality of Nabal, but Abigail softened his wrath (1 Samuel 25:9–35). Likewise, Jesus, son of David, advises reacting to an unwelcome reception by shaking the dust from their feet.

They anointed many with oil—Saint Mark recounts one of the two instances in the Gospels, in which oil is used for the sick (Mark 6:13). Saint Luke reports the parable in which a Good Samaritan tenderly cared for a robbed and beaten traveler. *When he saw him, he had compassion, and went to him and bound up his wounds, pouring on oil and wine* (Luke 10:33–34). Later, Saint James advises the presbyters (literally "elders;" this word came to be used for the Christian priests, instead of the pagan word for priest [ερευς]) that referred to the Old Testament priesthood) of the early Christian community to use oil to anoint the sick. *Is any among you sick? Let him call for the elders of the Church, and let them pray over him, anointing him with oil in the name of the Lord* (James 5:14). The Catholic Church offers suffering believers the Sacrament of the Anointing of the Sick, which was instituted by Christ in His commissioning of the apostles. It was further explained and clarified by the Apostle James, and remains today the sacrament of healing in the Church.

Previously, the Anointing of the Sick was called "The Last Rites," and was reserved for those in imminent danger of death. For many it was the last rite of the Church, the sacrament that prepared the Catholic for his or her final journey into the next world. The dying person would hear the words of the priest, saying, "By this holy anointing, may the Lord help you by the grace of the Holy Spirit. May the Lord who forgives your sins, save you and raise you up." Today, the Church also offers this beautiful sacrament to those whose life is in danger because they are seriously ill or facing major surgery.

The death of John the Baptist—Sandwiched in between Jesus' sending out and the return of the apostles, Mark inserts a flashback. By placing the narrative of the death of John the Baptist within the first missionary outreach of the apostles, Mark reveals the cost of discipleship. The death of John the Baptist prefigures the death of Jesus, and the martyrdom of the apostles and many subsequent Christians.

A royal family leaves a trail of blood—The full name of Herod was "Herod Antipas," the son of Herod the Great. Herod the Great had at least nine sons and five daughters by ten wives; not all sons actually ruled. Herod the Great ruled during the time of Jesus' birth and was responsible for the slaughter of the Holy Innocents (Matthew 2:16–18). As tetrach (Matthew 14:1; Luke 9:7; literally "quarter") the Romans allowed Herod Antipas to rule over one quarter of the territory of his father. King Herod Antipas, ruler during the lifetime of Jesus, is responsible for the murder of John the Baptist. One son of Herod Antipas, King Herod Agrippa I, was king during the early years of the Church, and is responsible for the first persecutions of Christians and the death of the apostle James by the sword (Acts 12:1–2).

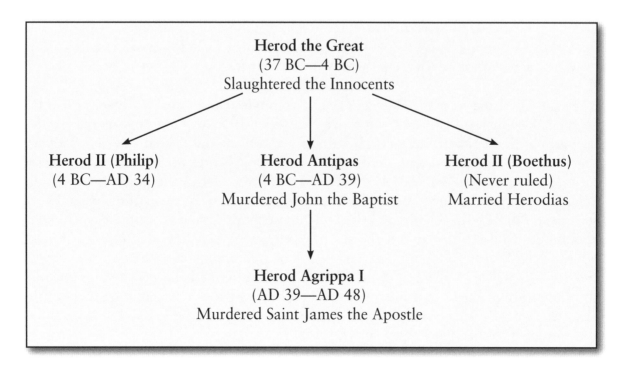

King Herod heard (**Mark 6:14**)—Although translators usually make the text flow by adding "of it," Saint Mark mentions only that Herod *heard*. There is some logic to that: the disciples of Jesus are on their way, and the name of Jesus is continually on their lips. There is no real difference between King Herod and the reader, who also just "hears" when the Gospel is read. The quality of life of the reader/hearer and his/her fruitfulness depends on how one hears (Mark 4:3–9). Ultimately, on Mount Tabor, all that God asks of the disciples is that they listen to His Son (Mark 9:7).

Herodias, a niece of Herod Antipas, had been married to one of the half-brothers of Herod Antipas. Saint Mark calls this half-brother, who never actually held any power by the name of "Philip" (Mark 6:17), but Saint Luke correctly drops that name (Luke 3:19), since Herod Philip was another half-brother and actually a powerful co-ruler of Herod Antipas. Both Herod Antipas and Herodias divorced their respective spouses to come together in what was both an adulterous, and according to Mosaic Law, an incestuous relationship (Leviticus 18:6ff). John the Baptist was imprisoned for publicly renouncing this illicit union. Herodias held a grudge against John and wanted to kill him, but could not, *for Herod feared John, knowing that he was a righteous and holy man, and kept him safe* (Mark 6:20a).

When he heard him, he was much perplexed, and yet he heard him gladly (**Mark 6:20b**)—Herod is not really hearing what John says. The not-hearing of Herod Antipas is the flip-side of his boasting. He calls himself a king, but actually he rules over a small territory (one fourth of his father's kingdom); and even that small area is in danger of being cut in half at a banquet, when Herodias' daughter Salome's dance pleases him, Herod boasts: *"Whatever you ask me, I will give you, even half of my kingdom"* (Mark 6:23), as if he were a grand king.

His boast also recalls the language of King Ahasuerus: *"What is it, Queen Esther? What is your request? It shall be given you, even to the half of my kingdom"* (Esther 5:3). While Queen Esther begs for her life, and the lives of her Jewish people to be spared (Esther 7:3), Salome asks for a holy and innocent man to be murdered. She makes a gruesome request—the head of John the Baptist on a platter.

Divided against himself—While his small kingdom faced possible division on account of his rash oath, Herod Antipas himself is really a divided person: interiorly divided against himself. He thinks John is a holy man, but he cannot stand being corrected by him. A divided person *"cannot stand, but is coming to an end"* (Mark 3:26). Herod Antipas is a pathetic king. He throws big parties while others manipulate him. In the Gospel, he is really an anti-king who is only big in his boasting. The portrayal of this ruler in the Gospel challenges the reader to reflect on whether pride or boasting emerges in one's personal life. Is that pride or boasting something that fits in with the Gospel of Jesus, or not? While Herod Antipas is interiorly torn apart and divided, John the Baptist is a man of undivided character, never changing his testimony to the truth of God's law.

Herod regrets his rash oath. Similarly, in the Old Testament, Jephthah makes a rash vow, which results in disaster for his daughter (Judges 11:30–39). Herod exhibits the descending spiral of unrepentant sin. Following adultery, Herod plunges into debauchery, then rash oaths, cowardice, and finally the murder of an innocent man. Even though Herod knows that John the Baptist is a righteous and holy man, and regrets his oath, he lacks the courage to repent of his folly and spare the innocent.

Good intentions amount to nothing—Hearing the Gospel is always a matter of simplicity. Simply obey the truth of the Gospel, and do not complicate it. Complicit in Herod's sin are many others—his wife, her daughter, banquet guests, who express no outrage, guards and executioners, who might have intervened. Evil triumphs when good people do nothing to stop it. Hearing the Gospel is always a matter of simply letting the seed of the Word fall on good soil, take root, and bear fruit. "Root" in Latin, is *radix:* hearing the Gospel is being radical in the truth.

There are many parallels in the death of John the Baptist and Jesus, innocent, righteous and holy men. Even though Pilate knows that Jesus is innocent, he does nothing to save Him. All of the bystanders in Jesus' Passion and death, indeed all of sinful humanity are somehow complicit in the death of Jesus. The disciples of John the Baptist hear of his murder. They come and claim his body and reverently lay it in a tomb. Similarly, Joseph of Arimathea will claim the body of Jesus, wrap it in a linen shroud, and reverently place it in his own tomb (Mark 15:42–47).

The apostles return—Imagine the excitement of the Twelve, returning to Jesus and recounting all that they had done and taught. They experience the great joy of proclaiming the good news and advancing the kingdom of God. And Jesus says to them *"Come away by yourselves to a lonely place, and rest a while." For many were coming and going, and they had no leisure even to eat* (Mark 6:31–32).

Jesus models the importance of prayer and rest in ministry. Christians must remain with Jesus, pray to God the Father, and rest in the Holy Spirit, in order bear fruit. The importance of regular prayer, Adoration of the Blessed Sacrament, retreats, and leisure, keep a Christian grounded, and in the center of God's will. A grave danger for the Christian is to neglect prayer, and to proceed on merely human effort. Without faithful prayer and proper rest, a person may simply burn out, or revert to a secular or personal agenda. Jesus says *"He who abides in me, and I in him, he it is that bears much fruit, for apart from me you can do nothing"* (John 15:5b).

Many people sought after Jesus, and observed Him getting into a boat. They ran on foot to meet Jesus when He arrived on the shore. And they arrived before Jesus and the apostles. When Jesus saw the great throng of people, *he had compassion on them, because they were like sheep without a shepherd* (Mark 6:34). Just before Moses died, he was concerned that the people not be abandoned—*that the congregation of the*

LORD *may not be as sheep which have no shepherd* (Numbers 27:17). Similarly, Ezekiel prophesied God's concern for His scattered sheep. *"So they [my sheep] were scattered, because there was no shepherd . . . I myself will be the shepherd of my sheep, and I will make them lie down, says the Lord GOD"* (Ezekiel 34:5, 15). Jesus reveals, *"I am the good shepherd. The good shepherd lays down his life for the sheep"* (John 10:11).

Teaching is feeding—Jesus proceeds to teach the people many things. People are hungry for truth. Even today, people are hungry for God's Word. They long for solid teaching. When the multiplication of loaves (Mark 6:41) is compared to the Eucharist of the Last Supper because of the similar wording—*took bread . . . blessed . . . broke it . . . gave it to them* (Mark 14:22), then it is easy to see that there is a Liturgy of the Word preceding the Liturgy of the Eucharist! It might be more accurate to speak of a miraculous nourishing (spiritually and bodily) than of (just) a multiplication of loaves. Nourishment begins when Jesus teaches and continues when He multiplies the loaves. The truth of Jesus is that God has something to say to us, and what He has to say to us through His Son is what lets us live. Hearing what Jesus says, means becoming aware of one's hunger.

Jesus prepares for plenty—When it grows late, the disciples take the initiative and suggest that Jesus send the people away to buy food. But, Isaiah foretold a time when there would be free food and drink. *"Come, buy wine and milk without money and without price"* (Isaiah 55:1). The lack of food prepares for a revelation: human beings are always needy in many ways, and when that happens, God in His mercy comes to their aid. If a person would walk away from want or dryness, in order to look for a bite somewhere he might miss out on God's mercy! What matters in life is to trust God even in the desert of life. He took care of His people in the desert with manna, and will do so now. Actually, a reader might not experience God's mercy looking back twenty centuries in history, but rather find God's mercy by trusting in God in the desert of daily life now.

Jesus feeds five thousand—The Prophet Elisha once fed a hundred men with twenty barley loaves (2 Kings 4:42–44). Jesus' miracle will far surpass Elisha's. The miracle of the feeding of the five thousand anticipates the Institution of the Blessed Sacrament at the Last Supper (Matthew 26:26–29; Mark 14:22–25; Luke 22:17–19), and the Marriage Supper of the Lamb in the New Jerusalem (Revelation 19:7–9). When Jesus asks the disciples to offer what they have, they present five loaves and two fish. He directs the people to sit down in orderly groups. *And taking the five loaves and the two fish he looked up to heaven, and blessed, and broke the loaves, and gave them to the disciples to set before the people* (Mark 6:41). Jesus . . . took . . . blessed . . . broke . . . and gave. Jesus will repeat these same verbs and this ritual at the Last Supper when He institutes the Eucharist (Mark 14:22).

Disciples cooperate—Jesus does not distribute the bread to the hungry people Himself. Rather, the apostles feed the people, foreshadowing the role of the ordained priests in the Church in giving the bread of the angels, the Eucharist to hungry souls. The disciples need to distribute the broken loaves, but obviously, the one who gives is Jesus. Similarly, in every good work, it is God who takes a believing person in his good service, but there should be no mistake that the one who gives is God. Knowing that God is behind every good work makes it easier to serve. A person doing a good work is not giving up something, but just passing on what has been received. This is the background of the one saying of Jesus that is found outside the Gospels: *"remembering the words of the Lord Jesus, how he said, 'It is more blessed to give than to receive'"* (Acts 20:35).

1. Where did Jesus go and what did He do? Mark 6:1–2

2. How was Jesus received? Mark 6:2–3

3. What do wisdom and mighty works indicate?

Mark 6:2
Jeremiah 10:12
Daniel 2:20

4. Who are the brothers and sisters of the Lord, and who are they *not*?

Mark 6:3
CCC 500

* Describe your closest "brothers and sisters in the Lord."

5. Why is Mary's virginity important in the plan of salvation? CCC 503–506

6. Explain aspects of the commission Jesus gave to the apostles.

Mark 6:7	
Mark 6:8–9	
Mark 6:10–11	
Mark 6:12	
Mark 6:13	

7. Why is Christian hospitality important? How do you do this? Hebrews 13:1–2

8. What sacrament is suggested in these passages?

Mark 6:13	
James 5:14–15	
CCC 1511–1517	

* How do you offer comfort to the sick?

9. Why was John the Baptist in prison? What did people think of him?

Mark 6:17–18
Mark 6:19–20

10. Compare the women at these banquets.

Esther 2:8–9, 17
Esther 5:3
Mark 6:22
Esther 7:3
Mark 6:24–25

11. What does John the Baptist's death foreshadow?

Mark 6:14–16
Mark 15:33–39
Acts 7:54–60
Revelation 20:4

* Why is it important for Catholics to pay respect to the deceased?

12. What can you learn from these passages?

Mark 6:29
Mark 15:42–46
CCC 1682–1683

13. How does God see Israel and the neediness of His people?

1 Kings 22:17
John 10:11, 14–18

14. Identify some human emotions of Jesus that Mark describes in these passages.

Mark 1:41
Mark 3:5
Mark 6:34
Mark 8:2
Mark 10:21
Mark 14:33–34

* What emotion do you most often manifest or display to others?

15. What do the disciples suggest to Jesus? Mark 6:35–36

16. What does Jesus ask them to do? Mark 6:37

17. What does Jesus do? What does this prefigure?

Matthew 14:19
Mark 6:39, 41
Luke 9:14–16
John 6:11
CCC 1335

18. Who distributes the bread to the people? Who does this prefigure?

Mark 6:37, 41b
CCC 1563–1564

19. Describe the wondrous result of this miracle. Mark 6:42–44

20. How do you share your bread with the hungry, and the Gospel with the needy?

CHAPTER 8

Purity Within
Mark 6:45–7:23

"This people honors me with their lips,
but their heart is far from me;
in vain do they worship me,
teaching as doctrines the precepts of men."
Mark 7:6-7

Again in the boat—After Jesus nourished the people first by His word and then by miraculously multiplying bread and fish, He *immediately* makes His disciples get into the boat. In contrast to the miraculous healings, no reaction to this incredible miracle is recorded. This sense of hurry and immediacy is on purpose—the reader is now reminded of the long day of nourishing and teaching on the shore of the Sea of Galilee when Jesus spoke in parables—that day too ended by Jesus initiating a boat trip across the lake. The similarity of the situation prepares for a new test both for the disciples and the readers. Will the disciples get it right this time? Are the readers getting what the Gospel is leading up to?

He saw that they were distressed—Jesus has the initiative. As He makes His disciples go, He dismisses the crowd, but not without taking leave of them. As is His custom (Mark 1:35), He goes to a lonely place, up the mountain (Mark 3:13), to pray (Mark 6:46). The lonely place and taking leave of the people indirectly shows what prayer is—to let go of others (of what they owe us, or of what we want to pay back to them) in order to be with God. Jesus lives from His relationship with the Father. The goal of reading about Jesus praying is to follow in His footsteps—to do the same as He does—pray.

The Gospel emphasizes that evening has come, that Jesus is alone on the land and that the disciples are out on the sea. Not withstanding the darkness and distance, He sees their distress and comes to their aid, walking on the water. In their distress, the disciples did not realize that He would see them, and when they do see Him, they think He is a ghost. Often the narrow perspective of immediate difficulties tricks people into thinking that God does not see or does not care.

He meant to pass them by—The multiplication of loaves reminds the reader of the manna with which God fed his people in the desert. But there is more that is reminiscent of the Old Covenant. When the apostles returned, it was Jesus' intention that they should come to a lonely place and rest awhile (Mark 6:31). This recalls the time when Moses led the people through the desert, and God said: *"My presence will go with you, and I will give you rest"* (Exodus 33:14). When Moses asked for confirmation of God's favor, *the LORD said, "Behold, there is a place by me where you shall stand upon the rock; and <u>while my glory passes by</u> I will put you in a cleft of the rock, and I will cover*

89

you with my hand <u>until I have passed by</u>" (Exodus 33:21–22). God let Moses see His goodness pass before him. Now, the apostles are permitted to see the glory of Jesus pass before them. But they are terrified and cry out to Him. Jesus explains this epiphany by identifying Himself with the same divine title that God used to identify Himself to Moses—"*I AM WHO I AM*" (Exodus 3:14). Jesus says, "*Take heart, it is I* (literally "I am"); *have no fear*" (Mark 6:50).

They did not understand—Again, as in the first stormy crossing of the lake, the disciples are utterly astounded. Saint Mark notes explicitly that they have failed to understand *about the loaves*. He even notes that *their hearts were hardened*, an expression that—until now—has only been applied to the scribes and Pharisees who plotted to kill Jesus (Mark 3:5–6). What is there to understand in the miraculous multiplication of loaves? Do you, reader, understand at what the Gospel is hinting?

The Gospel is revelation. On the one hand that is easy, for it teaches what we cannot see for ourselves. But on the other hand it is difficult, for we need to admit our inadequacy; as humans we are created in God's own image and likeness, yet there is a blind spot—original sin. This blind spot hinders us from seeing who Jesus truly is. On the lake, the disciples saw Him (with their eyes), but they did not really see Him (with their hearts), not even when He used God's own name. Disciples and readers need the faith of Abraham who pleaded: "*My lord, if I have found favor in your sight, do not pass by your servant*" (Genesis 18:3).

Do we understand? It is evident—especially since the parable of the sower and its explanation—that Saint Mark invites the reader to be part of the Gospel. In doing so, he only does what Jesus continually did with His disciples. Saint Mark did not write the Gospel for the disciples who, by that time, had already given their lives for Jesus in martyrdom. The Gospel is written for the reader and the not (yet) understanding of the disciples is highlighted to make us, the readers, think hard about who Jesus really is. It is easy to see that Jesus does what only God can do. *He made the storm be still, and the waves of the sea were hushed* (Psalm 107:29), but—as the first stormy crossing showed—that is not enough. The miracle of the loaves holds a clue. Which one? For now, we can only ponder and read on.

The Word of God versus words of men—In the land of Gennesaret people recognize Jesus, and wherever He goes they bring the sick. Just touching the fringe of His garment heals many; this seems to imply that they had the faith of the anonymous woman suffering from hemorrhage.

Great success draws great criticism. The Pharisees and their scribes find fault with the disciples for eating without ritual hand washing. This has nothing to do with hygiene per se, but the scribes interpret this omission as a neglect of the tradition of the elders. The scribes of the Pharisees had expanded the Mosaic Laws pertaining to ritual purification for the Levitical priests, and made their precise rituals an expectation for *all* Jews. The Pharisees do not accuse the disciples of bad hygiene, but of religious sloth.

A rite of purification in the Holy Mass—during the Liturgy of the Eucharist, the priest washes his hands. However, the priest already has clean hands when he enters to say the Mass. During this gesture, the priest silently prays: *Wash me thoroughly from my iniquity, and cleanse me from my sin* (Psalm 51:2). The Eucharist is the sacrifice of Jesus who is without sin. The hand-washing rubric lets the priest make a humble gesture of penitence for sin before he utters the words of Jesus.

"Why do your disciples not live according to the tradition of the elders, but eat with hands defiled?" (Mark 7:5). The Pharisees do not ask a question about adherence to the Law of God, but the traditions of the elders. Jesus gives them an exceptionally sharp rebuke. He quotes the prophet Isaiah (Isaiah 29:13) and calls them hypocrites, accusing them of ignoring God's commandments in order to keep their traditions. Jesus points out their "lip service" to God, while advancing their own human traditions on a par with the divine commandments.

Corban is an Aramaic word for "offering," a monetary gift or property donated to the temple. The donor would usually be publicly recognized for his generosity. While generosity is a good thing, and people should be good stewards of their resources, Jesus brings to light certain abuses. The first commandment for which God attaches a promise and blessing is: *"Honor your father and your mother, that your days may be long in the land which the* LORD *your God gives you"* (Exodus 20:12). Furthermore, *whoever honors his father atones for sins, and preserves himself from them. When he prays, he is heard; and whoever glorifies his mother is like one who lays up treasure* (Sirach 3:3–4). Honoring parents should begin in childhood and continue throughout life. *Help your father in his old age, and do not grieve him as long as he lives* (Sirach 3:12). God's commands are irrevocable.

The Sacred Scriptures clearly and repetitively command caring for parents in their declining years. However, the Pharisees provide a loophole. Some people pledge their resources to the temple, and then rationalize that their responsibility to help their parents has been absolved. Jesus mentions this obvious example of ignoring God's law in favor of the tradition of the elders. He also points out that they do many other such things. Jesus steers the discussion from hand washing, to the care of elderly parents, to defilement, and ultimately to the condition of one's heart.

Defilement—The Old Covenant has many dietary prescriptions. The basis for these laws is the holiness of God. In order to be light to the nations, God's chosen people need to set themselves apart from the Gentiles in their way of life (Leviticus 19–26). Practically, these laws prevented Jews and Gentiles from enjoying table fellowship. Jesus, in His own person, is now the light of the world (Mark 4:21–25; John 1:4–5; 8:12), inaugurating the kingdom of God. Introducing the New Covenant, He renders the Old Testament restrictions unnecessary. Now, both Jews and Gentiles can come to the table of the Lord. Nevertheless, defilement is still a reality. It is, however, not caused by food, but comes *from within, out of the heart of man* (Mark 7:21). Jesus has the power to cleanse the defilement of sin (Mark 2:10). Dietary laws caused serious discussion in the early Christian Community. God sent Peter a vision to resolve this dilemma. *"Rise, Peter; kill and eat." But Peter said, "No, Lord; for I have never eaten anything that is common or unclean." And the voice came to him again a second time, "What God has cleansed, you must not call common"* (Acts 10:13-15).

From within—*Heart* appears here three times (Mark 7:6, 19, 21). Jesus effects a radical change, and declares that all foods are clean. The heart of the matter is that defilement has not much to do with food and washing cups, vessels and so on. Defilement has to do with what is incompatible with the holy God. It is ***sin***, the conscious and deliberate turning away of one's heart from God that defiles a person.

Jesus masterfully offers parables. Some parables are stories. Others are riddles, or obscure sayings. Here, Jesus offers a parabolic saying. *"Hear me, all of you, and understand: there is nothing outside a man which by going into him can defile him; but the things which come out of a man are what defile him"* (Mark 7:14–16). You can almost imagine the scribes and Pharisees, and even the disciples, scratching their heads in wonder. What could this possibly mean? When Jesus enters a house, alone with the disciples, the parable is explained. The heart represents the essence of the person, the place where decisions are made. Moral judgment takes place in the heart. Foods and rituals do not make a person unclean. Sin brings defilement.

Hard Truth—Jesus lists a catalogue of thirteen serious sins. Saint Paul expands on these in his catalogue of sins in Romans. *They were filled with all manner of wickedness, evil, covetousness, malice. Full of envy, murder, strife, deceit, malignity, they are gossips, slanderers, haters of God, insolent, haughty, boastful, inventors of evil, disobedient to parents, foolish, faithless, heartless, ruthless* (Romans 1:29–31). Interestingly, Saint Paul adds to his list—haters of God, the faithless, and those who are disobedient to parents—the very commandment that Jesus highlighted in the Corban discussion, with the Pharisees.

The long list of sins in Mark 7:21–22 is one of the most difficult sayings of Jesus, for it forces the disciples and readers to look into their own hearts and recognize the truth. Sin is not born out of what others do, as if one were unable to prevent it, or as if it would be an excuse. What others do, can—at most—trigger a sin that comes from within a person, and is strictly his or her own. Getting to know Jesus inevitably involves getting to know one's self better. The disciples in the boat did not yet really see Jesus for who He truly is. Did they see themselves as they truly are?

It is a characteristic of God that He can see the heart—the intention, the will, the aim of a person: *"for the LORD sees not as man sees; man looks on the outward appearance, but the LORD looks on the heart"* (1 Samuel 16:7). Jesus knows the objectives of the Pharisees—Jesus sees the heart. Unlike the outward displays of ritual piety for show, Jesus wants to see moral goodness. *He has showed you, O man, what is good; and what does the LORD require of you but to do justice, and to love kindness, and to walk humbly with your God* (Micah 6:8).

The Evangelist Mark reports the following words of Jesus, which are inserted within the debate at that time regarding what is pure and impure: *"There is nothing outside a man which by going into him can defile him; but the things which come out of a man are what defile him . . . What comes out of a man is what defiles a man. For from within, out of the heart of man, come evil thoughts"* (Mark 7:14–15, 20–21).

Beyond the immediate question concerning food, we can detect in the reaction of the Pharisees a permanent temptation within man: to situate the origin of evil in an exterior cause. Many modern ideologies deep down have this supposition: since injustices comes "from outside," in order for justice to reign, it is sufficient to remove the exterior causes that prevent it being achieved. This way of thinking—Jesus warns—is ingenuous and shortsighted. Injustice, the fruit of evil, does not have exclusively external roots; its origin lies in the human heart, where the seeds are found of a mysterious cooperation with evil . . .

Man is weakened by an intense influence, which wounds his capacity to enter into communion with the other. By nature, he is open to sharing freely, but he finds in his being a strange force of gravity that makes him turn in and affirm himself *above* and *against* others: this is egoism, the result of original sin. Adam and Eve, seduced by Satan's lie, snatching the mysterious fruit against the divine command, replaced the logic of trusting in Love with that of suspicion and competition; the logic of receiving and trustfully expecting from the Other with anxiously seizing and doing on one's own (Genesis 3:1–6), experiencing, as a consequence, a sense of disquiet and uncertainty. How can man free himself from this selfish influence and open himself to love?

. . . What is needed is an even deeper "exodus" than that accomplished by God with Moses, a liberation of the heart, which the Law on its own is powerless to realize . . . What then is the justice of Christ? Above all, it is the justice that comes from grace, where it is not man who makes amends, heals himself and others . . . but the loving act of God who opens Himself in the extreme, even to the point of bearing in Himself the "curse" due to man so as to give in return the "blessing" due to God.

. . . Conversion to Christ, believing in the Gospel, ultimately means this: to exit the illusion of self-sufficiency in order to discover and accept one's own need—the need of others and God, the need of His forgiveness and His friendship. So we understand how faith is altogether different from a natural, good-feeling, obvious fact: humility is required to accept that I need Another to free me from "what is mine," to give me gratuitously "what is His." This happens especially in the sacraments of Reconciliation and the Eucharist. Thanks to Christ's action, we may enter into the "greatest" justice, which is that of love.

Pope Benedict XVI, *Message of His Holiness Benedict XVI for Lent 2010*, October 30, 2009.

1. What does Jesus do in these passages?

Mark 1:35	
Mark 6:31	
Mark 6:46	

2. How does Jesus pray? CCC 2602

* How, when, and where do you pray?

3. Compare the following scenarios.

Mark 4:35–36	Mark 6:45
Mark 4:37–38	Mark 6:48
Mark 4:39–40	Mark 6:49–50
Mark 4:41	Mark 6:51–52

4. How would the disciples know that Jesus is God?

Exodus 3:14
Exodus 33:21–22
Job 9:8; 38:16
Isaiah 41:4, 10
Mark 6:48–50

5. What was the reaction of the disciples? Mark 6:51–52

6. Identify some miracles in these passages.

Mark 1:40–44
Mark 2:3–12
Mark 3:1–6
Mark 5:1–15
Mark 5:25–42
Mark 6:54–56

7. What other signs and wonders can you find?

Mark 4:35–41	
Mark 6:34–44	
Mark 6:45–52	

*Share a contemporary healing or miraculous work of God.

8. Explain the conflict in Mark 7:1–6.

9. What did Jesus call the Pharisees?

Isaiah 29:13	
Mark 7:6	

** Define "hypocrite." Find a contemporary example of hypocrisy.

10. Contrast man's tradition with Sacred Tradition. 2 Thessalonians 2:15

*** What are some oral traditions handed down by the apostles to us?

11. What commandment does Jesus bring to mind?

Exodus 20:12; Leviticus 20:8–9
Deuteronomy 5:16
Sirach 3:3–4, 12, 16

* How have you been able to show honor to your parents?

12. What is "Corban?" For what did Jesus accuse them? Mark 7:11–13

13. How does Jesus relate to the Law?

Mark 7:9–14
CCC 581–582

14. What can you learn about the "heart?"

1 Samuel 16:7
Proverbs 4:23
1 John 3:19–21
CCC 1764

15. What does Saint Peter recommend? 1 Peter 1:22

16. Explain Jesus' parable in Mark 7:14.

17. Compare Jesus' catalog of sins with Saint Peter and Saint Paul's lists.

Mark 7:21–22	1 Peter 4:3–4	1 Timothy 1:9–10

18. What problem did the disciples experience? Mark 6:52; 7:18

19. What radical change did Jesus authorize? Mark 7:18–19

20. What can you do about the human heart problem? CCC 1432, 1456

* When was your last confession? When could you plan to go again?

Answer these Questions Personally

Mark 1:27	*What is this?*	*A new teaching! Jesus has authority over even the unclean spirits and me.*
Mark 2:7		
Mark 2:16		
Mark 3:4		
Mark 3:33		
Mark 4:13		
Mark 4:40		
Mark 6:2		
Mark 7:18		
Mark 8:11		

Monthly Social Activity

This month, your small group will meet for coffee, tea, or a simple breakfast, lunch, or dessert in someone's home. Pray for this social event and for the host or hostess. Try, if at all possible, to attend.

After a short prayer and some time for small talk, write a few sentences about "sharing who Jesus is." What evidence could you give to show that Jesus is the Messiah? Be personal if you can.

Examples

◆ *All of the stories in the Bible are very real to me. I can almost see Jesus walking on the water, healing the blind, multiplying bread for the hungry.*

◆ *When my child got sick and the doctors couldn't do anything, my faith was the only thing that pulled me through. I had nowhere else to turn but to Jesus.*

◆ *After praying and praying for a child in our family, a miracle occurred. Every child is a miracle and this child is an exceptional and tangible miracle of God's grace.*

CHAPTER 9

Belief and Unbelief
Mark 7:24–8:21

*And they were astonished beyond measure, saying
"He has done all things well;
he even makes the deaf hear and the mute speak."*
Mark 7:37

Across the border—Leaving the unbelieving and antagonist Pharisees behind, Jesus journeys to the area of Tyre, a Gentile city some forty miles northwest of the Sea of Galilee, in what is presently the coast of modern day Lebanon. Despite the confusion of the disciples, and the belligerence of some religious leaders, Jesus continues on His mission advancing the kingdom of God, and inviting people to repentance and conversion. A surprising number of unexpected people come to have faith in Jesus. One of these is an anonymous woman of non-Jewish birth.

The Gospel hardly introduces her, but her presence follows naturally after the discussion on purity, in which Jesus leveled external barriers between Jews and non- Jews. The woman has a little daughter who is possessed by a demon. When she hears about Jesus and His miraculous healing powers, she "immediately" hurries to meet Jesus and begs Him to cast the demon out of her daughter. Jesus' first goal is to proclaim the good news to the children of Israel. This woman and her daughter are not part of the chosen people. Jesus explains in an incredibly harsh statement: *"Let the children first be fed, for it is not right to take the children's bread and throw it to the dogs"* (Mark 7:27).

Salvation in terms of bread—Jesus speaks of salvation in terms of bread. While customarily most attention is dedicated to the precise meaning of "dogs," it is really astonishing that Jesus pictures God's mercy in terms of bread. There is no Old Testament parallel that prepares for this imagery. The Old Testament passages that come closest involve the manna, the bread from heaven, which saved the people in the desert (Exodus 16; Numbers 11; Deuteronomy 8). Ultimately, salvation from God is Jesus, who says of Himself: *"I am the bread of life"* (John 6:35).

Dogs and their master—It is possible to search for an explanation for this choice of words so uncharacteristic of Jesus. There is, for instance, history: in the eighth century BC the northern territory of Israel was conquered by Tiglath Pileser III and many were deported to Assyria. The land was left practically undefended and neighbors could roam and scavenge at will. The inhabitants of Tyre and Sidon were among the scavengers, and thus earned the nickname "dogs." The Psalms recall those difficult years (Psalm 44:13; 79:4, 12; 80:6). *All that pass by despoil him; he has become the scorn of his neighbors* (Psalm 89:41). However, history is not the reason for Jesus' choice of words; something else is at work here. Sometimes *dogs* is translated as "puppies" or "household pets," in order to soften the words of Jesus, but there is really no reason to make these words say something other than what they actually mean. It sounds rough, but the Gospel has an effective pedagogy for the reader. In this way the unshakeable faith of the woman shines all the more clearly. The woman turns what sounds like a rude refusal into an invitation! She is willing to be counted among the "dogs" as long as Jesus is willing to be her Master, implying that He takes care of her! *"Yes, Lord; yet even the dogs under the table eat the children's crumbs"* (Mark 7:28). The Syrophoenician woman is the first person in the Gospel of Mark to address Jesus by the title "Lord."

Exemplary response—The woman doesn't take no for an answer, but rather she persists in her entreaty with cunning. She takes Jesus up on His word and just turns it around. Perhaps Jesus smiled at her quick retort. Certainly her hope and unconditional trust contrast with the unbelief that Jesus encounters from others. She has heard what Jesus has done and knows that He has the power to do likewise for her. The contrast with the disciples is striking. Full baskets with leftovers from the five loaves of bread were not enough for the disciples to understand (Mark 6:52), but this woman has enough with just a few crumbs. When Saint Mark wrote the Gospel, the Church was already celebrating the Eucharist. The exemplary faith of the anonymous foreigner should give pause and make the reader wonder: how many times must one receive Holy Communion before he or she lets the Lord take care?

The kingdom of God abroad—Jesus recognizes the woman's faith and grants her request. *And he said to her, "For this saying you may go your way; the demon has left your daughter"* (Mark 7:29). The Gospel does not label the woman's response as "faith." Faith requires knowledge, which must come through Israel. Nevertheless, there is salvation for the Gentiles. As the outcome demonstrates, Jesus did not intend to restrict the kingdom of God to Israel. He does have a programmatic strategy for advancing the kingdom of God, which Saint Paul will explain later. *For I am not ashamed of the gospel: it is the power of God for salvation to every one who has faith, to the Jew first and also to the Greek* (Romans 1:16).

Miraculous healing—Taking a circuitous route, Jesus proceeds twenty miles northeast to the town of Sidon, and then journeys southward, toward the cities of the Decapolis, staying close to the eastern shore of the Sea of Galilee, in fact covering all of southern Phoenicia. The Gerasene demoniac, who has been delivered from a legion of demons, has proclaimed in the Decapolis how much Jesus had done for him (Mark 5:20), and prepared the landscape. People now bring their sick to Jesus, and He miraculously heals a deaf mute. With this miracle, Jesus certainly fulfills the prophecy of Isaiah: *Then the eyes of the blind shall be opened, and the ears of the deaf unstopped* (Isaiah 35:5). Similarly, the Wisdom literature testifies to the divine power at work in Jesus: *wisdom opened the mouth of the mute,* (Wisdom 10:21). But there is a lot more going on in this miraculous healing, than meets the eye.

Strategy of the Gospel—The only evangelist to report the healing of the deaf mute is Saint Mark. Both the presence and the location of this miracle in this Gospel are significant, as intuited from the elaborate way in which it is reported. Saint Mark recounts the healing in such detail that the reader should be alert to what really is happening. It seems as if the healing is very difficult for Jesus. All the gestures He makes and especially the sighing point to enormous effort. Jesus sighs—is there any conceivable reason why Jesus should sigh? He healed Peter's mother-in-law with a touch. He healed countless others without even touching them, and cast out demons with a single word. What can be so hard for Jesus that He should sigh? Here the reader can begin to see a connection with what is going on in the Gospel with regard to the disciples, who so far are not very successful in understanding Jesus, while others with faith and complete trust immediately find access to Him.

What is in a sigh? The effort involved in the healing has to do with Jesus working with the disciples and the Gospel working with the reader; the Syrophoenician effortlessly stepping over even the barrier that Jesus has set up, is likewise part of the same strategy. As before, Saint Mark makes use of an inclusion to make his point:

A	Mark 7:31–37	Jesus *sighs* at the healing of the deaf mute.
B	Mark 8:1–10	Disciples do not know what they should know.
A*	Mark 8:11–13	Jesus *sighs* at the unbelief of the scribes.

Deafness—The Jewish creed (*Shema*) starts with a quotation, *"Hear, O Israel: The Lord our God is one"* (Deuteronomy 6:4). If one does not hear, how then could one believe? Intentional deafness equals unbelief; unintentional deafness functions as a symbol of unbelief. Being unable to speak means one cannot answer to the word of salvation that God has spoken, not even confirm it with an *"Amen"* (*"It is so"*).

A keyword in the miraculous healing is *Eph'phatha*, another Aramaic word, meaning, "be open." Right from the beginning of the Gospel Jesus is open to the plan of God and the path it involves. At the baptism of Jesus in the river Jordan, the heavens open and the Holy Spirit descends upon Him. And right from the beginning, Jesus has called disciples to share in His mission and be open to this plan of God and the path involved: *"Whoever does the will of God is my brother, and sister, and mother"* (Mark 3:35). Being open to Jesus and joining Him in the new family of God means listening to Him and acknowledging Him and His words (Mark 4:14-20). It involves opening one's eyes, and ears, and tongue and heart.

Who is deaf? Jesus takes the deaf mute *aside from the multitude privately* (Mark 7:33). Notice the connection with the storyline of the Gospel. Jesus usually takes His chosen followers aside for privileged instruction. Do they hear what He says and do they respond appropriately? What do they really believe? Time and again the disciples do not know who Jesus is (Mark 4:41; 6:49); and the words that an anonymous foreigner in Tyre was able to express—*Yes, Lord* (Mark 7:28), have never crossed their lips. Deafness can be healed, but what about unbelief?

Disciples and readers—Jesus has been with the disciples every day since He called them (Mark 3:13-14) and He instructs them. At the same time, the Gospel instructs the reader. The healing of the deaf mute in the Decapolis has a meaning that transcends the historical facts—it symbolizes what goes on in the Gospel and what goes on between the Gospel and the reader. Jesus is working to "open" the disciples for the Good News, for He is the Good News. The historical fact of the healing of the deaf mute acquires an extra meaning in the Gospel view of the reader. Saint Mark exploits the external senses (eyes, ears) to signify insight, understanding, and the heart. In the Gospel physical deafness and blindness are the occasion to go beyond what can be heard or seen. And this is not an invention of Saint Mark. Jesus quotes the cynical words of Isaiah to explain this: *"so that they may indeed see but not perceive, and may indeed hear but not understand"* (Mark 4:12).

Left to their own resources, the disciples do not understand who Jesus is. Jesus needs to work hard to get them to comprehend. What about the reader? Can he or she understand what the Gospel is about without Jesus working hard to reveal Himself? The truth about Jesus is not a purely human insight; it does not depend on the intelligence of the disciples or readers. The Gospel is a divine revelation, and it is Jesus who works hard to open up disciples and readers alike.

Tell no one—The man's ears are opened by Jesus. He is now able to hear and to speak clearly. Nevertheless, Jesus charges people not to speak about the miracle. Until the heart opens for Him and the route He is following is followed, it is better not to speak about the miracles. Miracles are certainly a part of who Jesus truly is. But half a truth, without the other half, could become a lie. Not surprisingly, in spite of what Jesus says, people zealously recount the signs and wonders they see. However, what does come as a surprise is that the Gospel is just doing what Jesus charged everyone not to do! Why would the Gospel inform the reader about the miracle when miracles alone are insufficient? There is a connection between what goes on within the Gospel and what goes on between Gospel and reader.

Jesus multiplies bread for the Gentiles—Previously, Jesus had multiplied five loaves and two fish to feed five thousand men, for what was probably a predominantly Jewish audience (Mark 6:35–44) in the area of Tabgha. Now, in Gentile territory, a large crowd gathers to hear His teaching, which satisfies their spiritual hunger. However, these people have been with Jesus for three days, and they are also physically hungry. Jesus has compassion on the hungry people. The scene is familiar but the way in which the situation evolves is totally different from the previously reported multiplication of loaves. The difference is in Jesus taking the initiative.

Mark 6:35	*His disciples came to him and said . . . "send them away"*
Mark 8:1, 3	*He called his disciples to him, and said to them . . . "if I send them away"*

Clueless—Who takes the initiative may seem to be insignificant, but it is all revealing. The disciples may have been unaware of what was coming the first time, but there is no reason they should not know what to expect the second time. First, the disciples had a question and Jesus provided the answer. Now, Jesus has *the same question* and the disciples should therefore know the answer. Especially since they themselves were directly involved in the first occasion—bringing the five loaves, distributing what Jesus had blessed and broken, and collecting the left over pieces. The disciples should know what is coming. If all the disciples can say is, *"How can one feed these men with bread here in the desert?"* (Mark 8:4), the reader might rightly ask, "Who has a problem—the man in the Decapolis, or the disciples?" The unspoken question remains—What would the reader say about Jesus?

Eucharist—Just as before, Jesus asks the disciples to offer to Him what little they have, in this case seven loaves. He then commands the crowd to sit down. Previously, Jesus *looked up to heaven, and blessed, and broke the loaves* (Mark 6:41). Here, the Greek verb *eucharisteō ("gave thanks")* is used (Mark 8:6), from which the word Eucharist derives. Once again, this miracle recalls God providing manna in the desert for Moses and the hungry people. This miracle also anticipates the Last Supper (Mark 14:22), the Blessed Sacrament in the Church, and the Marriage Supper of the Lamb to come in the New Jerusalem (Revelation 19:7–9).

Jesus draws the disciples into the action. He *gave them to his disciples to set before the people; and they set them before the crowd* (Mark 8:6). The disciples are a kind of intermediary between Jesus and the people, but it is evident that Jesus is the one who takes the initiative and who gives. Jesus is the one who has compassion. Sending people away because of shortage would mean sending them away from God's compassion and mercy. Can the disciples fathom the extent of God's compassion in Jesus? Can the reader? After Jesus sent the people away, He immediately got into the boat with his disciples. No reaction to the miracles is reported: but no reaction is also a reaction, and it is not a good one. They come to the district of Dalmanutha, the location of which is uncertain.

Pharisees demand a sign—While Jesus works amazing signs and wonders for Jews and Gentiles alike to see so clearly, some Pharisees continue to antagonize Him. The motivation and belligerence of the Pharisees emerges clearly from the words *to argue* and *to test. The Pharisees came and began to argue with him, seeking from him a sign from heaven, to test him* (Mark 8:11). The bad will of the Pharisees recalls Satan's testing and tempting Jesus in the wilderness (Mark 1:13). Since Jesus has been performing one miracle after another, their demand for a sign can only result from their stubborn, hardhearted refusal to see and believe.

> For those with faith, no sign is necessary.
> For those without faith,
> no sign will ever be enough.

Wrong question—Like the devil tempting Jesus, the Gospel reveals that this demand for a sign is not a sincere search for understanding. Questions may be asked for various reasons, not all of which are good. Some questions betray a hidden agenda. The aim of the Pharisees is *to destroy Him* (Mark 3:6). The Pharisees do not really want Jesus to perform some sort of cosmic spectacle of nature to prove that He is the Messiah. They do not believe Him and have hardened their hearts against Him. If the Gospel unmasks the demand for a sign so clearly, what does that mean for the questions the reader may want to put to God? Humbly considering the awesome character of God, it is never appropriate to put God to the test, or demand that God should act in a certain way, or impose human criteria upon God. God is God, and human beings are His creatures. As Isaiah reasoned: *"Woe to him who strives with his Maker, an earthen vessel with the potter! Does the clay say to him who fashions it, 'What are you making?'"* (Isaiah 45:9). Rather, take a humble stance, *O* Lord, *you are our Father, we are the clay, and you are our potter; we are all the work of your hand* (Isaiah 64:8).

Blatant unbelief—In the Old Testament, people grieve God by demanding signs and wonders, despite the miraculous ways in which God has delivered them from slavery, and provided for all their needs. *And the Lord said to Moses, "How long will this people despise me? And how long will they not believe in me, in spite of all the signs which I have wrought among them?"* (Numbers 14:11). Jesus refuses to acquiesce to the Pharisees and give them the sign that they demand. He walks away from them, and departs in a boat to go to the other side of the lake.

Strictly speaking, the only thing Jesus does on the other shore after the second multiplication of loaves is to *sigh deeply in his spirit* (Mark 8:12). In the Gospel, not-understanding parallels not-believing. The deaf mute and the Pharisees frame the second miraculous multiplication of loaves, in which the disciples manifest that they do not understand. Twice Jesus sighs—both the deaf mute, who is closed-off, and the hypocritical Pharisees shed light for the disciples. What do they really believe? And, by extension, what does the reader really believe?

The way of the Gospel—The Gospel does not just reveal blatant unbelief in order that the reader may cope with it on his or her own. The Gospel reveals how Jesus, in the midst of unbelief and not-understanding, continues on the path His Father has marked out for Him, and how He takes disciples with Him, tirelessly addressing them and instructing them. Jesus sees them and deals with them in a way they do not perceive. It should be a comfort for any reader that God works with humans in ways they cannot fully comprehend themselves, but which are very real nonetheless.

One bread—The apostles continue to relate to Jesus on a material plane, while Jesus tries to elevate them to a level of spiritual understanding; simultaneously the Gospel tries to bring the reader to deeper understand and faith. In the Gospel, God works in and through Jesus increasingly in terms of bread. This began with the miraculous multiplication of loaves and continued when Jesus said that the children's bread should not be given to the dogs, and the Syrophoenician woman replied that dogs do eat the crumbs that fall from the table. Now it continues in the apparently casual remark, *they had forgotten to bring bread; and they had only one loaf with them in the boat* (Mark 8:14). Even if the situation of Jesus together with the disciples in the boat does not remind the reader of the two previous significant crossings of the Sea of Galilee (Mark 4:40–45: 6:45–52), the statement is still illogical. If they had forgotten to bring bread, then they would have no bread at all with them.

Beware of the leaven of the Pharisees and Herod—The Gospel, however, does not just speak physically about the one loaf of bread the disciples have brought with them. This becomes evident when Jesus, remaining within the same word field of bread, warns the disciples of the leaven of the Pharisees and Herod. The leaven of the Pharisees and the leaven of Herod symbolize an evil and wicked influence that could spread and infect the disciples. The way of thinking of the Pharisees and the way of acting of Herod is contagious (and life-threatening for Jesus) as long as the disciples fail to see who Jesus is. The one bread with them in the boat is Jesus, but they do not know Him well enough to recognize how He is going to be their salvation.

Questions to be answered—When there is lack of knowledge, Jesus helps by asking the right questions. His questions make an unmistakable connection between the outer senses (eyes and ears) and the inner sense of the heart. *"Why do you discuss the fact that you have no bread? Do you not yet perceive or understand? Are your hearts hardened? Having eyes do you not see, and having ears do you not hear? And do you not remember? When I broke the five loaves for the five thousand, how many baskets full of broken pieces did you take up? . . . And the seven for the four thousand, how many baskets full of broken pieces did you take up? . . . Do you not yet understand?"* (Mark 8:17–21).

Broken bread—The last two questions are intended to help bring understanding. The disciples know the material answers: twelve and seven baskets. Still they do not understand what Jesus is getting at, and the question remains: *"Do you not yet understand?"* Does the reader understand how these questions should help? The point is not in the correct number but in what is contained in the baskets—pieces of broken bread, crumbs.

After these questions, *bread* is not mentioned again until the disciples find themselves at table with Jesus at the Last Supper. There He will take bread, break it, and identify Himself with the broken bread: *"This is my body"* (Mark 14:22). Jesus will say this in anticipation of what is going to happen the next day in Jerusalem, on Golgotha, where His body will be broken for the salvation of the world—that is how He is Messiah. Until the disciples accept this truth, they are unable to recognize the One Bread who is with them all the time. When Mark writes the Gospel, the question—who Jesus is—cannot be answered apart from the Eucharist.

The questions posed to the apostles prepare them and the reader of the gospel for the next section of the Gospel of Saint Mark, in which they will have to grapple with the concept of Jesus' suffering, dying and rising from the dead. Disciples and readers alike still have a way to go to understand.

1. Where does Jesus go? What territory is this? Mark 7:24

2. Describe the drama below.

Mark 7:24	
Mark 7:25	
Mark 7:26	
Mark 7:27	
Mark 7:28	

* How do you think the woman felt about Jesus' denial of her request?

3. Compare the following verses to explain Mark 7:27.

Matthew 15:24	
Romans 1:16; 9:4–5	
CCC 839	

4. What do you think of the woman's retort to Jesus? Mark 7:28

5. Find some parents for whom Jesus shows compassion.

Matthew 19:13–15
Mark 5:22–43
Mark 9:17–27
Luke 7:11–15

6. How does Jesus response to the woman's clever remark? Mark 7:29

* Recall a time when you used a clever remark to a good end.

7. What was the result of the woman's persistence? Mark 7:30

8. Where is Jesus and what happens in Mark 7:31–32?

** If someone prays over you for healing, would you care about privacy or not?

9. Explain the sequence of events in this narrative. Find seven things Jesus does.

Mark 7:33
Mark 7:33
Mark 7:33
Mark 7:33
Mark 7:34
Mark 7:34
Mark 7:34

10. What happened as a result of Jesus' efforts above? Mark 7:35

11. Why does Jesus uses physical measures and matter to heal people?

Mark 7:33–34
CCC 1151
CCC 1504

* What physical matter is used in the sacraments?

12. What emotion does Jesus display in these passages?

Mark 1:41	
Mark 6:34	
Mark 8:2	

13. Identify some problems in the following verses.

Mark 8:1–2	
Mark 8:3–4	

14. How much do the disciples have to offer? Mark 8:5, 7

15. What can you learn from these passages?

Mark 8:6	
1 Corinthians 11:23–24	
CCC 1328	
CCC 1329	
CCC 1335	

* What do you have to offer to the Lord?

16. How much was left over? What does this signify? Mark 8:8

** What does the Eucharist mean to you?

17. Explain the following passages. Find two verbs to reveal the Pharisees' intent.

Numbers 14:11
Mark 8:11
CCC 548

18. How does Jesus respond to the Pharisees demand for a sign? Mark 8:12–13

19. What can you learn about leaven? Mark 8:15, 1 Corinthians 5:8

20. List the questions that Jesus asks in Mark 8:17–21 and give your answers.

Chapter 10

On the Way
Mark 8:22–9:29

And he asked them, "But who do you say that I am?"
Peter answered him, "You are the Christ."
Mark 8:29

On the Way—The prophet Isaiah foretold: *the eyes of the blind shall be opened, and the ears of the deaf unstopped* (Isaiah 35:5). This prophecy is fulfilled in Jesus who cures the blind and the deaf. Saint Mark—and also other Gospel authors—report these healings. Saint Mark mentions just two of many healings and places them at strategically chosen moments—at the beginning and at the end of Jesus' journey to Jerusalem. First, Jesus heals a blind man in Bethsaida in a special manner (Mark 8:22–26). Later, Jesus gives sight to the blind beggar Bartimaeus as He is leaving Jericho (Mark 10:46–52). These two miracles of Jesus curing blind men serve as bookends to frame Mark's middle narrative of Jesus' ministry.

From the very beginning of the Gospel, Jesus' ministry has been characterized as being *on the way* (Mark 1:2-3). Since the call of the first disciples, Jesus has gone from synagogue to synagogue all over Galilee and even to the surrounding pagan territories. At this point in the Gospel, after crossing the lake with His disciples for the third time, Jesus comes to Bethsaida, and He will proceed on to the northern tip of Palestine from where He will begin His journey towards Jerusalem. Once in Jerusalem, Jesus will stay in the city or its immediate vicinity—the town of Bethany. Other Gospels mention Jesus coming repeatedly to Jerusalem, but Saint Mark emphasizes only this last journey and frames it with two healings of blind men. The phrase *on the way* occurs both in the first and in the last verse of this middle section of the Gospel (Mark 8:27; 10:52).

Do you see anything? The fact that the blind man knows what trees and men look like indicates that he was probably not blind from birth, but suffered blindness through some accident or illness, after having once been sighted. Friends bring the blind man to Jesus and beg for Jesus to touch him.

The cure of the blind man in Bethsaida is quite elaborate and has many similarities with the healing of the deaf mute in Decapolis (Mark 7:31-37). In both healings Jesus uses His spittle. The healing of the deaf mute has a symbolic meaning for the disciples. The symbolism is evident in Jesus sighing here and sighing again with the unbelieving Pharisees. Likewise, *"Do you see anything?"* (Mark 8:23), is virtually the same question Jesus put earlier to his disciples: *"Having eyes do you not see?"* (Mark 8:18). They have not yet answered him. The cure of the blind man in Bethsaida is gradual and symbolizes the way in which the disciples slowly grow in understanding of who Jesus is. In this sense the gradual healing is programmatic.

The symbolic and programmatic value of the gradual healing in Bethsaida is also seen (in hindsight) in its relationship to the second and immediate healing at the end of the journey to Jerusalem. At the beginning of the journey Jesus mentions His suffering, death and Resurrection. But the disciples do not comprehend why He should die. During the journey, the disciples (and readers) are taken aside by Jesus and receive special instruction about what will happen in Jerusalem. At the end, they *see*. This repeated private instruction, away from the crowds, corresponds to the situation of the blind man in Bethsaida whom Jesus *led out of the village* (Mark 8:23). Only twice is instruction not reserved for the disciples—concerning following Christ and about divorce.

Saint Luke explains similarly how difficult it was for the disciples to *see* that Jesus should suffer, die and rise from the dead. At first the disciples on the road to Emmaus did not comprehend it either , and did not *see* Jesus until the end of their journey on which they received special instruction, so that their hearts began to burn within while he talked to them (Luke 24:13–32).

Time and place—Having received no answer from His disciples *"Having eyes do you not see?"* (Mark 8:18) and having healed the blind man gradually, Jesus now sets His face toward Jerusalem. Beginning in the northernmost area of Galilee, in what is now the Golan Heights, they continue through Caesarea Philippi (Mark 8:27), through Galilee (Mark 9:30), and stop for a time in Capernaum (Mark 9:33). They seem to travel through the eastern section of the Jordan valley (Mark 10:1) and by way of Jericho (Mark 10:46), they arrive at the Mount of Olives, and ultimately to the holy city of Jerusalem and the temple (Mark 11:11).

In spite of all the places mentioned, an exact reconstruction of the journey is not possible. Moreover, it is most unlikely that Jesus would have only gone once to Jerusalem. As mentioned, other Gospels report that He went regularly to Jerusalem. These observations on geography indicate that Mark's Gospel is not intended as a diary, and that geography is subordinated to a greater concern—discipleship.

Similar observations can be made on the time-line of the Gospel. The first half unrolls in Galilee and virtually all time references are lacking. During the journey to Jerusalem, some indications of time are given. It is only in Jerusalem (from Mark 11 onwards) that the reader can follow from day to day what happens. Note an astonishing observation— one third of the Gospel (Mark 11–16) takes up only one week, and the last day of the gospel takes up two long chapters (Mark 14–15).

Discipleship—As already mentioned, discipleship in Saint Mark's Gospel surpasses the importance of geography and chronology. Discipleship depends on one factor only— the identity of the Master—on who Jesus is. The identity of Jesus determines what the life of a disciple will look like. The slow movement from the northernmost area of Palestine to Jerusalem in the south is the backdrop for the definite revelation about the identity of Jesus. It all starts with Jesus taking initiative and asking first: *"Who do men say that I am?"*(Mark 8:27) and then: *"But who do __you__ say that I am?"* (Mark 8:29).

Responding for the Twelve, *Peter answered him, "You are the Christ"* (Mark 8:29) and this is traditionally called Peter's "profession of faith." Peter is charged *to tell no one about Him* (Mark 8:30) because although it is certainly true, it is not the full, complete truth. There is a complementary profession of Jesus revealing that He truly is a suffering Messiah (Mark 8:31–32a).

In the structure of the Gospel, Peter's profession of faith is connected with the second healing of a blind man. As Peter professed Jesus to be the Christ (Messiah), so blind Bartimaeus addresses Jesus with a messianic title: *"Son of David"* (Mark 10:47). Unlike Peter, who wanted to stop Jesus and is rebuked, Bartimaeus *sees* clearly immediately. Bartimaeus is the first person ever in the Gospel who is allowed by Jesus to follow Him *on the way*. At the beginning of the journey, Peter is more like the first blind man in Bethsaida—seeing something that is true (Jesus is the Christ), but not seeing clearly the whole truth (Jesus is a suffering Messiah, who will die and rise from the dead for the salvation of the world).

Who is Jesus?

The question *"Who is Jesus?"* resonates through the centuries. Many have responded to this question in a philosophical or academic manner. Intellectual speculation does not lead to a personal relationship with Jesus and commitment, and is not sufficient. C. S. Lewis offered three possibilities for the identity of Jesus, who claimed to be the Son of God. Jesus could be a lunatic, a liar, or the Lord. A man who claims to be God, but is not, would be deluded or insane. A man claiming to be God, knowing that he is not, would be a liar. A man who claims to be God, and is, in fact, God, is the Lord, worthy of all praise and adoration.

Peter's confession of faith (Mark 8:29), even in its incompleteness, marks a turning point, and a pivotal moment, in the Gospel of Mark. For the first time since the opening line of the Gospel—*The beginning of the Gospel of Jesus Christ, the Son of God* (Mark 1:1)—Jesus is called **"Christ."** It will take the entire second half of the Gospel before someone professes, *"Truly this man was the **Son of God!**"* (Mark 15:39). The opening line thus appears to be a programmatic statement and (in hindsight) the entire Gospel is revealed as focused on the true identity of Jesus.

The miracles of the first part of Mark's Gospel all highlighted the identity of Jesus. The last half of the Gospel transitions to difficult teachings about what kind of Christ He is. From this point on, Jesus travels toward Jerusalem. Although the city is not named explicitly, the mention of *elders and chief priests* points to the suffering and humiliation that await Him. While the disciples hoped for a Davidic warrior king to defeat their enemies and deliver them from suffering and oppression, Jesus would teach them about a different type of Messiah. Jesus would be a Suffering Servant, who would willingly embrace the Cross in order to save mankind. This would be a difficult concept for the disciples to grasp and accept.

> **The program**—Three main issues dominate the whole middle section of the gospel:
> 1) Thrice Jesus predicts His suffering, death and Resurrection (Mark 8:31; 9:31; 10:33–34).
> 2) Thrice the disciples respond negatively, either through denial (Mark 8:32) or through unbelief of Jesus' words (Mark 9:31–32; 10:35–37).
> 3) Thrice Jesus teaches His disciples what it means to follow Him as a disciple (Mark 8:33–9:1; 9:35–50; 10:38–45).

The journey is structured in three sections, each of which is characterized by a certain unity of location. In Mark 8:27–9:1 and 10:32–45 no change of location is mentioned, although they are on the move. In Mark 9:30–32, 33–50, there is a change from *way* to *house,* allowing the reader to recognize the following layout:

Mark 8:27–30	Peter's profession—(seeing something, but not well)	
	Mark 8:31–32a	Prediction—Jesus' profession
	Mark 8:32b	Not understanding—no commitment
	Mark 8:33–9:1	Instruction on discipleship
Mark 9:2–29	"On and around a high mountain"	
	Mark 9:30–31	Prediction—Jesus predicts suffering
	Mark 9:32–34	Not understanding—no commitment
	Mark 9:35–50	Instruction on discipleship
Mark 10:1–31	"In Judea and beyond the Jordan"	
	Mark 10:32–34	Prediction—Jesus predicts suffering
	Mark 10:35–37	Not understanding—no commitment
	Mark 10:38–45	Instruction on discipleship
Mark 10:46–52	Jesus heals Bartimaeus—(seeing clearly immediately)	

Jesus foretells His Passion—Previously, there have been subtle and veiled suggestions of Jesus' Passion, as Jesus mentioned the days *when the bridegroom is taken away from them* (Mark 2:20), as the Pharisees sought to destroy Him (Mark 3:6), and at the death of John the Baptist (Mark 6:14–29). The disciples would not know that the fate of John the Baptist, the forerunner of Jesus, would become the fate of the Messiah as well. From this point on, Jesus will speak plainly, not in veiled language, about His impending suffering and death. Now, more than ever, it is important for the disciples to *listen* (Mark 4:3.9). *And he said this plainly* (Mark 8:32). The word translated as *plainly,* literally means "saying all." Jesus complements what Peter did not yet see and did not profess.

The mystery of suffering was perhaps more difficult for the disciples of Jesus to understand than it is for readers of the Gospel today. You know how the story ends. You know that

Easter Sunday follows Good Friday. The apostles did not know this. The disciples did not understand the concept of redemptive suffering. They expected that God would bless good people, and punish the wicked ones. They were not prepared to see an innocent Man suffer the most humiliating and violent death imaginable for the sins of others.

The proper place—The first time that Jesus speaks clearly about the suffering to come, Peter cannot handle it and begins to rebuke Jesus. A good disciple follows Jesus. Peter moves out of his position of following behind Jesus, and tries to take the lead, and "give Jesus advice," but in fact, he tries to stop Jesus from following His course. Blocking Jesus is something that Satan attempts to do. What Peter does is therefore not a gentle correction, but something Jesus does to unclean spirits (Mark 1:25; 3:12). Peter maneuvers himself to the side of the adversary of God: it seems as if he wants to cast a spirit out of Jesus! Peter handles the *word* spoken by Jesus in the same way Satan would treat the word sown by the divine sower (Mark 4:15). This explains why Jesus gives Peter the sharpest rebuke imaginable, *"Get behind me, Satan! For you are not on the side of God, but of men"* (Mark 8:33).

For a disciple, Peter's reaction is unacceptable, but by no means rare; even after years of faithful discipleship it can still crop up. How many Christians have tried to *tell* God how to arrange matters, or taken matters into their own hands, instead of waiting on Him? Like any disciple, Peter must learn to follow Jesus. He must learn to think of the things of God, and not steer blindly on his spontaneous human perception. Jesus tells Peter to get back behind Him, where he belongs. The words with which Jesus calls Peter back in line recall the same words with which He first called him as a disciple: *"Follow me. [Come behind me]"* (Mark 1:17).

The cost—Jesus turns to all of them and clearly explains the cost of discipleship. *"If any man would come after me, let him deny himself and take up his cross and follow me"* (Mark 8:34). As before (Mark 3:3, 23), Jesus uses rhetorical questions that are evident for all who want to see: *"What does it profit a man to gain the whole world and forfeit his life? For what can a man give in return for his life?* (Mark 8:36–37). Jesus outlines three clear steps to discipleship:
1) Follow after Jesus.
2) Deny yourself, which will result in the discovery of your genuine self and everlasting worth as a child of God.
3) Take up the crosses that you encounter in life: betrayal, illness, financial troubles, relationship problems, loneliness, discouragement, exhaustion, or whatever else may come your way.

The Gospel is not neutral and puts a challenge to any reader about his or her relationship to Jesus: whether one accepts or is ashamed of Jesus and of His words. Reading superficially is also a way of answering. The Gospel has the inevitable effect of creating a division between people according to how they read and respond. The people in Mark's time were suffering for their faith. They would have known what it meant to take up one's cross for an eternal hope.

The Transfiguration—Peter, James, and John, who witnessed the resurrection of Jairus' daughter (Mark 5:37), again enjoy a rare privilege. Jesus leads them up a high mountain. Other Gospel authors identify the place as Mount Tabor. And this time, Peter seems to have the good sense to follow. On the mountaintop, the divine glory of Jesus is manifested before them. Saint Mark has a hard time describing what no eye has seen before and has found a roundabout way of describing what happened to the clothes: they are intensely shiny and white *as no fuller on earth could bleach them* (Mark 9:3), showing that God is at work on the mountaintop.

Moses and Elijah appear, representing the Law and the Prophets. Both Moses and Elijah received a special revelation on a mountaintop (Exodus 20; 1 Kings 19); Moses represents the giving of the Law, which sealed the covenant, and Elijah represents the prophetic zeal to call the people back to faithfulness to this covenant. The presence of both Moses and Elijah means that a great revelation is about to take place. They speak with Jesus but no words are reported. Since both Moses and Elijah have given their lives in the service of God, it is likely that they speak of the zeal that will consume Jesus. Saint Luke mentions that they *spoke of his exodus, which he was to accomplish at Jerusalem* (Luke 9:31), meaning His death.

Not knowing what to say—Once again, Peter puts his foot in his mouth. In suggesting three booths, he assigns Jesus parallel status with Moses and Elijah. Saint Mark forewarns the reader that this makes no sense, thereby helping the reader not to make the same mistake. The mistake is a common human reaction when God takes over the initiative. People try to divert the attention to what they can oversee and manage, and to where they can be in control. When God is at work and leaves one in doubt as to what to say, it is often wise to keep silent and to listen.

Listen to him—The first speech on the mountaintop is not reported. The second makes no sense, and so all emphasis falls on the third speech, in which God reveals to the disciples what the reader has known since the prologue—that Jesus is the Son of God. The words that Jesus heard during the baptism in the river Jordan are now audible for the disciples. There can no longer be any doubt in the minds of Peter, James, and John concerning the identity of Jesus. God the Father has revealed clearly that Jesus is the beloved Son of God. For the reader, not all is repetition, some words are added: *"Listen to Him"* (Mark 9:7), giving an explicit divine approval to the words of Jesus. His last words concern His going to Jerusalem to suffer, die and rise from the death. Will they listen this time? Will the reader listen?

Coming down—On the way down, the disciples are charged not to speak of what they witnessed, *until the Son of man should have risen from the dead* (Mark 9:9). Jesus repeats and emphasizes what He said in order to complement the profession of faith by Peter. They now have the opportunity to put into practice what God the Father told them—to listen to Jesus. Will they listen this time? They do not speak to others about Jesus' words concerning His death and Resurrection, but they question among themselves. What they really think becomes evident in what they say to Jesus. They ask a very suggestive question concerning the return of Elijah, of whom the Scriptures report was taken up to heaven without dying (2 Kings 2). They subtly suggest that Jesus should do as Elijah did—go away (if He must), but without suffering and dying, and then come back, as Elijah will do. They still have not listened and accepted what Jesus professed about the kind of Messiah He is! Jesus forces them to stay with His words by quoting Scripture about the suffering of the Son of Man, and by clarifying that Elijah did already come back in John the Baptist, whose death was foreseen by Scripture.

God allows Christians to enjoy some mountaintop experiences. An experience of the Eucharist, an ordination, a wedding, the birth of a child, or a retreat can provide a mountaintop experience of joy and intimacy with God. But then God calls the believer to come back down into the valley of everyday life. The challenge is to be as faithful to God in the valleys as on the mountaintops.

A mute spirit—When Jesus descends from the mountain, a crowd gathers, and the disciples and scribes are arguing. The father of a sick boy approaches Jesus and a dialogue ensues. A parent's worst nightmare is seeing his child suffer, and being powerless to help. The son's symptoms seem quite similar to the medical condition of epilepsy. Demonic possession can manifest itself through physical symptoms, mental torment, and self-abuse. Two facts are curious: the father ascribes the condition of his son to a *"mute spirit,"* but there is nothing in the description of the symptoms to warrant such a diagnosis. Also curious is the fact that the disciples are unable to help. This is truly remarkable, since the disciples have been sent out before and have successfully healed the sick and cast out demons (Mark 6:13).

An unclean spirit—Jesus shows some impatience with the situation, and exclaims: *"O faithless generation"* (Mark 9:19). The exasperation of Jesus is probably provoked by the presence of the scribes who have earlier falsely accused Jesus of driving out demons by being possessed Himself (Mark 3:22). Jesus tells the father to bring his son. And as soon as the spirit sees Jesus, the boy begins to manifest symptoms. The dialogue between the father and Jesus transitions from a recounting of the symptoms to questions of faith. The father pleads with Jesus for pity *"if you can do anything"* (Mark 9:22). The reader knows that Jesus was moved with pity when a leper acknowledged that Jesus can do these things (Mark 1:41). The father's doubt is justifiable since the disciples were unable to do anything. When Jesus challenges the man's depth of faith, he immediately says: *"I believe, help my unbelief"* (Mark 9:24). How good it would be if the disciples could say something like this! In response to the father's faith, Jesus rebukes the unclean spirit.

A mute and deaf spirit—The pivotal moment in the scene comes when Jesus addresses the unclean spirit as *"mute and deaf spirit"* (Mark 9:25). This marks the third naming of an unclean spirit and strongly recalls the situation of the deaf mute in Decapolis (Mark 7:31–37). This deaf mute symbolized unbelief, and his healing, together with the unbelief of the Pharisees (Mark 8:11–13), framed the disciples who should have known better (Mark 8:1–10). Saint Mark reports the exorcism in such a way that the reader can begin to suspect something about the situation of the disciples—they are following Jesus to Jerusalem, where He will suffer and die, but they are not yet ready to accept the kind of Messiah Jesus professes to be. Who is really deaf to what Jesus has been saying? And who is really mute when it comes to acknowledging the words of Jesus about Himself as a suffering Messiah? Even after God Himself admonished the disciples to listen to His beloved Son, they still have not gotten around to doing so! The exorcism is narrated in such a way that the life and death of Jesus can be intuited. The boy appears to be dead, but Jesus takes the boy by the hand and raises him up, prefiguring what will come to pass in Jerusalem.

Prayer and fasting—When the disciples are alone with Jesus in the house, they ask Him privately why they could not exorcize the evil spirit. *And he said to them, "This kind cannot be driven out by anything but prayer and fasting"* (Mark 9:29). Ministry is not magic. In order to do the works of God, the disciples must learn to be in communion with Jesus, to receive power from Him. Prayer is to fold one's hands and to invite God to work. Fasting is praying with the body: not seeking one's strength from food, but from the Lord.

You are the Christ!

Simon's confession takes place at a crucial moment in Jesus' life when, after preaching in Galilee, he resolutely set out for Jerusalem in order to bring his saving mission to completion with his death on the Cross and his Resurrection . . .

There are two ways of "seeing" and "knowing" Jesus: one—that of the crowd—is more superficial; the other—that of the disciples—more penetrating and genuine. With his twofold question: "What do the people say?" and "who do you say that I am?" Jesus invited the disciples to become aware of this different perspective.

The people thought that Jesus was a prophet. This was not wrong, but it does not suffice; it is inadequate. In fact, it was a matter of delving deep, of recognizing the uniqueness of the person of Jesus of Nazareth and his newness.

This is how it still is today: many people draw near to Jesus, as it were, from the outside. Great scholars recognize his spiritual and moral stature and his influence on human history, comparing him to Buddha, Confucius, Socrates and other wise and important historical figures. Yet they do not manage to recognize him in his uniqueness . . .

Jesus is often also considered as one of the great founders of a religion from which everyone may take something in order to form his or her own conviction. Today too, "people" have different opinions about Jesus, just as they did then. And as he did then, Jesus also repeats his question to us, his disciples today: "And who do you say that I am?" Let us make Peter's answer our own. According to the Gospel of Mark he said: *"You are the Christ"* (Mark 8:29).

. . . In the Synoptic Gospels Peter's confession is always followed by Jesus' announcement of his imminent Passion. Peter reacted to this announcement because he was not yet able to understand. Nonetheless, this was a fundamental element on which Jesus strongly insisted. Indeed, the title attributed to him by Peter—you are "the Christ," "the Christ of God," "the Son of the living God"—can only be properly understood in light of the mystery of his death and Resurrection.

And the opposite is also true: the event of the Cross reveals its full meaning only if "this man" who suffered and died on the Cross "truly was the Son of God," to use the words uttered by the centurion as he stood before the Crucified Christ (Mark 15:39). These texts clearly say that the integrity of the Christian faith stems from the confession of Peter illumined by the teaching of Jesus on his "way" toward glory, that is, on his absolutely unique way, being the Messiah and the Son of God. It was a narrow "way," a shocking "manner" for the disciples of every age, who are inevitably led to think according to men rather than according to God.

Today too, as in Jesus' day, it does not suffice to possess the proper confession of faith: it is always necessary to learn anew from the Lord the actual way in which he is Savior and the path on which we must follow him. Indeed, we have to recognize that even for believers, the Cross is always hard to accept.

Instinct impels one to avoid it and the tempter leads one to believe that it is wiser to be concerned with saving oneself rather than losing one's life through faithfulness to love, faithfulness to the Son of God made man. Who do you say I am? What was it that the people to whom Jesus was speaking found hard to accept? What continues to be hard for many people also in our time?

It is difficult to accept that he claimed not only to be one of the prophets but the Son of God, and he claimed God's own authority for himself.

Listening to him preaching, seeing him heal the sick, evangelize the lowly and the poor and reconcile sinners, little by little the disciples came to realize that he was the Messiah in the most exalted sense of the word, that is, not only a man sent by God, but God himself made man.

. . . In Peter's profession of faith, dear brothers and sisters, we can feel that we are all one, despite the divisions that have wounded the Church's unity down the centuries and whose consequences are still being felt . . .

May the Holy Mother of God always guide us and accompany us with her intercession: may her unswerving faith, which sustained the faith of Peter and of the other Apostles, continue to sustain that of the Christian generations, our own faith: *Queen of Apostles, pray for us!* Amen.

Pope Benedict XVI, *Homily,* June 29, 2007

1. Explain the miracle in Mark 8:22–25.

2. What is the significance of Jesus' touching people?

CCC 699
CCC 1504–1505

3. Why is the significance of Jesus healing the blind man in stages? Mark 8:25

4. What did Jesus' humanity gain from his question in Mark 8:27? CCC 472

5. Who answered Jesus' question? How did he answer it?

Matthew 16:16
Mark 8:29
Luke 9:20
John 6:68–69

6. What can you learn from the following passages?

Mark 8:31
Mark 9:30–31
Mark 10:32–34
CCC 557
CCC 572
CCC 649

* How would you answer Jesus' question—*"Who do you say that I am?"*

7. What three things must a disciple of Jesus do? Mark 8:34

** What evidence do you look for in a disciple of Jesus?

8. Why would someone follow Jesus? Mark 8:35–38

9. In your own words, explain what happened in Mark 9:2–8.

*** Have you ever had a mountaintop experience with God?

10. What is the significance of Peter answering Jesus and being here? CCC 552

11. What is the significance of the Transfiguration? CCC 554–556

12. Explain the Most Holy Trinity. Mark 9:7–8, CCC 233–234

13. Compare and contrast these two events in the life of Jesus. Mark 1:9–11; 9:2–8

14. Explain the situation in Mark 9:14–27.

15. Are demons real? Mark 1:32–34; 9:38

16. What can you learn about demons? CCC 391, 1707, 2851

17. When and how does the Church first deal with sin and the devil? CCC 1237

18. How does the Catholic Church deal with demonic possession? CCC 1673

19. How can you deal with the devil in your own life? James 4:6–8

20. What can you say to someone who says: "the Trinity is not in the Bible"?

Chapter 11

The Way of the Disciple
Mark 9:30–10:27

They were exceedingly astonished, and said to him: "Then who can be saved?"
Jesus looked at them and said,
With men it is impossible, but not with God;
for all things are possible with God."
Mark 10:26-27

Speechless—Saint Mark used Jesus' deliverance of the young boy from evil spirits to interweave in the Gospel an instruction on listening and responding to Jesus' announcement of His death and Resurrection. Jesus and the disciples now continue on their way, passing through Galilee. And Jesus, for the second time, foretells His impending death and Resurrection (Mark 9:31–32). *"They did not understand the saying, and they were afraid to ask him"* (Mark 9:32). This is not much better than trying to go against Jesus as Peter did, and from trying to go around Jesus as the three apostles did when descending the mountain.

On the way to Capernaum, Jesus knows that the disciples are talking with one another. They do not speak with Him, but when they stop in a house in Capernaum, Jesus takes the initiative and questions them about what they were discussing. *But they were silent; for on the way they had discussed with one another who was the greatest* (Mark 9:34). The contrast between Jesus' profession that He must suffer and die with the apostles' desire for personal greatness is very stark. A new occasion for instruction arises.

More than an example—Sitting down signifies that Jesus is a teacher about to impart instruction to His disciples (Mark 4:1–2); by the same token it means that the Gospel is imparting instruction to the reader. As a good teacher uses the right didactical means, so Jesus knows how to drive His point home by adducing the right visual example. He puts a child in their midst, embraces him and says: *"Whoever receives one such child in my name receives me"* (Mark 9:37). In fact, Jesus identifies Himself with *"one such child,"* which must mean that the child is really much more than an example—something of Jesus Himself is seen in that child. Jesus' words and His gesture are aimed at the difficulty that the disciples have in understanding and accepting what kind of Messiah Jesus is. The reader too is invited to understand and accept the consequences of this teaching, and to ponder what it means that Jesus identifies Himself with a small child.

The teaching of Jesus is based on the essential condition of any child. To be a child is a relative condition—being a child has in itself nothing to do with age but everything with having parents. Any person is a child to his parents, irrespective of age. Being a child is having a relationship. The disciples discussed "who is the greatest?" Jesus applies and deepens their question: "Who is greater, a child or the parents?" In the natural sense the parents are obviously the greater, but precisely because they are greater, they (should) provide food, shelter, security, warmth and love. In fact, in order to do all this, parents often must deny themselves! So who really is the servant? In the human condition of this world it is understood that the parents, who are greater, are serving their children.

A Father's love—Jesus elevates what is normal on the natural level to the supernatural level by inserting Himself into the equation. On the mountain the disciples have heard the voice of His Father and therefore know that Jesus too is a child, the beloved Son. Jesus recalls this revelation for His disciples and shows them the real meaning of it. When it comes to answering the question "who is the greatest" in their company, it is evident that Jesus is the greatest. And just as for human parents to be the greatest really means to serve the small ones, so for Jesus, being the greatest naturally means that He serves them! His service, though, surpasses any service rendered by human parents—He will save them and give them access to eternal life. Jesus explicitly links Himself to the One who sent Him (Mark 9:37). Being the beloved Son, His service models His Father: Jesus has that love of the heavenly Father that makes it evident for Him that He must deny Himself. He **must** go to Jerusalem, suffer, die and rise from the dead!

Servanthood—The disciples and readers are invited to ponder their situation. Ultimately, God is the greatest and, in what really matters, all people are as helpless as children. No one can save himself, and no one has a right to demand salvation (Mark 8:36-37). Each individual must acknowledge his sinfulness and powerlessness and accept God's gift of redemption through the death and Resurrection of Jesus. What goes for Jesus also goes for His disciples. Discipleship entails this divine kind of servanthood: serving everyone, the weak, the sick, and the poor. The reader is reminded of the new type of community that Jesus began: *"Whoever does the will of God is my brother, and sister, and mother"* (Mark 3:35). The Christian community welcomes the rich and the poor, the young and the old. The Catholic Church announces: "Here comes everybody." There is no place for exclusivity, competitiveness, or pride in the Church.

Application—The teaching of Jesus is made more concrete by its application. Jesus spoke of receiving "one such child *in my name*" (Mark 9:37). John, one of the disciples, who was with Jesus on the mountain, addresses Jesus as "Teacher" and brings up the meaning of *in my name*. They were unable to cast out the demon from the sick boy, but they saw a man casting out demons *in your name*. John reports that they forbade him because he was *not following us*. The disciples freely make use of *us*, meaning—*us and Jesus*. This is correct up to a point. Jesus Himself has drawn them into the new family of God, but they should never forget that the order is really reversed: *Jesus and us*. In the new family of God Jesus takes the lead and the disciples follow Him. This is what Jesus' reply means: He first speaks of *in my name* and of *Me*, and only then there can be *us*. Jesus is always the point of reference in the Christian community, in the Church, that consists of the ones bearing *the name of Christ*. The consequence of this constitution of the Christian community is that when the way of Jesus entails suffering, so the way of the disciple will also involve suffering. Jesus foretells this situation of the Church by mentioning *a cup of water* given to them by whomever.

Consequences—The kind of Messiah Jesus is, is so important for the disciples to understand that Jesus explains the consequence of failure to understand and apply His teaching: *"Whoever causes one of these little ones who believe in me to sin, it would be better for him if a great millstone were hung round his neck and he were thrown into the sea"* (Mark 9:42). Jesus speaks of the scandal that arises when someone who professes to be His follower is in fact not following Him and thereby misleading and giving a false signal. The self-evident definition of being a disciple has a double consequence—with regard to others and with regard to oneself.

With triple hyperbole—an exaggeration or overstatement, Jesus spells out the consequences of such scandalous behavior for oneself:

Mark 9:43   *if your hand causes you to sin, cut it off;*
            it is better for you to enter life maimed . . .
Mark 9:45   *if your foot causes you to sin, cut if off;*
            it is better for you to enter life lame . . .
Mark 9:47   *if your eye causes you to sin, pluck it out;*
            it is better for you to enter the kingdom of God with one eye.

If Christians took these words literally, perhaps the whole world would be tongueless, handless, and maimed. The point Jesus makes is that the scandal of *appearing to be* a disciple but *not being* one must be eradicated. Just as disciples should not mislead others, so *they should not mislead themselves*—they should not divide up their lives in compartments and continue to sin in one area as if nothing were wrong. In other words, every reader should get serious about removing temptations to sin. For instance: if the problem is pornography, you may need to throw out your computer, or move it to a common area of the house. If gossip is a problem, you may need to restrict your use of the phone. If alcohol presents a problem, you need to stay out of the bars and the liquor stores.

Have salt in yourselves, and be at peace with one another (Mark 9:50)—Salt is a purifying agent, as well as a preservative, and a seasoning. Jesus takes discipleship very seriously. He mentions *hell* three times in Mark 9:43–47, explaining that hell is a place to avoid at all costs. He does not want us to enter there: if we do enter, it will be our choice and we will have to go over His dead body! These Gospel teachings of Jesus could be the necessary inducement for any reader who desires to be a disciple to reconsider his or her way of life. One way to deal with the problem of sin and evil is to identify sin patterns. While avoiding near occasions of sin, a disciple should also try to develop the opposite virtues. For example, if greed or materialism is a problem, one should try to develop the opposite virtue of generosity. Instead of shopping and buying more than what is needed, take that money and give it to the poor. If pride is a temptation, seek out a humble service. If gluttony is a besetting sin, embrace fasting, go on a diet, or give food away to the hungry. If lying is the problem, be vigilant in always speaking the truth. One of the best ways to make progress in discipleship is to find someone to hold you accountable: two persons see more than one, and no one has a complete view of him or herself. Habitual sins will not disappear immediately, but require strong measures and God's grace to overcome.

Testing Jesus—As Jesus continues on His way, through the region of Judea and beyond the Jordan, crowds gather and He teaches as usual. The Pharisees, who from the beginning refused to believe (Mark 2:1–3:6), also try to challenge Jesus. Seeking to entrap Jesus and get Him into trouble with Herod, they question Jesus on the acceptability of divorce. They know that Herod Antipas has divorced his wife, and Herodias has divorced her husband, the brother of Herod, so that Herod and Herodias can be together. John the Baptist had already denounced this sinful relationship (Mark 6:18). For this criticism, John the Baptist was imprisoned and then beheaded. Perhaps the Pharisees plan the same fate to befall Jesus.

Scripture explained by Scripture—The painful and complex situation of divorce prompted debates in the Jewish community, which continue to the present day. Divorce causes immense suffering, even beyond the couple to their children and others. The Pharisees use this situation for their own purpose and ask *"Is it lawful for a man to divorce his wife?"* (Mark 10:2). Jesus sees through their scheme. Their concern for God's law is insincere; it is, in fact, a badly concealed hardness of heart, which is far from God (see Mark 7:5–6). Jesus refuses to enter into the snare. Instead, like a wise teacher, Jesus asks a question in order to improve their question: *"What did Moses command you?"* (Mark 10:3). Sometimes people get the wrong answers because they ask the wrong questions. By using Scripture as a commentary on Scripture Jesus shifts the focus of the discussion from *what is permissible,* to *what is God's plan and perfect will.*

Discipleship in marriage—At the core of Jesus' reply to the Pharisees is a radical return to God's original plan for marriage. *God created man in his own image ... male and female he created them* (Genesis 1:27). For God, man and woman are equal and the inequality implied by the letter of divorce, of which Moses spoke in Deuteronomy, is a concession to the human hardness of heart. Jesus restores the original equality. God intends one man and one woman to leave their parents, and cleave to one another until death. Jesus is well aware that weak and sinful human beings will marry, and find it difficult to fulfill God's perfect plan. Jesus teaches that the way marked out by God for Him, also applies to disciples in marriage: they should be guided by God's plan, not by their own plan (Mark 8:34). Jesus' teaching about denying one's self, taking up a cross, and serving others, finds a new application here. God's grace is available to those who freely choose to enter into this most intimate of human relationships.

Jesus blesses the little children—A logical progression from the teaching about marriage moves to the consideration of the fruit of marital love—children. The only time in Mark's Gospel that Jesus becomes indignant appears here. People want to bring their children to Jesus for a blessing, or healing, or affection. Not unlike modern culture, many people find children to be a nuisance and an inconvenience in their lives. The apostles do not seem to hinder others from coming to Jesus, not even ritually unclean or violent persons (Mark 5:1–13), but they hinder the children. Jesus is indignant with them. *"Let the children come to me, do not hinder them; for to such belongs the kingdom of God. Truly, I say to you, whoever does not receive the kingdom of God like a child shall not enter it"* (Mark 10:14–15).

Children are models of helplessness and receptivity. They simply accept what adults offer to them. Children cannot provide for their own shelter or nourishment. Rather they accept the food and comfort provided. And they cannot reciprocate. Similarly, salvation and entrance into the kingdom of God can only be received. People can accept God's love, the forgiveness of sins, and the offer of eternal life. They cannot earn or achieve it any other way. When Jesus holds the children, He provides an illustration of how God the Father relates to the sons and daughters He has created. The early Church used this example of Jesus inviting the little children to come to Him, along with the example of Peter baptizing the entire household of Cornelius (Acts 10) including children and servants, as a basis for the practice of infant baptism, which continues in the Catholic Church today.

Only God is good—A rich man approaches Jesus: *"Good Teacher, what must I do to inherit eternal life?"* (Mark 10:17). It is remarkable that the rich man addresses Jesus as *Good teacher*; it implies that he is willing to learn from Jesus, which at this point is something the disciples are still struggling with. When Jesus answers: *"Why do you call me good? No one is good but God alone"* (Mark 10:18), this does not mean that Jesus is not good; instead it means that the man needs to learn more about real goodness. Here too, as always, the first reply of Jesus is to refer back to God the Father, the source of all that is good. With His first response Jesus invites the rich man to focus his mind and heart on God; only in this openness for God will the true but relative goodness of everything else be seen.

After Jesus recalls the commandments, the rich man makes an astonishing claim. Addressing Jesus this time as *Teacher,* showing that he learned the first lesson, he claims to have obeyed all the commandments from his youth! Although he is obviously not perfect, there is no reason to doubt the man's sincerity; he is serious about doing good with his life. He has been practicing the commandments since his youth and is honest enough to acknowledge that something is lacking, that keeps him from attaining the kingdom of God (which is a synonym for eternal life). He asks the right question: he has the ultimate goal in mind and is asking for directions. The disciples have yet to do that. The reader is invited to make a decision whether this question could also be his or her personal question. The answer that Jesus will give has to be understood in the light of this question.

A special look—The incredible but serious claim brings the man a loving gaze from Jesus. Jesus has a special way of looking at people, which is often noted in the Gospel. Jesus sees people and He sees through them: they do not need to hope for His understanding, for He knows them (John 2:25). He knows their faith and heart (Mark 2:5, 8); He sees as God sees (1 Samuel 16:7). He sees in some the capacity to become disciples (Mark 2:13). In people who do the will of God He sees his brother, sister and mother (Mark 3:34). Loving the rich man, Jesus points out his weakness and invites him to follow. *"You lack one thing; go, sell what you have, and give to the poor, and you will have treasure in heaven; and come, follow me"* (Mark 10:21). Jesus identifies the man's attachment to wealth, but promises him the treasures of heaven and offers him the privilege of becoming a disciple.

Delight in riches—Wealth itself is not the man's problem but his inordinate attachment to possessions. *For the love of money is the root of all evils; it is through this craving that some have wandered away from the faith and pierced their hearts with many pangs* (1 Timothy 6:10). From the beginning there have been rich disciples. Saint Mark notes that women followed Jesus from Galilee to Jerusalem even unto Golgotha, providing for Him and His disciples from their own means (Mark 15:41). They were rich, but attached to Jesus rather than to their money. Explaining the parable of the sower Jesus indicated that riches can hinder a person to listen to God and respond well: *"They are those who hear the word, but the cares of the world, and the delight in riches, and the desire for other things, enter in and choke the word"* (Mark 4:18-19). If not wealth but an inordinate attachment hinders a person to inherit eternal life, then the reader is invited to think not only of possessions, but also of other inappropriate attachments—to work, hobbies, other persons, and so on. More precisely, the one thing necessary is to be first of all attached to God (Matthew 6:33; Luke 10:42), *for where your treasure is, there will your heart be also"* (Matthew 6:21).

The right question—The rich man goes away sad, but it is not over yet. *Jesus looked around.* The disciples have witnessed all and their instruction now continues. Jesus surprises them by explaining the difficulty for those who trust in riches to enter the kingdom of God. Like many people, the disciples believe that the rich are those who are blessed and favored by God. They are amazed, for they have not considered the difference between being rich and trusting in riches.

Jesus now addresses them as *children*, reminding them of what He said earlier about the kingdom of God in connection with children: *"To such belongs the kingdom of God. Truly, I say to you, whoever does not receive the kingdom of God like a child shall not enter it"* (Mark 10:14-15). In order to drive His point home Jesus makes a comparison—a camel, the largest animal in Palestine, passing through the eye of a needle, the tiniest hole imaginable. The disciples know this is impossible and are astonished. As He looked lovingly at the rich man and at His disciples before, so Jesus now looks at them again. He *helped* them reach an obvious conclusion and now they ask the correct question: *"Then who can be saved?"* (Mark 10:26). Only with God are all things possible.

Nothing compares with God—God is good; wealth is good too, but the goodness of riches is not absolute. As soon as wealth competes with God, then what needs to be kept in mind are the words Jesus said the moment He laid eyes on the rich man: "God alone is good." If one trusts in wealth *more* than in God, then attachments to material possession become a hindrance. Riches choke the divine word, and the life of the person remains fruitless (Mark 4:18). Jesus has shaken His disciples and forces them to think outside their box, to think as He thinks: *"With men it is impossible, but not with God; for all things are possible with God"* (Mark 10:27). For Jesus this is not just theory: at Gethsemane He will face death with precisely these words, *"Abba, Father, all things are possible to you; . . . yet not what I will, but what you will"* (Mark 14:36). A rich man cannot buy his way into heaven, nor can he enter if he loves material possessions more than God. But the good news is, with God even a rich man can enter the kingdom.

Peter insists that the apostles have given up everything to follow Jesus. And Jesus assures him that those who have given up everything for His sake and for the Gospel will receive a hundredfold in this time, and in the age to come eternal life. Jesus adds something to houses, relatives and lands—*with persecutions.* Some people promote a prosperity gospel, promising riches and blessings in following Christ. But they ignore the part about suffering and persecution.

---

1. What did Jesus foretell in Mark 9:30–31?

2. How did the disciples react to this information? Mark 9:32?

3. What were the disciples discussing on the way to Capernaum? Mark 9:33–34

4. How would you describe their behavior after the news of Mark 9:31?

* How would you respond to the news that Jesus would die for your sins?

5. How does Jesus define true greatness? Mark 9:35–37

** What practical measures could you take to be a servant?

6. Explain the scenario in Mark 9:38–41.

*** What lesson can you apply from the above passage to your own life?

7. What warning does Jesus give in Mark 9:42–47?

8. Is hell real? Mark 9:43–47

**** How many times does Jesus mention hell in Mark 9:43–47?

9. Describe hell.

Isaiah 66:24
Mark 9:48
Revelation 20:9–15

10. How can you deal with sin and temptation? 1 Corinthians 10:13

* Identify a recurrent sin in your life and find an opposite virtue to counter it.

11. Explain the scene in Mark 10:1–9.

12. What can you learn about marriage? Whose idea was it?

Genesis 1:27–28
Genesis 2:24
CCC 1601–1602
CCC 1603–1605

13. What do Jesus and the Catholic Church say about divorce?

Mark 10:7–9
CCC 1640

14. What does a married couple need to strengthen their unity? CCC 1641–1642

* Think of a couple in a difficult marriage and commit to pray for them.

** Find a divorced person to pray for, encourage or help in some practical way.

15. What can you learn from these passages?

Mark 10:14
CCC 1244
CCC 1261

*** How does your parish welcome children?

16. What three things did Jesus do physically in Mark 10:16?

* What special opportunities are offered to bring children to Christ?

** Find a way to help or encourage a couple with young children this week.

*** Does your Bible Study offer a Children's Program and babysitting?

17. Explain the drama in Mark 10:17–22.

17b. What did the rich man insist? Mark 10:20

**** How reasonable is it to obey everything? Name some sins of omission.

18. What can you learn about money from these passages?

Ecclesiastes 5:10
Sirach 5:1; 31:5–7
1 Timothy 6:10
Hebrews 13:5

19. Find an anecdote to greed and materialism.

Sirach 35:4–11
Malachi 3:10
CCC 2443

20. What can you learn about salvation from these passages?

Mark 10:26–30
Acts 2:38; 3:19
CCC 1257
CCC 1260

* Compare Mark 10:29 and Mark 10:30, and identify one difference in the lists.

CHAPTER 12

Questions and Answers
Mark 10:1–52

"You know that those who are supposed to rule
over the Gentiles lord it over them,
and their great men exercise authority over them.
But it shall not be so among you;
but whoever would be great among you must be your servant,
and whoever would be first among you must be slave of all.
For the Son of man also came not to be served but to serve,
and to give his life as a ransom for many."
Mark 10:42–45

Backtracking into Mark 10, reflect and ponder more deeply how Jesus answers some very challenging questions, and how they apply to the world and your life today. The discussion of these questions precedes the third instance of Jesus foretelling His Passion and death and the healing of blind Bartimaeus.

The Pharisees ask *"Is it lawful for a man to divorce his wife?"* (Mark 10:2). Are the Pharisees really interested in the institution of marriage? Do the Pharisees actually want to better interpret the law? Or, are they interested in creating a stumbling block? Jesus uses their ploy to entrap Him as an opportunity to give a catechesis on marriage, and diverts the discussion to God's original plan. As marriage goes, so the society goes. Strong marriages make a strong society.

Jesus begins the discussion with a reflection of God's original plan, described in Genesis 1–2, and then goes on to acknowledge the accommodation that Moses made in allowing divorce, due to the hardness of a man's heart. Hardness of heart occurs in the Old Testament when God's people stubbornly refuse to follow God's commands (1 Samuel 6:6; Job 9:4; Psalm 95:8). *"When a man takes a wife and marries her, if then she finds no favor in his eyes because he has found some indecency in her, and he writes her a bill of divorce and puts it in her hand and sends her out of his house . . ."* (Deuteronomy 24:1) indicates that Moses made a provision for divorce in the case of immorality. This allowance came as a concession to human frailty and weakness.

God's original plan for humanity, providing for the union of a man and woman, and the procreation and education of children involved the faithful marriage of one man with one woman, until death. Contemporary research confirms that children do best on every measurable social variable, when they live in a household with their married parents. No other social arrangement in any culture in history has functioned as well as a stable, loving, sacramental marriage. God intends one man and one woman to leave their parents, and cleave to one another until death. Sadly this does not always happen, but it remains the ideal.

The answer Christ gave to the Pharisees, zealots of the Old Testament, is especially important for them. Those who seek the accomplishment of their own human and Christian vocation in marriage are called, first of all, to make this theology of the body, whose beginning we find in the first chapters of Genesis, the content of their life and behavior. How indispensable is a thorough knowledge of the meaning of the body, in its masculinity and femininity, along the way of this vocation!

A precise awareness of the nuptial meaning of the body, of its generating meaning, is necessary. This is so since all that forms the content of the life of married couples must constantly find its full and personal dimension in life together, in behavior, in feelings! This is all the more so against the background of a civilization which remains under the pressure of a materialistic and utilitarian way of thinking and evaluating. Modern bio-physiology can supply a great deal of precise information about human sexuality. However, knowledge of the personal dignity of the human body and of sex must still be drawn from other sources. A special source is the Word of God himself, which contains the revelation of the body, going back to the beginning.

How significant it is that Christ, in the answer to all these questions, orders man to return, in a way, to the threshold of his theological history! He orders him to put himself at the border between original innocence, happiness and the inheritance of the first fall. Does he not perhaps mean to tell him that the path along which he leads man, male and female, in the sacrament of marriage, the path of the redemption of the body, must consist in regaining this dignity? In it there is simultaneously accomplished the real meaning of the human body, its personal meaning and its meaning of communion.

Blessed John Paul II, *Theology of the Body*
(Boston, MA: Pauline Books and Media, 1997), 89.

The radical transformation of the question presented to Jesus allows Him to present the ideal of marriage envisioned by God from the beginning of Creation. The marriage bond should involve a free and total giving of self to the beloved, exclusively until death. Jesus is well aware that weak and sinful human beings will marry and find it difficult to fulfill God's perfect plan. Jesus was no stranger to suffering or betrayal. He dealt with imperfect situations. But God's grace is available to those who freely choose to enter into this most intimate of human relationships.

Are children a blessing or a burden? People brought children to Jesus. God's very first commandment in the Bible is: *"Be fruitful and multiply, and fill the earth and subdue it"* (Genesis 1:28). Fruitful marital love involves procreation and ideally results in children. Throughout the Bible, children are seen as a blessing. *Behold, sons are a heritage from* *the* LORD, *the fruit of the womb a reward. Like arrows in the hand of a warrior are the sons of one's youth. Happy is the man who has his quiver full of them! He shall not be put to shame* (Psalm 127:3–5). Children are a gift from God, created in love for love. Not all people see children as a blessing from God. Many people in Jesus' time, and also today, see a child as a burden or a nuisance, rather than a treasure. Sometimes self-centered people become so busy enjoying themselves during their childbearing years that they neglect to consider a family. When their later years come, they are surprised at their loneliness, and the fact that they have no one to care for them.

A good question—*"Good Teacher, what must I do to inherit eternal life?"* (Mark 10:17). Jesus again uses the Socratic method, and poses a question in response to a question: *"Why do you call me good?"* (Mark 10:18). Jesus invites the man to recognize the goodness of the One who stands before him. Jesus' goodness stems from His divine nature and His perfect conformity to the will of God the Father. After Jesus recalls the commandments, the rich man makes an incredible claim. He has obeyed all of the commandments from his youth! Really? He was perfectly obedient to God in all of his thoughts, words and actions? The rich man stands before the Perfect One and claims himself to be perfectly obedient!

> Perhaps a modern parallel would be helpful. Once, the worst gossip in town told the parish priest that she would certainly go to confession, *if* she had any sins! Sometimes relatively good people have difficulty seeing their own sins, weaknesses, and failings. It is so much easier to see the sins of others!

The questions posed to Jesus and the questions posed by Jesus inspire the reader of the Gospel to self-reflection. What are my attitudes toward marriage, divorce, the commandments, wealth, and discipleship? Are my thoughts, beliefs, and attitudes formed by God's Word or by the world, the culture, popular opinion, or the media? How do the answers to these questions reflect God's perfect plan?

People in biblical times believed that the rich were blessed and favored by God, while God punished the poor and suffering because of some sin. If the rich cannot get into heaven, who can? The disciples don't understand that material wealth can exist alongside spiritual poverty. Wealth and attachments to material possession can be hindrances to total abandonment to divine providence. Wealth is not the root of all evils. Rather, inordinate attachment to wealth and material possessions can be obstacles. Jesus does not ask everyone to sell everything. He gives a radical invitation to some people to sell everything and embrace poverty. But to other rich people, like Zacchaeus, and Joseph of Arimathea, He does not. The disciples want to know who can be saved. Wealth and poverty are not insignificant factors. When Jesus announces the kingdom of God, He invites everyone—rich and poor—to become a disciple. Total trust in God requires detachment from money, treasures, and material things.

An inordinate attachment to wealth and material possessions can be troubling for people living in the wealthiest nations on earth. Even middle income and poor Americans enjoy more of the world's resources than people in developing countries enjoy. One way to avoid attachment to material things and the accompanying guilt is to embrace the Old Testament practice of tithing. *Glorify the Lord generously, and do not stint the first fruits of your hands. With every gift show a cheerful face, and dedicate your tithe with gladness. Give to the Most High as he has given, and as generously as your hand has found* (Sirach 35:8–10).

When Christians give the first portion of their income to the Lord, through the Church and various missions, they are freed from the burden of attachments. Some people may be even more generous to the Lord and give a larger percentage of their income, but a tithe provides a good starting point for many.

The apostles gave up everything to follow Jesus. Jesus promises that those who have given up everything for His sake and for the Gospel will receive a hundredfold in this time, and in the age to come eternal life. Jesus adds something to houses, relatives and lands—*with persecutions.* The so-called prosperity gospel promises that if someone believes in God, he or she will be materially blessed. But many saints suffer in this world, awaiting their reward in the next world. Do not ignore the part about suffering for Christ and the Gospel. As Jesus foretells His Passion, death and Resurrection for the third time (Mark 10:33–34), He also tells the disciples that they should expect suffering and persecution. In this most detailed prediction, Jesus reveals that both the Jews and the Gentiles will conspire to put Him to death, with mocking, spitting, and scourging.

Once again, after the foretelling of His Passion in even more detail than earlier, the disciples insensitively focus on their own glory. James and John, the sons of thunder (Mark 3:17), want to sit at His right and left hand in glory (Mark 10:37). Jesus asks about their willingness to drink the chalice that He drinks, which is the chalice of suffering. The baptism with which Jesus is baptized is the baptism into His Passion and death. Saint Paul says: *We were buried therefore with him by baptism into death, so that as Christ was raised from the dead by the glory of the Father, we too might walk in newness of life* (Romans 6:4).

The Savior calls martyrdom a baptism, saying: "Can you drink the cup which I drink and be baptized with the baptism with which I am to be baptized." Indeed, the martyrs too confess, by being made a spectacle to the world, both to angels and to men.

Saint Cyril of Jerusalem (AD 315–386), *Catechetical Lectures,* 3.10

Servanthood—The apostles expect to enjoy certain special perks and privileges as disciples of Jesus. But Jesus reveals a different concept. *"Whoever would be great among you must be your servant, and whoever would be first among you must be slave of all. For the Son of man also came not to be served but to serve, and to give his life as a ransom for many"* (Mark 10:43–45). Jesus died for all men and even the worst sinner can be saved, if he repents. Even though Jesus died for all, not all will choose to accept the salvation that He freely offers.

Jesus and the disciples proceed on to Jericho, the lowest city in the world, some eight hundred fifty feet below sea level. Blind Bartimaeus sits by the roadside, begging alms from people passing by. Twice he cries out *"Jesus, Son of David, have mercy on me!"* (Mark 10:47–48). For the first time in Mark's gospel the messianic title of Jesus as "Son of David" is proclaimed, clearly indicating that Jesus is the long-awaited Messiah. Jesus does not silence Bartimaeus. Like the children, Bartimaeus seems like a nuisance to those who try to silence him.

But Jesus calls Bartimaeus to Himself. Bartimaeus responds immediately, springing up and throwing off his cloak, which represents casting off his old way of life to follow Jesus. He asks Bartimaeus what he wants Him to do. Rather than asking for power and glory, as James and John had done, Bartimaeus asks for his sight to be restored, *"Master, let me receive my sight"* (Mark 10:51). Bartimaeus calls Jesus "Master," just as Peter had done at the Transfiguration (Mark 9:5).

Bartimaeus asks Jesus for mercy, and he receives mercy. He asks for sight, and he receives his sight. Unlike the blind man in Mark 8:22–26, who received his sight gradually, Bartimaeus receives his sight "immediately." And after receiving his sight, Bartimaeus follows Jesus *"on the way"* (Mark 10:52). Unlike many of the disciples, who are slow to realize exactly who Jesus is, Bartimaeus the blind man sees Jesus, the Son of David, suddenly and clearly. Bartimaeus receives healing and salvation at the same time. He comes to know who Jesus is, and he drops everything to follow Jesus on His way to Jerusalem.

—◦◦◦—

1. What was the motive of the Pharisees' question in Mark 10:2?

* How appropriate or fair is it for someone (a Pharisee) to ask a general question, without considering the particular circumstances of a person or situation?

2. What can you learn about marriage? What does it pre-figure?

Genesis 1:27–28
Genesis 2:24
Sirach 25:1
Sirach 26:1–4
Ephesians 5:21–33
Revelation 19:7–9
CCC 757
CCC 1602, 1612

* Describe the most beautiful marriage you have ever encountered.

3. How does Jesus speak about marriage and divorce? Matthew 19:4–6

* What does the Catholic Church offer to couples in troubled marriages?

4. What practical things can you do to promote Christian marriage today?

5. How does God feel about children? Are children a blessing or a burden?

Genesis 1:28
Psalm 127:3–5
Psalm 128:3–6
Proverbs 17:6

6. What promise does God offer to children who honor parents? Exodus 20:12

7. What special things can you learn about parents and children?

Proverbs 22:6
Sirach 3:1–15
Colossians 3:20–21

8. How and of what special family can you become a member? John 1:12

9. List three special things about your family and family of origin.

10. Share three special things about your parish family.

11. What emotion did Jesus feel for the rich man? Mark 10:21

12. What did Jesus offer and promise to the rich man? Mark 10:21b

13. What can you learn about riches from these passages?

Psalm 37:4–6
Psalm 49:5–9
Psalm 52:7
Psalm 62:10b

14. Find one way to prevent greed and materialism? Philippians 4:11

15. Find hope in these passages. Job 42:2; Mark 9:23; Mark 10:27

16. What does Jesus reveal in the third prediction of His Passion? Mark 10:33–34

17. What does Jesus teach the disciples about greatness? Mark 10:42–45

18. How does Bartimaeus address Jesus? What does he ask? Mark 10:46–51

19. What happens to Bartimaeus? Mark 10:52

20. Compare the cures of the blind men in Mark 8:22–26 and Mark 10:46–50.

* What would you ask from Jesus right now? Ask your group to pray for you.

Monthly Social Activity

This month, your small group will meet for coffee, tea, or a simple breakfast, lunch, or dessert in someone's home. Pray for this social event and for the host or hostess. Try, if at all possible, to attend.

After a short prayer and some time for small talk, write a few sentences about fruit in your personal life, your family, your work, and your parish ministry. Where can you find good fruit? Where do you need to prune or fertilize to make the fruit a bit better?

Examples

◆ *My prayer life needs a lot of work. Sometimes I don't schedule enough time for prayer. Sometimes we are late for Mass.*

◆ *My marriage is bearing pretty good fruit. We have kindness, affection, and good communication.*

◆ *My ministry in the parish is bearing good fruit. I am helping to feed the poor. People really appreciate what our parish provides for them.*

CHAPTER 13

On to Jerusalem
Mark 11:1–33

And when they drew near to Jerusalem . . .
those who went before and those who followed cried out,
"Hosanna! Blessed is he who comes in the name of the Lord!
Blessed is the kingdom of our father David that is coming!
Hosanna in the highest!"
And he entered Jerusalem, and went into the temple . . .
Mark 11:1, 9–11

Two events highlight Jesus' sovereignty, and frame the Jerusalem period of His ministry. First, Jesus' triumphal entry into Jerusalem (Mark 11:1–10) fulfills the Old Testament prophecies of the Davidic king, and finally, the Resurrection of Jesus (Mark 16) shows His triumph over sin and death. Prior to His Passion and death, Jesus works in Jerusalem over a period of three days, encountering some conflicts and controversies preceding His arrest.

Jesus enters Jerusalem—The prophet Zechariah had foretold that the Messianic king would come in a specific manner. *Rejoice greatly, O daughter of Zion! Shout aloud, O daughter of Jerusalem! Behold, your king comes to you; triumphant and victorious is he, humble and riding on a donkey, on a colt the foal of a donkey* (Zechariah 9:9). Even earlier, Jacob's last words to his sons included: *The scepter shall not depart from Judah, nor the ruler's staff from between his feet, until he comes to whom it belongs; and to him shall be the obedience of the peoples. Binding his foal to the vine and his donkey's colt to the choice vine, he washes his garments in wine, and his vesture in the blood of grapes* (Genesis 49:10–11).

Bethany and Bethpage are small cities southeast of Jerusalem. The Mount of Olives stands parallel to the Holy City. As Jesus draws near to these cities, He sends two disciples on ahead into the village to procure a colt, on which to ride in order to fulfill the Old Testament prophecies. The fact that no one has ever sat on this particular beast indicates that it has been set apart for a sacred purpose. Jesus gives specific instructions to the two disciples, and they find everything exactly as He had foretold it would be.

Jesus triumphantly enters the Holy City—Jesus enters Jerusalem on the colt and people spread their garments and leafy branches before Him. *And those who went before and those who followed cried out, "Hosanna! Blessed is he who comes in the name of the Lord! Blessed is the kingdom of our father David that is coming! Hosanna in the highest!"* (Mark 11:9–10). *Hosanna* is a transliteration from the Greek, meaning: "save us, please." In this case, it is used as a prayer of homage to Jesus, rather than a cry for mercy, help or deliverance.

Hosanna in the highest points to the heavens, the sovereign realm in which God dwells. *Praise the* LORD *from the heavens, praise him in the heights!* (Psalm 148:1). As Jesus rides into Jerusalem, the people praise Him with one of the Hallel Psalms, a song of victory: *Blessed is he who enters in the name of the* LORD! *We bless you from the house of the* LORD (Psalm 118:26). Jesus comes to Jerusalem in the name of the Lord. The people celebrate and hope for the restoration of the kingdom of David, but Jesus ushers in a kingdom far greater than what they imagine. The kingdom of God involves more than a restoration of Israel.

Mark presents the activity of Jesus in Jerusalem, prior to His passion and death in the framework of a three-day sequence of time.

Day One—Jesus enters Jerusalem, goes to the temple, and returns to Bethany
    (Mark 11:1–11).
Day Two—Jesus curses a barren fig tree, and cleanses the temple
    (Mark 11:12–19).
Day Three—Peter observes that the fig tree Jesus cursed has withered.
    Jesus enters the temple and is confronted by the chief priests,
    scribes, and elders
    (Mark 11:20ff).

The cleansing of the temple is sandwiched in between a curious narrative about Jesus cursing a barren fig tree. Why would Jesus curse a tree that is not blooming, when it isn't even the season for bearing fruit? Fig trees in the Holy Land usually bloom in the summer, starting around June. Some keys that help to unlock the meaning of this passage involve Israel. Figs and fig trees were a symbol for Israel in the Old Testament. *It has laid waste my vines, and splintered my fig trees* (Joel 1:7). *"I laid waste your gardens and your vineyards; your fig trees and your olive trees the locust devoured; yet you did not return to me"* (Amos 4:9).

Israel demonstrated fruitlessness in prayer, worship, and temple piety. The corruption of the temple officials, and the display of greed and materialism precipitate righteous anger in Jesus. *Woe is me! For I have become as when the summer fruit has been gathered, as when the vintage has been gleaned: there is no cluster to eat, no first-ripe fig which my soul desires. The godly man has perished from the earth, and there is none upright among men* (Micah 7:1–2). God desires mercy, justice, and righteousness. But when Jesus comes into the temple, He instead finds greed, avarice, commercialism, and hypocrisy.

The prophet Isaiah used the image of the fig tree to illustrate God's wrath against the nations. *All the host of heaven shall rot away, and the skies roll up like a scroll. All their host shall fall, as leaves fall from the vine, like leaves falling from the fig tree* (Isaiah 34:4). Because Jesus finds no fruit on the fig tree, and because He does not find the fruit of righteousness in the temple, judgment will follow. The fig tree will be cursed and will wither. The temple and temple officials: chief priests, scribes, and elders will experience God's judgment as well.

Jerusalem, the Holy City

Jerusalem—*the city of our God; the holy mountain, fairest of heights, the joy of the earth . . . the city of the great king* (Psalm 48:2–4)—was identified in Jewish tradition as the site of Mount Moriah, where Abraham had been willing to offer his son Isaac in sacrifice (Genesis 22:2; 2 Chronicles 3:1), a prefigurement of the ultimate sacrifice of the Beloved Son (Romans 8:32). Jerusalem was also identified as the Salem of the mysterious priest-king Melchizedek, who offered bread and wine (Genesis 14:18), foreshadowing the Eucharist.

King David conquered the city in about 1000 BC and chose it as his capital. One of the great moments in Israel's history was when David brought the Ark of the Covenant into the city in procession, with music, sacrifices, and dancing for joy before the Lord (2 Samuel 6:12–19). His son Solomon built the magnificent temple to house the Ark, and the Holy City became the center of religious life for the Israelites and the place of God's special favor.

After the Jews' exile and return from Babylon, the city and temple were rebuilt, but without attaining their former glory. Through the prophets God promised a new and glorious Jerusalem, a place of overflowing joy and center of worship for the entire world (see Isaiah 2:2–3; 60:1–22; Zephaniah 3:14–17: Haggai 2:7–9).

At the time of Jesus, the temple had been renovated and Jerusalem was near the pinnacle of her earthly splendor. On each of the three great Jewish feasts—Passover, Weeks (Pentecost), and Booths—the city was flooded with pilgrims, more than tripling its normal population of about 40,000. Yet as Jesus' words and prophetic gestures make clear, the Holy City was marred by corruption and religious hypocrisy. His warning of great devastation (Mark 13:1–30) was tragically fulfilled when Jerusalem was leveled to the ground by Roman legions in AD 70.

Mary Healy, *The Gospel of Mark*,
(Grand Rapids, MI: Baker Academic, 2008), 221.

Agricultural imagery emerged earlier in the Gospel of Mark. When Jesus compared the kingdom of God to a mustard seed, which grows into a large tree, He was offering a preview into the spread of the New Covenant (Mark 4:30–32), and the advancement of the kingdom of God. The barren fig tree, representing the Old Covenant stands in sharp contrast to the fruitful mustard seed of faith. With the covenant, the Law, and the prophets, opportunities abounded to bring forth good fruit. Perhaps it is important for each believer to examine the fruit in one's own life. What can you do today to advance the kingdom of God? Are the fruits of righteousness evident in your personal life, your work, your family, and your parish?

On the second day, when Jesus enters the temple, He displays righteous anger. He begins to drive out the merchants, and overturn the tables of the moneychangers. Imagine the scene of coins flying all over the floor, and people scrambling to recover their money. Jesus turns over the seats of those selling pigeons. Perhaps Jesus recalls, or has been told about the incident in which Mary and Joseph brought Jesus to the temple, eight days after His birth, and bought two pigeons, as the acceptable offering for the poor.

And he taught, and said to them, "Is it not written, 'My house shall be called a house of prayer for all the nations'? But you have made it a den of robbers" (Mark 11:17). Jesus recalls the quote from the prophet Jeremiah: *"Has this house, which is called by my name, become a den of robbers in your eyes? Behold, I myself have seen it, says the* LORD*"* (Jeremiah 7:11). Isaiah indicated, *"for my house shall be called a house of prayer for all peoples"* (Isaiah 56:7b). The early Christian community would reflect on the words of Jesus in Mark *for all the nations*, would include Gentiles in worship.

When Zechariah prophesied concerning the coming of the day of the Lord, he foretold that: *there shall no longer be a trader in the house of the* LORD *of hosts on that day* (Zechariah 14:21b). The chief priests and scribes would have known this prophecy. The words and actions of Jesus have been carefully observed and scrutinized by the chief priests and elders. Their comfortable positions and habits are in danger of change. Jesus' words should bring repentance and conversion.

---

*Jesus' words
comfort the afflicted,
and afflict
the comfortable.*

Because of Jesus' outburst in the temple, the chief priests and scribes become quite uncomfortable. They enjoy their status quo, just as it is. Their positions are secure, and they don't relish having someone come in to criticize their operations. Therefore, they seek out ways to get rid of Jesus permanently. People flock to Jesus and listen to His teaching. While the multitudes are astonished at Jesus' teaching and crowd to Him for miracles, the chief priests are indignant.

Interestingly, from this point in the Gospel on, Jesus works no more exorcisms. Satan and the evil spirits seem to leave Jesus alone for the moment. Earlier, Jesus had many confrontations with Satan and demons. From now on, wickedness will confront Jesus through the circles of religious power and politics. The plot to destroy Jesus will even enter into the close circle of His twelve apostles (Mark 14:10–11). Even the crowds, who once crowded to hear Jesus teach, tried to touch Him to obtain healing, and threw their garments and branches before Him as He entered Jerusalem, will ultimately turn against Him (Mark 15:13–14).

Peter speaks for the Twelve when he observes the withered fig tree. Ultimately, like the demise of the tree, temple worship and the once magnificent temple itself will also come to an abrupt end. *"There will not be left here one stone upon another, that will not be thrown down"* (Mark 13:2). The Romans sack and level Jerusalem in AD 70, and the temple has remained in ruin since that time. Only the western wall of the temple remains today—the Wailing Wall.

Subsequently, Jesus offers a catechesis on prayer. He enjoins the apostles to have faith, believe, persevere in prayer, and forgive one another. Without forgiving others, one cannot expect to receive mercy from God. Unforgiveness blocks a person from experiencing God's mercy and peace, and prevents one from drawing close to God in prayer. Unforgiveness binds the one who will not forgive.

Have faith in God (Mark 11:22).

Believe that it will come to pass (Mark 11:23–24).

Forgive if you have anything against anyone (Mark 11:25).

Just as Jesus dealt with conflicts and controversies earlier in Mark 2–3, once again Jesus will be confronted with more controversies. The chief priests, scribes, and elders come to Jesus and demand: *"By what authority are you doing these things?"* (Mark 11:28). It is not clear what specific things they mean. Does the question concern Jesus' teaching, His miracles, His cleansing of the temple? Rather than answering their question directly, Jesus poses a question to them, concerning John the Baptist. *"Was the baptism of John from heaven or from men? Answer me"* (Mark 11:30). "Answer me," throws down the gauntlet. God has the right to demand an answer. *"O my people, what have I done to you? In what have I wearied you? Answer me!"* (Micah 6:3).

While the chief priests had planned to trap Jesus into uttering blasphemy, they find themselves trapped instead. Jesus' clever question forces them into a corner. And Jesus asks His question with authority, demanding an answer from them. If the temple officials admit that John the Baptist's authority was divine, they would have to admit that Jesus' authority is also divine, and in fact Jesus is greater than John. On the other hand, the disciples of John the Baptist recognize him as a prophet and a martyr. There could be an uprising of John's disciples if the chief priests speak against him. Therefore, the chief priests, scribes, and elders are trapped in the snare they created for another. Jesus has silenced them. But they will return again.

1. Where is Jesus now? Mark 11:1

2. What does Jesus ask the disciples to do? Mark 11:2–3

3. By what title does Jesus refer to Himself here? What does this mean?

Mark 11:3
CCC 209
CCC 446

4. What happened to the disciples' errand? Mark 11:4–7

5. How will the king of Israel come? Zechariah 9:9

6. What can you learn from these passages?

Psalm 118:26
Mark 11:7–10
CCC 559
CCC 560

* When do Catholics celebrate Jesus' triumphal entry into Jerusalem?

7. What happened when Jesus entered Jerusalem? Mark 11:11

8. Describe the events of Jesus' three days in Jerusalem.

Mark 11:1–11
Mark 11:12–19
Mark 11:20–33

9. What can you learn from these passages about fig trees?

Amos 4:9
Micah 7:1–2
Isaiah 34:4
Mark 11:12–14
Mark 11:20

10. Who is the spokesman for the apostles? Mark 11:21

*Describe some good fruit in your own personal life, family, job, and your parish.

Personal Life
Family
Work
Parish

11. Describe the scene in Mark 11:15–17.

12. Compare the following passages.

Isaiah 56:7b
Jeremiah 7:11
Zechariah 14:21b
Mark 11:17

** What is the significance of God's house being a house of prayer for all nations?

13. Describe the four "marks" of Christ's Church.

CCC 813
CCC 823–824
CCC 830
CCC 857

14. How do the chief priests and the multitudes react to Jesus? Mark 11:18

15. What does Jesus teach the disciples about prayer?

Mark 11:22
Mark 11:23–24
Mark 11:25

* Is there anyone that you have been unable or unwilling to forgive?

** If so, ask your group to pray that God will give you the grace to forgive.

16. Who confronts Jesus? What do they ask? Mark 11:27–28

17. How does Jesus spring their trap? Mark 11:29–30

* How can you respond to someone who tries to entrap you with words?

18. Explain the discussion of the chief priests, scribes and elders. Mark 11:31–32

19. What was their final response to Jesus? Mark 11:33

20. How does Jesus end the confrontation? Mark 11:33b

** What can you learn from the way Jesus deals with adversaries?

CHAPTER 14

Love the Lord
Mark 12:1–44

Jesus answered,
"The first [commandment] is,
'Hear O Israel: The Lord our God, the Lord is one;
and you shall love the Lord your God with all your heart,
and with all your soul,
and with all your mind, and with all your strength.'
The second is this,
'You shall love your neighbor as yourself.'
There is no other commandment greater than these."
Mark 12:29–31

The parable of the wicked tenants represents the last parable that Mark records. Controversy and confrontations continue to plague Jesus. Following the temple authorities' demand for Jesus to present credentials and indicate by what authority He acts, Jesus presents a parable concerning a vineyard. Jesus' listeners would remember the Old Testament references to Israel as the vineyard.

In Psalm 80, the prayer for Israel's restoration, the psalmist says: *Restore us, O God of hosts: let your face shine, that we many be saved! You brought a vine out of Egypt; you drove out the nations that planted it* (Psalm 80:7–8). The Prophet Isaiah offers a parable of the vineyard: *My beloved had a vineyard on a very fertile hill. He dug it and cleared it of stones, and planted it with choice vines; he built a watchtower in the midst of it, and hewed out a wine vat in it; and he looked for it to yield grapes, but it yielded wild grapes* (Isaiah 5:1–2). Similarly, the Prophet Jeremiah laments: *"Yet I planted you a choice vine, wholly of pure seed. How then have you turned degenerate and become a wild vine?"* (Jeremiah 2:21).

Parable of the Wicked Tenants

Vineyard = God's kingdom entrusted to Israel

Vineyard Owner = God

Hedge = the Law, protecting people from evil influences

Tenants = Israel's religious leaders

Tower = the temple

Wine press/servants = Prophets calling for repentance

Beloved Son = Jesus

The religious leaders recognize that Jesus speaks about them. God entrusted the religious leaders with the care of the chosen people, hoping that they would model piety, righteousness, and justice. However, a certain formalism and ritualistic religiosity prevent many of the leaders from recognizing God's provision in Jesus. Although, it should be remembered that some of the religious leaders listen to Jesus with humility and an open mind, others seek to entrap and kill Him.

After the owner of the vineyard sends servants to collect the fruit, he decides to send his beloved son. *He had still one other, a beloved son* (Mark 12:6). The term *beloved son* appears three times in Mark. At Jesus' baptism in the Jordan River: *a voice came from heaven, "You are my beloved Son; with you I am well pleased"* (Mark 1:11). Then, at the Transfiguration, *a cloud overshadowed them, and a voice came out of the cloud, "This is my beloved Son; listen to him"* (Mark 9:7). This third use of the term *beloved son* in Mark 12:6 leaves no ambiguity that Jesus is the beloved Son of God the Father. The idea in the parable of killing the son and casting him out of the vineyard foretells the crucifixion of Jesus outside of the city of Jerusalem. *So Jesus also suffered outside the gate in order to sanctify the people through his own blood* (Hebrews 13:12).

The Parable of the rejected stone—This parable was frequently quoted in the early Church. Jesus recalls a victory song of ancient Israel and quotes it here to refer to Himself, and His relationship with the temple leaders. *The stone which the builders rejected has become the cornerstone. This is the LORD's doing; it is marvelous in our eyes* (Psalm 118:22–23). The religious leaders reject Jesus, who is the cornerstone of the Church. Both Saint Peter (Acts 4:11) and Saint Paul use the cornerstone imagery to proclaim that Jesus is the foundation of the Church. *Come to him, to that living stone, rejected by men but in God's sight chosen and precious* (1 Peter 2:4). Similarly, Saint Paul invites new believers: *So then you are no longer strangers and sojourners, but you are fellow citizens with the saints and members of the household of God, built upon the foundation of the apostles and prophets, Christ Jesus himself being the cornerstone* (Ephesians 2:19–20).

Should we pay taxes? Usually, Pharisees and Herodians were enemies. The Pharisees set themselves apart from Gentiles, in an effort to preserve their Jewish identity, while the Herodians cooperated with Herod Antipas. But both groups came together in their opposition to Jesus. They approach Jesus with false flattery and a seemingly surefire way to entrap Him. What they say in approaching Jesus is true, but insincere. *"Teacher, we know that you are true, and care for no man; for you do not regard the position of men, but truly teach the way of God"* (Mark 12:14). If they truly believe that, why do they not listen to Jesus and put their faith in Him? Is it because they care too much for their positions, and the opinions of men, and too little for the truths of God? Jesus recognizes their hypocrisy and knows that they are testing Him. They play the role of the tempter, Satan.

The answer to the question of paying taxes provides an inescapable dilemma for Jesus. If He tells the people to pay their taxes, He will disappoint the humble, common people, who have been following, listening, and believing Him. Poor people are being over-taxed and gouged by the Roman authorities. If Jesus tells the people not to pay taxes, He will be denounced to the Roman occupiers as a rebel and a revolutionary. They will have grounds to imprison Him as an instigator. The leaders seem to have set an excellent, foolproof trap for Jesus.

Jesus asks for a coin. The denarius presented to Jesus would probably have had the image of the emperor Tiberius, and the inscription would likely have read: "Tiberius Caesar divine son of Augustus." Masterfully, Jesus turns a question about paying taxes into a spiritual catechesis. The coin has the image of Caesar on it. But, what belongs to God? *So God created man in his own image, in the image of God he created him, male and female he created them* (Genesis 1:27). All humanity has been created in the image and likeness of God. Even Caesar has been created by God, and owes God something. Each person must give God an accounting for his life. Jesus skillfully turns a political question into a spiritual reflection. What return will a person make to God, who has given him life and grace?

Sadducees confront Jesus with an absurd question—The Sadducees come onto the stage to make their one and only appearance in Mark's Gospel. Sadducees were an elite and aristocratic group within Judaism. The origin of their name may derive from the Hebrew word *tsaddiq* for righteous, or from the priest Zadok, who served King Solomon (1 Kings 2:35). Zadok's descendants received exclusive rights to minister in the temple in Jerusalem. No love was lost between the Pharisees and the Sadducees. The Sadducees held some very divergent beliefs.

Sadducees Deny

1) The validity of any other Scriptures beyond the Torah.

2) The immortality of the soul.

3) The resurrection of the body.

4) Angels and other spirits.

5) The afterlife, with rewards and punishment for behavior.

Pharisees accepted the Pentateuch, the prophets, and the writings. But the Sadducees only recognized the first five books of the Bible, the Torah—Genesis, Exodus, Leviticus, Numbers, and Deuteronomy. Therefore, any discussion with the Sadducees required limiting the dialogue to those five books. Most often, Pharisees and Sadducees are cast in a negative light, as they cling to old ways and refuse to consider Jesus, His teachings and His power. The Pharisees and Sadducees believed that they had God all figured out. They could not conceive that God might want to act in new or unexpected ways.

When the Sadducees approach Jesus, they present a bizarre scenario and expect that Jesus will be unable to answer their ridiculous question. Because they did not accept other books of the Sacred Scriptures, the Sadducees might not have known that a similar drama actually does emerge in the book of Tobit. Sarah, the only daughter of Raguel, is given in marriage to seven husbands, but the evil demon Asmodeus kills each husband before he takes her as his wife (Tobit 3:7–8). The righteous Tobias and the Archangel Raphael come to rescue Sarah.

How will Jesus answer their conundrum, using only the Pentateuch? Jesus confronts their ignorance of Scripture, and accuses them of not understanding the power of God. God is the originator of life, and has power over life and death. Jesus explains that marriage exists for this life. The unitive and procreative purposes of marriage are accomplished in life here on earth. When we die, we will not be angels, who are merely disembodied spirits, but we will be *like* angels, in glorious immortality. Jesus quotes Exodus to provide light on the afterlife. *"I am the God of your father, the God of Abraham, the God of Isaac, and the God of Jacob"* (Exodus 3:6). Jesus proclaims that God is the God of the living, not the dead, and the Sadducees are quite wrong in their thinking.

Which is the greatest commandment? Finally, a righteous scribe approaches Jesus without the hostility and animosity of previous questioners. This scribe has listened to Jesus' answers to the Pharisees and Sadducees. He recognizes that Jesus has answered them well. He seems sincere when he asks Jesus about the greatest commandment. Observant Jews pray the Shema twice a day. And, as good, pious Jews, Joseph, Mary and Jesus would have prayed the Shema, twice a day as well. Jesus quotes the beginning of the Shema, Deuteronomy 6:4, for the questioner.

Loving God with your whole heart, mind, soul, and strength involves the entire person, loving God with every available resource. The heart represents the depth of the person, the source of will, decision, and emotion. The mind involves knowing, studying, and learning about God, His ways and commands. The soul is that essence of the person that will live forever, either happily with God, or tragically separated from Him. Strength involves muscular vitality and conditioning. Following God is not for wimps. A genuine faith commitment requires every bit of one's will and energy. The martyrs exhibited the strength of faith and a commitment to God that prevailed through suffering and death.

Added to the first sentence of the Shema, Jesus quotes another Old Testament passage: *you shall love your neighbor as yourself* (Leviticus 19:18b). Jesus sums it all up by adding, *There is no other commandment greater than these* (Mark 12:31). The Jews recognized six hundred thirteen commandments. There would be plenty of opportunity to discuss the relative importance of each. But Jesus cuts through the red tape, simplifies, and clarifies. Loving God and one's fellow man sums up the commandments and directs the heart in right relationship to God and others. While the scribe applauds Jesus' answer, and is not *far* from the kingdom, he still needs to take that courageous, giant step to *enter* the kingdom of God.

Shema
Hear O Israel

"Hear, O Israel: The LORD our God is one LORD; and you shall love the LORD your God with all your heart, and with all your soul, and with all your might. And these words which I command you this day shall be upon your heart; and you shall teach them diligently to your children, and shall talk of them when you sit in your house, and when you walk by the way, and when you lie down, and when you rise. And you shall bind them as a sign upon your hand, and they shall be as frontlets between your eyes. And you shall write them on the doorposts of your house and on your gates" (Deuteronomy 6:4–9).

"And if you will obey my commandments which I command you this day, to love the LORD your God, and to serve him with all your heart and with all your soul, he will give the rain for your land in its season, the early rain and the later rain, that you may gather in your grain and your wine and your oil. And he will give grass in your fields for your cattle, and you shall eat and be full. Take heed lest your heart be deceived, and you turn aside and serve other gods and worship them, and the anger of the LORD be kindled against you, and he shut up the heavens, so that there be no rain, and the land yield no fruit, and you perish quickly off the good land which the LORD gives you.

"You shall therefore lay up these words of mine in your heart and in your soul, and you shall bind them as a sign upon your hand, and they shall be as frontlets between your eyes. And you shall teach them to your children, talking of them when you are sitting in your house, and when you are walking by the way, and when you lie down, and when you rise. And you shall write them upon the doorposts of your house and upon your gates, that your days and the days of your children may be multiplied in the land which the LORD swore to your fathers to give them, as long as the heavens are above the earth" (Deuteronomy 11:13–21).

The LORD said to Moses, "Speak to the sons of Israel, and bid them to make tassels on the corners of their garments throughout their generations, and to put upon the tassel of each corner a cord of blue; and it shall be to you a tassel to look upon and remember all the commandments of the LORD, to do them, not to follow after your own heart and your own eyes, which you are inclined to go after wantonly. So you shall remember and do all my commandments, and be holy to your God. I am the LORD your God, who brought you out of the land of Egypt, to be your God: I am the LORD your God" (Numbers 15:37–41).

Jesus provides a complicated exegesis of a victory psalm of King David, the priest king. *The* LORD *says to my lord: "Sit at my right hand, till I make your enemies your footstool"* (Psalm 110:1). Teaching in the temple, Jesus explains that the Holy Spirit inspired David to write the words of this psalm. The question remains—how is the Messiah the son of David, and yet David calls him Lord? Jesus shows that although the Messiah is the son of David, he is more than that. If David is speaking in Psalm 110, then logically, he is speaking to someone other than himself. The Messiah is the son of David, and He is also the Lord of David. Jesus is David's son in His humanity. He is also the beloved Son of God in His divinity, and thus David's Lord. After theological reflection, the truth emerges that Jesus is true God and true man, fully divine and fully human.

Jesus denounces the scribes and exalts a poor widow—Two incidents at the end of Mark 12 form a diptych, by which to contrast different characters. First, Jesus denounces the hypocrisy of the scribes, who parade around in long robes and seek out places of honor. Scribes were able to read, write, and draw up documents. Jesus does not criticize all scribes, but He does criticize those whose piety is a pretense, and who devour widow's houses and further empoverish them.

Scribes in antiquity could draw up wills and trusts, much as estate planning lawyers do today, although it was probably far simpler then. Most widows could not read. If the scribe was the trustee of the widow, he could take a portion of her estate as his fee. A lawyer who paraded around in luxurious clothing and occupied a choice seat in the synagogue would have a good chance of demonstrating his importance and advertising his services. Greed could be a great temptation for the scribe. *"You shall not afflict any widow or orphan"* (Exodus 22:22).

Jesus watches the offering in the temple treasury. Coins were used in antiquity. So, there would be lots of noise when large coins clanged into the treasury. Jesus observes the rich and the poor. Widows in antiquity were needy in more ways than one can imagine today. Without a husband or children to care for her, she could be without food and shelter. A widow could also be vulnerable to the unscrupulous, if she had any means at all. In any culture, widows, especially elderly widows must deal with loneliness, and sometimes, social isolation. After the death of Saint Joseph, Mary would have faced the fears and loneliness of widowhood.

The rich give from their abundance, but the poor widow gives from her poverty. She gives back to the Lord all that she has. She trusts God to provide for her. Jesus contrasts their greed with her generosity. While rich people are often generous and some poor people can be greedy, here an obvious contrast emerges. The scribes are *takers*, focusing their attention on themselves. The poor widow *gives* generously, giving all for others. *Each one must do as he has made up his mind, not reluctantly or under compulsion, for God loves a cheerful giver. And God is able to provide you with every blessing in abundance, so that you may always have enough of everything* (2 Corinthians 9:7–8). God gave us everything. The poor widow foreshadows Jesus, who gives everything, His very lifeblood, to redeem sinful humanity.

God is Love

We have come to believe in God's love: in these words the Christian can express the fundamental decision of his life. Being a Christian is not the result of an ethical choice or a lofty idea, but the encounter with an event, a person, which gives life a new horizon and a decisive direction . . .

In acknowledging the centrality of love, Christian faith has retained the core of Israel's faith, while at the same time giving it new depth and breadth. The pious Jew prayed daily the word of the *Book of Deuteronomy* which expressed the heart of his existence: *"Hear, O Israel: the Lord our God is one* LORD, *and you shall love the* LORD *your God with all your heart, and with all your soul and with all your might"* (Deuteronomy 6:4–5). Jesus united into a single precept this commandment of love for God and the commandment of love for neighbor found in the *Book of Leviticus: "You shall love your neighbor as yourself"* (Leviticus 19:18; cf. Mark 12:29–31) . . .

God's love for us is fundamental for our lives, and it raises important questions about who God is and who we are . . .

There is only one God, the Creator of heaven and earth, who is thus the God of all. Two facts are significant about this statement: all other gods are not God, and the universe in which we live has its source in God and was created by him. Certainly, the notion of creation is found elsewhere, yet only here does it become absolutely clear that it is not one god among many, but the one true God himself who is the source of all that exists; the whole world comes into existence by the power of his creative Word. Consequently, his creation is dear to him, for it was willed by him and "made" by him.

The second important element now emerges: this God loves man. The divine power that Aristotle at the height of Greek philosophy sought to grasp through reflection, is indeed for every being an object of desire and love—and as the object of love this divinity moves the world—but in itself it lacks nothing and does not love: it is solely the object of love. The one God in whom Israel believes, on the other hand, loves with a personal love. His love, moreover, is an elective love: among all the nations he chooses Israel and loves her—but he does so precisely with a view to healing the whole human race. God loves, and his love may certainly be called *eros,* yet it is also totally *agape.*

Pope Benedict XVI, *God Is Love [Deus Caritas Est],*
(December 25, 2005), 1, 2, 9

1. What can you learn about vineyards?

Psalm 80:7–15
Isaiah 5:1–7
Jeremiah 2:21
Hosea 10:1
Mark 12:1–2

2. What fruit does God desire?

Hosea 10:12
John 15:1–10
Galatians 5:22–23
CCC 2447

* Which fruit of the spirit are evident in your life right now?

** Which works of mercy do you do regularly?

3. What motivation for sin can you find in the following passages?

Genesis 37:18–20	
Mark 12:6–7	

4. Compare the following verses.

Mark 12:8	
Hebrews 13:12	

5. What can you learn from these passages?

Psalm 118:22–23	
Mark 12:10–11	
Acts 4:10–11	
Ephesians 2:19–20	
1 Peter 2:4	
CCC 756	

6. How did the religious leaders respond to Jesus' parable? Mark 12:12

7. Identify words that indicate the Pharisees and Herodians' motivation.

Mark 12:13	
Mark 12:15	

8. What do they say about Jesus? Is it true? Mark 12:14

9. What does Jesus ask them? Is Jesus on to them? Mark 12:15

10. Explain how Jesus skillfully gets out of the conundrum? Mark 12:15–17

11. What principal is offered below?

Mark 12:17
Romans 13:7
CCC 450

* How do people respond to Jesus? Mark 12:17b. What response does He want?

12. What one thing do the Sadducees not believe in? What do they ask?

Mark 12:18
Mark 12:23
CCC 993–994

* Why would someone ask about something in which they don't believe?

13. How does Jesus answer their question? What is repeated? Mark 12:24–27

14. What question does the scribe ask Jesus? Mark 12:28

15. How does Jesus answer?

Deuteronomy 6:4
Mark 12:29–30 Mark 12:31
CCC 202

16. What does Jesus explain in the temple?

Mark 12:35–37
CCC 479–482

17. What did Jesus say about the scribes? Mark 12:38–39

18. What did Jesus accuse the scribes of doing?

Exodus 22:22
Mark 12:40

19. What contrast did Jesus point out?

Mark 12:40, 41, 44
Mark 12:42, 43, 44

20. Who else gave everything as the widow had? John 3:16, Romans 8:32

* List three practical ways that you could be more like the widow than the scribes.

CHAPTER 15

Final Discourse
Mark 13:1–37

"Watch therefore—for you do not know when the master of the house will come,
in the evening, or at midnight, or at cockcrow, or in the morning—
lest he come suddenly and find you asleep.
And what I say to you I say to all: Watch."
Mark 13:35–37

Jesus' final discourse—His longest discussion in Mark's Gospel, concludes the teaching ministry of Jesus. This speech is *eschatological,* in that it discusses the "last things" or the "end times." Jesus foretells the destruction of the temple in Jerusalem (Mark 13:1–4), an approaching time of suffering (Mark 13:5–13), the great tribulation (Mark 13:14–23), and the triumph of the Son of Man (Mark 13:24–27). Finally, Jesus exhorts us to watch and persevere (Mark 13:28–37).

Mark 13:1–4	Jesus foretells the destruction of the temple.
Mark 13:5–13	Apostasy and sufferings will follow.
Mark 13:14–23	A great tribulation will come.
Mark 13:24–27	The Son of Man will return in glory.
Mark 13:28–37	Jesus exhorts disciples to watch and pray.

Solomon's Temple in Jerusalem—King David's son, King Solomon built the first temple in Jerusalem in the tenth century BC. He imported huge quarried stones and cedars from Lebanon to build the magnificent structure. The temple platform spanned over thirty acres. Nebuchadnezzar II of Babylon destroyed the temple on the ninth day in the month Av (August 10th) in the year 586 BC.

After the Babylonian exile ended, King Cyrus of Persia authorized the rebuilding of the temple in Jerusalem (Ezra 1:1–4). The temple was rebuilt in 516 BC, but the second temple lacked the first temple's original grandeur. Nevertheless, the eastern wall facing the Mount of Olives ascended three hundred feet. Some of the stones of the temple, quarried limestone or marble, were over thirty feet long, and weighed hundreds of tons. Architects and archeologists still marvel at the remaining foundation of the structure, and are stymied as to how the enormous stones were ever put into place.

Herod the Great embarked upon an extensive remodeling project for the temple around the year 20 BC. The white marble façade of the open-air temple was gilt with gold, making the structure dazzle in the sun. Malachi foretold that the Lord would come to the temple, and Jesus fulfilled his prophecy. *"Behold, I send my messenger to prepare the way before me, and the Lord whom you seek will suddenly come to his temple"* (Malachi 3:1). After Jesus denounced the hypocrisy of the religious leaders, He would leave the temple area for the last time.

When the disciples gaze back upon this spectacular, breath-taking edifice, Jesus predicts that the temple will be destroyed. *"Do you see these great buildings? There will not be left here one stone upon another, that will not be thrown down"*(Mark 13:2). The destruction that Jesus predicted must have been mind-boggling to the disciples, for it was such an immense, imposing structure. However, the apostles believe Jesus. They ask when the destruction will take place, and what signs they should anticipate. Jesus says: *"But when you see the desolating sacrilege set up where it ought not to be (let the reader understand), then let those who are in Judea flee to the mountains"* (Mark 13:14).

The desolating sacrilege had been foretold by Daniel, and appeared in the temple in the past. *"Forces from him shall appear and profane the temple and fortress, and shall take away the continual burnt offering. And they shall set up the abomination that makes desolate"* (Daniel 11:31). In 167 BC, the evil Antiochus Epiphanes IV *plundered the city, burned it with fire, and tore down its houses and its surrounding walls* (1 Maccabees 1:31). Antiochus Epiphanes entered the temple and placed an idolatrous statue of the Greek god Zeus on the altar of burnt offering, profaning the temple.

About ten years after Jesus' death and Resurrection, the Emperor Gaius Julius Caesar Germanicus, nicknamed *Caligula,* "little boots," attempted to desecrate the temple by having his statue placed on the altar. His attempt was denounced by faithful Jews and was thwarted. About twenty-five years later, the Zealot party took over the temple, appointed their own high priest, and made their military headquarters within the temple. Both of these events were sacrilegious. One of them may have been the sacrilege that Jesus discussed with the apostles.

Beginning in April AD 70, forty years to the week from the time of the Jesus' Passion and death, thirty thousand Roman troops began a systematic slaughter of the Jews in Jerusalem. The walls of the temple were breached on the ninth day of Av in AD 70, just as the first temple had been burned on the ninth day of Av in 586 BC. The Roman siege lasted one hundred forty three days. The historian Josephus reports that 1,100,000 Jews were slaughtered, and another 97,000 Jews were captured and subsequently enslaved. Titus, the son of Vespasian, delivered the final blows to the Jews and to their holy city. The Romans torched the temple and the city, and the fires were reported to be still burning one month later.

The destruction of the temple and the city of Jerusalem was devastating and total, just as Jesus had predicted. Whatever veiled language Jesus used to warn the disciples might have been, it was understood and heeded by the early Christians. Apparently, Jewish Christians living in the city of Jerusalem listened to and obeyed Jesus' warnings and fled the city. As a result, there are no reports of a single Jewish Christian perishing in the massacre in Jerusalem in AD 70. The destruction of the temple marks the sudden end of the old covenant sacrificial system.

Trials and tribulations will come—Jesus warns that Christians will be persecuted. They will be beaten and handed over to religious and government authorities. They will bear witness for Jesus' sake and preach the Gospel to all nations. Disciples will share in the sufferings of Christ. False prophets and false messiahs will arise. Some false messiahs named Theudas, James, and Simon emerged in the first century. In preaching the Gospel, disciples must not be anxious, for the Holy Spirit will be with them. Baptism in the Holy Spirit will empower believers to witness: *"And when they bring you to trial and deliver you up, do not be anxious beforehand about what you are to say; but say whatever is given you in that hour, for it is not you who speak, but the Holy Spirit"* (Mark 13:11).

Even close, intimate family relationships will suffer. Faithfulness to Christ and to the Gospel will supersede even the sacred duties of family loyalty. Fathers, children, and brothers will forsake all others in their devotion to Jesus. *But he who endures to the end will be saved* (Mark 13:13). Faithfulness to Christ comes before all else.

There will also be cataclysmic signs of wars and natural disasters. The death of Jesus was marked by extraordinary phenomena—darkness falling over the earth, an earthquake accompanied by tombs opening and the dead walking about, and the temple curtain being torn in two. Similarly, the early Church endured adversity. Several significant natural disasters and calamities struck in the time of the early Church.

Disasters

Famine — Israel AD 46–48

Earthquake — Laodicea AD 60

Volcano — Pompeii AD 62

War and Fire — Jerusalem AD 70

Old Testament prophets frequently predicted wars and natural disasters as signs of God's judgment against wicked and perverse people. *And in an instant, suddenly, you will be visited by the LORD of hosts with thunder and with earthquake and great noise, with whirlwind and tempest, and the flame of a devouring fire* (Isaiah 29:6). Jeremiah also predicts God's judgment on the wicked: *"Behold, I will punish them; the young men shall die by the sword; their sons and their daughters shall die by famine; and none of them shall be left"* (Jeremiah 11:22–23).

Daniel predicted the great tribulation. *And there shall be a time of trouble, such as never has been since there was a nation till that time; but at that time your people shall be delivered, everyone whose name shall be found written in the book* (Daniel 12:1b). Similarly, Jesus reiterates: *"For in those days there will be such tribulation as has not been from the beginning of the creation which God created until now, and never will be"* (Mark 13:19). The triumph of those who remain faithful in the time of tribulation emerges clearly in the Apocalypse of Saint John. *"These are they who have come out of the great tribulation; they have washed their robes and made them white in the blood of the Lamb"* (Revelation 7:14).

The age of the Church emerges as an age of evangelism and suffering. Many Christian martyrs follow Jesus, and offer their lives for the truth of the Gospel. After Jesus warns the disciples not to be led astray, one finds a bit of comfort in having been forewarned. *"But take heed, I have told you all things beforehand"* (Mark 13:23). The age of the Church, the age in which we now live, follows Mark 13:23. This age will continue until Jesus comes again in glory to judge the living and the dead. The gap between Mark 13:23 and Mark 13:24 is already about two thousand years long! The early Church and Christians throughout the ages eagerly await the coming of the Son of Man in glory.

The triumphant Son of Man will come in glory—Daniel predicts the triumph of the son of man. *And behold, with the clouds of heaven there came one like a son of man, and he came to the Ancient of Days and was presented before him. And to him was given dominion and glory and kingdom, that all peoples, nations, and languages should serve him; his dominion is an everlasting dominion, which shall not pass away, and his kingdom one that shall not be destroyed* (Daniel 7:13–14). In a certain sense, the triumph of Jesus is the triumph of the Cross. After the crucifixion, Jesus ascends to heaven and is enthroned at the Father's right hand.

The triumph of Christ continues in the Church, as Jesus draws repentant men and women to Himself, and transforms their lives by His grace. The final triumph of Christ will occur in His Second Coming. Jesus describes it clearly. *"But in those days, after the tribulation, the sun will be darkened, and the moon will not give its light, and the stars will be falling from heaven, and the powers in the heavens will be shaken. And then they will see the Son of man coming in clouds with great power and glory. And then he will send out the angels, and gather his elect from the four winds, from the ends of the earth to the ends of heaven"* (Mark 13:24–27).

Joel described the day of the Lord: *The earth quakes before them, the heavens tremble. The sun and the moon are darkened, and the stars withdraw their shining* (Joel 2:10). Saint Peter reminded the early Christians of the promise of the Lord's return, which would indicate the end of this world. *But the day of the Lord will come like a thief, and then the heavens will pass away with a loud noise, and the elements will be dissolved with fire, and the earth and the works that are upon it will be burned up* (2 Peter 3:10). Saint Paul offers a vivid picture of the coming of the Lord. *For the Lord himself will descend from heaven with a cry of command, with the archangel's call, and with the sound of the trumpet of God. And the dead in Christ will rise first; then we who are alive, who are left, shall be caught up together with them in the clouds to meet the Lord in the air; and so we shall always be with the Lord. Therefore comfort one another with these words* (1 Thessalonians 4:16–18). But, when will this event happen?

Jesus exhorts believers to watch and pray—*"But of that day or that hour no one knows, not even the angels in heaven, nor the Son, but only the Father. Take heed, watch and pray; for you do not know when the time will come"* (Mark 13:32–33). Just as a servant doesn't know when his master will return from a journey, no one knows when the Lord will return in glory. So, the prudent believer waits in hope and prays. *Pray at all times in the Spirit, with all prayer and supplication. To that end keep alert with all perseverance, making supplication for all the saints* (Ephesians 6:18). Wait in faithfulness, watch, and pray. *Continue steadfastly in prayer, being watchful in it with thanksgiving* (Colossians 4:2). When will Jesus return triumphantly in glory? Who will be waiting faithfully?

Of the Son it is said: *"Of that day and hour no one knows, except the Father; not the angels in heaven and not the Son"* (Mark 13:32). If we receive Baptism equally in the Father, Son, and Holy Spirit, we must believe there is one name for Father, Son, and Holy Spirit, which is God. If God is one, how can there be a diversity of knowledge in one divinity? What is greater, to be God or to know all things? If He is God, how does He not know?

In the Apostle we read about Christ: *"In whom are hidden all the treasures of wisdom and knowledge"* (Colossians 2:3). See what he says: *"all the treasures of wisdom and knowledge."* Not that some are and some are not: but *all* the treasures of wisdom and knowledge; but they are *hidden.*

So what is in Him is not lacking to Him, even though it be hidden from us. But if all the treasures of wisdom and knowledge are hidden in Christ, we must ask why they are hidden. If we men were to know the day of judgment, which is the subject of the statement, and that the day of judgment is to come after two thousand years, knowing that it is so far in the future, we would only become more negligent. We would say, "What difference does it make to me if the day of judgment is to come after two thousand years?" When it is said that the Son does not know the day of judgment, it is so stated for our sake, so we do not know when the day of judgment is to come.

Finally, see what follows that statement: *"Take care, watch and pray: for you do not know when that time will come"* (Mark 13:33).

Saint Jerome (347–420 AD),
Homilies on the Gospel of Mark, 10, 13, 32.

1. What is foretold in the following passages?

Micah 3:12
Mark 13:1–2
Luke 19:41–44

2. Where was Jesus? Who was with Him? Mark 13:3

3. What can you learn about the coming of the kingdom of God?

Mark 13:4
1 Thessalonians 5:2

4. Identify some warnings in these passages.

Mark 13:5–6
Mark 13:21–23
John 8:24
1 John 2:18–19

* Where would you hope to be when Jesus comes again?

5. What will happen to the disciples?

Mark 13:9
Acts 4:1–4
Acts 5:40
Acts 12:1–4
Acts 21:30–36

6. What does Jesus compel us to do?

Mark 13:10
Matthew 28:19–20
CCC 849
CCC 905

* When have you shared the Gospel with someone, or invited someone to Church?

7. Who will help you to find the words to share the Gospel? Mark 13:11

8. What will happen to families of believers? Mark 13:12–13

9. What is the sign that people should leave Jerusalem? Mark 13:14

10. What comfort did Jesus give? Mark 13:23

11. What are we eagerly awaiting?

Isaiah 13:9–10
Daniel 7:13–14
Mark 13:26
1 Thessalonians 4:16-17
Revelation 1:4–7
CCC 673

12. How could someone prepare to meet the Lord? Acts 2:38, 3:19

13. What can you learn about God's Word? Mark 13:31

* Why is it important for you to study God's Word?

14. When will the Lord return?

Mark 13:32
Matthew 24:36
CCC474

15. What signs will precede the Lord's return?

Isaiah 13:9–10
Joel 2:1–10
Amos 8:9
Mark 13:24–27

16. In the end, who will be saved? Mark 13:13

17. What must people be prepared to do?

Mark 13:14–16
2 Corinthians 5:9–10
1 Thessalonians 1:10

18. What does Jesus ask believers to do?

Mark 13:33
CCC 2612
CCC 2849

19. What verb is repeated three times in Mark 13:33–37? What must you do?

20. What can you learn from these passages?

1 Corinthians 16:13–14
Colossians 4:2, 6
1 Peter 5:8

* Share some ways that you can be attentive to the Lord and watchful in prayer.

CHAPTER 16

Bread that is Broken
Mark 14:1–31

He took bread, and blessed, and broke it, and gave it to them, and said,
"Take; this is my body."
And he took a chalice, and when he had given thanks
he gave it to them and they all drank of it.
And he said to them,
"This is my blood of the covenant, which is poured out for many.
Truly I say to you, I shall not drink again of the fruit of the vine until that day
when I drink it new in the kingdom of God."
Mark 14:22–25

The Passion narrative provides the climax of Mark's Gospel. Each event and detail leads up to the Cross of Christ. Contrast the elevation of Jesus on the Cross in supreme sacrifice, with the depth of betrayal of the people. They hand Him over, deny, and abandon Him. Everything in the Gospel of Mark has been leading up to these final three chapters, and the purpose of Jesus' mission.

Two beautiful events fall in between three evil situations. The anointing of Jesus is sandwiched between the chief priests and scribes conspiracy to arrest and kill Jesus, and Judas' betrayal. The religious leaders do not want to arrest Jesus during the feasts of Passover and Unleavened Bread, when the city of Jerusalem will swell with pilgrims. They do not want to cause a riot of thousands of people. However, the sacrifice of Jesus will take place on God's timetable, not theirs. The Last Supper falls after Judas' plot to betray Jesus and before Jesus predicts Peter's denial.

Mark 14:1–2	Leaders plot to kill Jesus.
Mark 14:3–9	*A woman anoints the Messiah.*
Mark 14:10–11	Judas seeks to betray Jesus.
Mark 14:12–25	*Jesus eats His Last Supper with the apostles.*
Mark 14:26–31	Peter's denial is foretold.

While Jesus dines in the home of Simon the leper (perhaps someone who had been healed of leprosy), in Bethany, an unnamed woman comes, bringing an alabaster jar of costly ointment and anoints the Lord's head with oil. John identifies Mary, the sister of Martha and Lazarus of Bethany (John 12:1–8), pouring nard on Jesus' feet. Nard perfumed the couch of the king in the Song of Solomon. *While the king was on his couch, my nard gave forth its fragrance* (Song of Solomon 1:12). Nard, a costly perfume from India, was worth three hundred denarii. Since one denarius equaled a full day's wage, the cost of this ointment was almost an entire year's earnings. In ancient Israel, pouring oil over someone's head reflected the anointing of a king. *So he arose, and went into the house; and the young man poured the oil on his head, saying to him, "Thus says the LORD the God of Israel, I anoint you king over the people of the LORD, over Israel"* (2 Kings 9:6).

Some observers are indignant at this financial waste in anointing Jesus with such a costly perfume. They insist that the nard should have been sold, and the money given to the poor. But Jesus insists that she has done a noble thing. *"Let her alone; why do you trouble her? She has done a beautiful thing to me. For you always have the poor with you, and whenever you will, you can do good to them; but you will not always have me. She has done what she could; she has anointed my body beforehand for burying. And truly, I say to you, wherever the gospel is preached in the whole world, what she has done will be told in memory of her"* (Mark 14:6–9). Jesus knows that His death and burial are imminent. Jesus praises the woman, who has recognized His identity, and anointed Him the Messiah and King.

Just as the woman's act of love and devotion was pleasing to Jesus, so acts of love and charity for the poor are always pleasing to God. God remains hidden in the poor and marginalized. Mother Teresa of Calcutta's charism was to serve Jesus in the distressing disguise of the poor. However, her sisters, the Missionaries of Charity begin each day with Mass and Adoration of the Blessed Sacrament. In spending time with Jesus they find the strength to serve the poorest of the poor, the dying and destitute. They lavish attention on Jesus and the poor.

Judas conspires to betray Jesus—Contrasted with this woman's extravagant devotion the religious leaders and one of the apostles conspire to kill Jesus. Judas Iscariot, one of the Twelve, goes to the chief priests and offers to betray Jesus. They offer Judas money for his betrayal. Other evangelists expose Judas' motivation for betrayal. Matthew reveals that Judas was greedy (Matthew 26:15). Luke discloses that Satan influenced Judas' life (Luke 22:3). John provides insight from Judas' reaction to the costly nard used to anoint Jesus. *"Why was this ointment not sold for three hundred denarii and given to the poor?" This he said, not that he cared for the poor but because he was a thief, and as he had the money box he used to take what was put into it* (John 12:5–6). Judas was a thief plagued by greed. John also reveals that the devil had entered the heart of Judas (John 13:2). Judas' sins provided an opening for Satan's influence to enter.

Judas had walked with Jesus, talked with Jesus, and shared meals with Him. He watched Jesus perform miracles of healing and multiply food for the hungry. Perhaps they shared laughter and touching moments. And yet, Judas makes a conscious, premeditated decision to hand Jesus over to enemies. Mortal sin involves grave matter, full knowledge of the evil of the act, and full consent of the will. Judas does not commit an impulsive crime of passion, without thinking. Judas plans out his treachery. Jesus feels betrayed. *Even my bosom friend in whom I trusted, who ate of my bread, has lifted his heel against me* (Psalm 41:9).

Jesus' last supper with the apostles—Mark places the Last Supper (Mark 14:22–25) between Judas' conspiracy to betray Jesus and the prediction of Peter's denial (Mark 14:30). Passover, a yearly Jewish feast, recalls Israel's deliverance from slavery in Egypt. God told Moses to celebrate this feast annually to recall God's powerful act of redemption (Exodus 12). Along with the Feast of Unleavened Bread, the celebration continued for seven days from the fifteenth until the twenty-first day of the month of Nissan (March/April). Homes are cleaned from all leaven. Unblemished, firstling Passover lambs would be sacrificed in the temple courts. At sundown, each family or household eats the Seder meal of roasted lamb, unleavened bread, bitter herbs, and wine.

When the disciples ask Jesus where they will eat the Passover, they learn that all of the preparations have been made. Jesus instructs them to go into the city and follow a man, carrying a jar of water, to a large, upper room. Women ordinarily drew and carried water: *by the well of water at the time of evening, the time when women go out to draw water* (Genesis 24:11). A man carrying a water jug is an unusual occurrence. Everything has been prepared exactly as Jesus foretold.

When the apostles gather, Jesus announces that one of them will betray Him, and they are distressed at these words. Jesus knows all things. He knows what will take place. God can achieve His purposes without human cooperation. Perhaps Judas receives this one last opportunity to examine his heart and repent. The disciples reflect and question as they dip their bread into the dish of *maror* "bitter herbs," recalling the bitter bondage of slavery. Similarly, the bondage of sin brings bitterness. *See to it that no one fail to obtain the grace of God; that no "root of bitterness" spring up and cause trouble, and by it the many become defiled* (Hebrews 12:15). Saint Paul admonishes those who approach the table of the Lord: *Let a man examine himself, and so eat of the bread and drink of the cup. For any one who eats and drinks without discerning the body eats and drinks judgment upon himself* (1 Corinthians 11:28–29).

Mark tightly weaves past, present and future events into the Last Supper account. The Seder is not complete without the Passover Lamb. Jesus becomes the Lamb of sacrifice in His Passion and death. Presently, Jesus identifies His own flesh with the bread of the Passover feast. Jesus institutes the sacraments of the Eucharist and Holy Orders. He anticipates the messianic banquet in God's kingdom. Earlier Jesus had foretold, *"For the Son of man also came not to be served but to serve, and to give his life as a ransom for many"* (Mark 10:45). Now Jesus announces, *"This is my blood of the covenant, which is poured out for many"* (Mark 14:24).

Bread that is broken—Consistent with Jesus' actions at the multiplication of the loaves, *he took bread, and blessed, and broke it and gave it to them* (Mark 14:22). In feeding the five thousand, Jesus performed a similar ritual. *And taking the five loaves and two fish he looked up to heaven, and blessed, and broke the loaves, and gave them to the disciples to set before the people* (Mark 6:41). Similarly, in feeding the four thousand, *he took the seven loaves, and having given thanks he broke them and gave them to his disciples to set before the people* (Mark 8:6).

Jesus institutes the Blessed Sacrament

*He **took** bread, and **blessed**,*
*and **broke** it,*
*and **gave** it them,*
and said,
"Take; this is my body"
(Mark 14:22).

Jesus likewise takes the chalice, gives thanks, and offers it to the apostles, saying, *"This is my blood of the covenant, which is poured out for many"* (Mark 14:24). Wine symbolizes an abundance of joy: *You have put more joy in my heart than they have when their grain and new wine abound* (Psalm 4:7). Old Testament covenants were sealed in blood, and Jesus seals the New Covenant between Christ and His Church in His own blood. Jesus restores the broken relationship between sinful humanity and God the Father by pouring out His precious blood in atonement for our sins. *But God shows his love for us in that while we were yet sinners Christ died for us. Since, therefore, we are now justified by his blood, much more shall we be saved by him from the wrath of God* (Romans 5:8–9).

This last supper will be the last time that Jesus will eat a meal with His apostles until He has completed His mission. The drama of the Passion of Christ unfolds exactly in the way it has been ordained. Jesus purposefully explains to the apostles how they will continue His mission, after He is gone. Holy Orders and the Eucharist were initiation by Jesus. The Eucharist was celebrated in the early Church, and is offered continually, every hour, every day, in Catholic Churches all around the world for the sustenance of the followers of Jesus.

Jesus predicts Peter's denial—Following the Last Supper, Jesus and the disciples sing hymns, probably some of the Hallel Psalms (Psalms 113-118) sung on joyous occasions, as they proceed to the Mount of Olives. Zechariah prophesied that there would be a wounded shepherd. *"Strike the shepherd, that the sheep may be scattered"* (Zechariah 13:7). Jesus recounts this prophecy, and then says: *"But after I am raised up, I will go before you to Galilee"* (Mark 14:28). Peter loves Jesus, but he does not yet understand that faithfulness to God requires more than good intentions and strong will. Fidelity is a pure gift of grace. Peter must learn to deny himself (Mark 8:34) in humble submission to God. Denial of Christ is the opposite of discipleship. Jesus knows all things. Peter will learn to trust in God's Word, and to follow. Peter will learn to trust Jesus, rather than his own strength, in leading the flock. Similarly, believers must learn self-discipline and self-mastery, but must ultimately rely on God's grace to remain faithful.

The Eucharist, the Heart of Life

Two immeasurably profound sayings . . . stand for all time at the heart of the Church, at the heart of the Eucharistic celebration, the sayings from which we draw our life, because these words are the presence of the living God, the presence of Jesus Christ in our midst, and thereby they tear the world free from its unbearable boredom, indifference, sadness and evil. *"This is my Body, this is my Blood"*: these are expressions taken from the Israelite language of sacrifice, which designated the gifts offered in sacrifice to God in the Temple. If Jesus makes use of these words, then he is designating *himself as the true and ultimate sacrifice,* in whom all these unsuccessful strivings of the Old Testament are fulfilled.

What had always been intended and could never be achieved in the Old Testament sacrifices is incorporated in him. God does not desire the sacrifice of animals; everything belongs to him. And he does not desire human sacrifice, for he has created man for living. God desires something more: he desires love, which transforms man and through which he becomes capable of relating to God, giving himself up to God . . .

"This is my body, which is given for you; my blood, which is shed for you and for many." . . . At the Last Supper, Jesus takes this saying into his own mouth: He is suffering for the many . . . it has always been clear that God desires that everyone should be saved and that Jesus died, not just for a part of mankind, but for everyone . . . he loves everyone because he has created everyone . . . A second point to add to this is that God never, in any case, forces anyone to be saved. God accepts man's freedom . . . That is why God's all-embracing desire to save people does not involve the actual salvation of all men. He allows us the power to refuse.

On the Cross, Christ saw love through to the end . . . Jesus died praying, and in the abyss of death he upheld the First Commandment and held on to the presence of God. Out of such a death springs this sacrament, the Eucharist . . . So let us be ready to hear the call of Jesus Christ, who achieved the great success of God on the Cross; he who, as the grain of wheat that died, has become fruitful down through all the centuries; the Tree of Life, in whom even today men may put their hope. . . . Receiving Communion means entering into communion with Jesus Christ; it signifies moving into the open through him who alone could overcome the limits and thus, with him and on the basis of his existence, becoming capable of resurrection oneself . . . What is given us here is not a piece of a body, not a thing, but him, the Resurrected one himself—the person who shares himself with us in his love, which runs right through the Cross. This means that receiving Communion is always a personal act. It is never merely a ritual . . . In Communion I enter into the Lord, who is communicating himself to me.

Joseph Cardinal Ratzinger (Pope Benedict XVI), *God is Near Us*
(San Francisco, CA: Ignatius Press, 2003), 32–37, 40–41, 81.

The Church draws her life from the Eucharist. This truth does not simply express a daily experience of faith, but recapitulates *the heart of the mystery of the Church.* In a variety of ways she joyfully experiences the constant fulfillment of the promise: *"Lo, I am with you always, to the close of the age"* (Matthew 28:20), but in the Holy Eucharist, through the changing of bread and wine into the body and blood of the Lord, she rejoices in this presence with unique intensity. Ever since Pentecost, when the Church, the People of the New Covenant, began her pilgrim journey towards her heavenly homeland, the Divine Sacrament has continued to mark the passing of her days, filling them with confident hope . . .

The Eucharistic sacrifice is "the source and summit of the Christian life." "For the most holy Eucharist contains the Church's entire spiritual wealth: Christ himself, our Passover and living bread. Through his own flesh, now made living and life-giving by the Holy Spirit, he offers life to men." Consequently the gaze of the Church is constantly turned to her Lord, present in the Sacrament of the Altar, in which she discovers the full manifestation of his boundless love . . .

Reading the account of the institution of the Eucharist in the Synoptic Gospels, we are struck by the simplicity and the "solemnity" with which Jesus, on the evening of the Last Supper, instituted the great sacrament. There is an episode, which in some way serves as its prelude: *the anointing at Bethany.* A woman, whom John identifies as Mary the sister of Lazarus, pours a flask of *costly ointment* over Jesus' head, which provokes from the disciples—and from Judas in particular—an indignant response, as if this act, in light of the needs of the poor, represented an intolerable "waste." But Jesus' own reaction is completely different. While in no way detracting from the duty of charity towards the needy, for whom the disciples must always show special care—*"the poor you will always have with you"* (Mark 14:7)—he looks towards his imminent death and burial, and sees this act of anointing as an anticipation of the honor which his body will continue to merit even after his death, indissolubly bound as it is to the mystery of his person.

The account continues . . . with Jesus' charge to the disciples to *prepare carefully the "large upper room"* needed for the Passover meal and with the narration of the institution of the Eucharist. Reflecting at least in part the *Jewish rites* of the Passover meal leading up to the singing of the Hallel, the story presents with sobriety and solemnity, even in the variants of the different traditions, the words spoken by Christ over the bread and wine, which he made into concrete expressions of the handing over of his body and the shedding of his blood . . . In the humble signs of bread and wine, changed into his body and blood, Christ walks beside us as our strength and our food for the journey, and he enables us to become, for everyone, witnesses of hope. If, in the presence of this mystery, reason experiences its limits, the heart, enlightened by the grace of the Holy Spirit, clearly sees the response that it demanded, and bows low in adoration and unbounded love.

Blessed John Paul II, *Ecclesia de Eucharistia,* April 17, 2003, 1, 47, 62.

1. Find the word *betray, betrayed,* or *betrayer* in Mark 14:1–72.

2. What can you learn about the incident in Mark 14:2–9?

2 Kings 9:3–6
Psalm 23:5
Song of Solomon 1:12
Song of Solomon 4:12–14
Mark 14:3–5
John 12:1–5

3. How did Jesus evaluate the woman's action? Mark 14:6–7

* Why is it appropriate to waste time and treasure on Jesus?

** How is it possible to be lavish to God, and still show charity to the poor?

4. What did the woman accomplish, and how is she remembered? Mark 14:8–9

* What are some things that you would like people to remember about you?

5. What can you learn about Judas?

Matthew 26:15
Mark 14:10–11
Mark 14:43–46
Luke 22:3
John 6:70–71
John 12:6; 13:2

6. Explain the preparations for celebrating the Passover in Mark 14:12–16.

7. What can you learn about the celebration of Passover?

Exodus 12:1–7
Exodus 12:8
Exodus 12:14–15
Exodus 12:24–28

8. Find some unusual aspects of the Passover in Mark 14.

Genesis 24:11
Mark 14:13
Mark 14:14–15
Mark 14:16

9. What title is used to refer to Jesus? Mark 14:14

* What titles for God do you usually use in prayer?

10. What information does Jesus share with the apostles?

Psalm 41:9	
Mark 14:18	
John 13:18	

11. How did the apostles respond to this news? Mark 14:19

* The apostles seem to examine their consciences. How can you do that?

12. Did the apostles learn who would betray Jesus? John 13:21–30

13. What does Jesus say about His betrayer? Mark14:20–21

14. Compare the following accounts.

Matthew 26:26–29
Mark 14:22–25
Luke 22:17–19
1 Corinthians 11:23–26

15. How does Jesus explain sacrament?

John 6:35
John 6:51
John 6:53
John 6:56

16. How did people respond to Jesus' teaching? John 6:66–69

17. Explain the sacrament that Jesus institutes at the Last Supper.

CCC 1323
CCC 1324–1327
CCC 1328–1330
CCC 1335
CCC 1339–1340

18. What other sacrament did Jesus initiate? What did He command? CCC 1337

19. Explain the Holy Orders necessary for the Eucharist to continue.

CCC 1555–1556
CCC 1564–1566

20. What does Eucharist mean? Share your favorite Communion prayer or hymn.

* Name your bishop and priests. Pray for them.

CHAPTER 17

Trials and Crucifixion
Mark 14:32–15

And Jesus uttered a loud cry, and breathed his last.
And the curtain of the temple was torn in two, from top to bottom.
And when the centurion, who stood facing him,
saw that he thus breathed his last, he said,
"Truly this man was the Son of God!"
Mark 15:37–39

Jesus prays—Mark reveals Jesus at prayer. Christian artists capture the most familiar of these prayer times in Jesus' agony in the garden of Gethsemane, on the western slope of the Mount of Olives. One can assume that Jesus spent the forty days in the wilderness (Mark 1:12–13), preceding His public ministry, fasting and praying intently. Mark also relates that after calling the disciples, exorcizing the first demon, preaching, and healing in Galilee, Jesus took time alone in the early morning to pray. *And in the morning, a great while before day, he rose and went out to a lonely, place, and there he prayed* (Mark 1:35). After feeding five thousand, Jesus sent the disciples into a boat, dismissed the crowd, and went alone to pray (Mark 6:46). Prayer sustains and energizes Jesus, and prayer animates His entire ministry. Jesus appoints twelve special men, the apostles to remain with Him. *And he appointed twelve, to be with him* (Mark 3:14). On the last night of His earthly life, Jesus invites the apostles to remain with Him in prayer. He invites, Peter, James, and John to draw near Him to watch and pray with Him.

Jesus ponders and confronts the reality of His imminent, horrific suffering and death. He also suffers under the weight of the enormity of human sin, so deserving of God's punishment and wrath. *He was despised and rejected by men; a man of sorrows, and acquainted with grief; and as one from whom men hide their faces he was despised, and we esteemed him not. Surely he has borne our griefs and carried our sorrows . . . he was wounded for our transgressions, he was bruised for our iniquities; upon him was the chastisement that made us whole* (Isaiah 53:3–5).

Mark is the only evangelist to reveal Jesus using the intimate Aramaic word *Abba* "Father" to address God the Father. *And he said "Abba, Father, all things are possible to you; remove this chalice from me; yet not what I will, but what you will"* (Mark 14:36). The psalmist recognized the fatherhood of God. *As a father pities his children, so the* LORD *pities those who fear him* (Psalm 103:13). Paul uses the term "Abba, Father" in two of his epistles. *When we cry "Abba! Father!" it is the Spirit himself bearing witness with our spirit that we are children of God* (Romans 8:15–16). Jesus' submission to the Father enables sinful humanity to be reconciled to God. Those who believe in Jesus and are baptized are adopted into the family of God. *But when the time had fully come, God sent forth his Son, born of woman, born under the law, to redeem those who were under the law, so that we might receive adoption as sons. And because you are sons, God has sent the Spirit of his Son into our hearts, crying, "Abba! Father!"* (Galatians 4:4–6).

Jesus submits to the will of the Father, even as He knows that God can do all things. God can remove this suffering. Jesus had previously told the father of a possessed boy, *"All things are possible to him who believes"* (Mark 9:23). When Jesus spoke with His disciples about the difficulties that the rich encounter in entering the kingdom of God, *Jesus looked at them and said, "With men it is impossible, but not with God; for all things are possible with God"* (Mark 10:27). God could remove the chalice of suffering, if it is His will to do so.

Jesus seeks solace and comfort from His three closest apostles, Peter, James, and John. The humanity of Jesus desires human contact and support. People suffering from serious illness can be greatly comforted by having family or friends nearby to visit them and keep them company. But Jesus' closest friends prove to be fickle. Jesus asks them to watch and pray, but three times they disappoint Him.

"My soul is very sorrowful, even to death; remain here, and watch" (Mark 14:34).
"Simon are you asleep? Could you not watch one hour?" (Mark 14:37).
"Are you still sleeping and taking your rest?" (Mark 14:41).

The Church views Jesus' question to Peter to watch one hour as an invitation to all Christians to set aside time for daily prayer. Religious pray throughout the entire day. But even busy laypeople can get up early to pray, or stop in their workday to attend daily Mass and take a prayer time. On Holy Thursday night, churches remain open, so that the faithful can watch and pray with Jesus, even though the disciples could not. Prayer and watchfulness are essential in warding off the temptations of the evil one. God's grace enables perseverance in prayer.

Judas betrays Jesus with a kiss—And "immediately," a term that Mark uses over forty times in his Gospel, Judas approaches Jesus with a crowd of armed soldiers. This is the first time that a crowd does not relate to Jesus in a favorable way. Previously, crowds of people thronged around Jesus, trying to touch the hem of His garment to obtain healing, or to see Him, or hear a word from Him. Now this crowd wants to seize, antagonize, and abuse Jesus.

Usually, a kiss signifies love and affection. In the early Church, Saints Peter and Paul encourage the Christians to greet one another with a holy kiss. *Greet one another with the kiss of love* (1 Peter 5:14). *Greet one another with a holy kiss* (Romans 16:16). When Jesus dined with Simon, the Pharisee, a sinful woman came into the house to anoint Jesus with oil. *"You gave me no kiss, but from the time I came in she has not ceased to kiss my feet. You did not anoint my head with oil, but she has anointed by feet with ointment"* (Luke 7:45–46). Judas turns what should be a gesture of affection into the mark of betrayal. *Faithful are the wounds of a friend; profuse are the kisses of an enemy* (Proverbs 27:6). One of the intimate Twelve becomes the adversary, and seals it with a kiss.

Violence erupts—An impulsive disciple mistakenly thinks that he can stop violence with more violence. *Then Simon Peter, having a sword, drew it and struck the high priest's slave and cut off his right ear. The slave's name was Malchus. Jesus said to Peter, "Put your sword into its sheath; shall I not drink the chalice which the Father has given me?"* (John 18:10–11). Luke tells us that Jesus works another healing miracle, restoring the man's ear. *But Jesus said, "No more of this!" And he touched his ear and healed him* (Luke 22:51–52). Jesus has been in the temple publicly preaching, and yet they come to seize Him with swords and clubs, as if Jesus were a robber. Why did they not approach Jesus in plain daylight when He was preaching in the temple?

They all deserted him and fled (Mark 14:50). The apostles who walked, talked, and ate with Jesus, all flee. No one stays with Jesus. The prophet Zechariah predicted about a coming wounded prophet. *"And if one asks him, 'What are these wounds on your back?' he will say, 'The wounds I received in the house of my friends.'" Awake, O sword, against my shepherd, against the man who stands next to me," says the* LORD *of hosts. "Strike the shepherd, that the sheep may be scattered"* (Zechariah 13:6–7). They strike Jesus, and the disciples flee. Peter follows at a distance, as Jesus is led to the house of the high priest.

Kangaroo court—Jesus is brought before the chief priests and Sanhedrin in the middle of the night. Mark uses a framing technique to arrange the silent faithfulness of Jesus in contrast with the cowardice of Peter. Trumped up charges are brought against Jesus. Finding no valid reasons to put Jesus to death, the chief priests and the whole council hear false witnesses and liars, whose testimony does not agree. They accuse Jesus of: 1) blasphemy, and 2) threatening to destroy the temple. The chief priests know that Mosaic Law demands two or more credible witnesses. *"A single witness shall not prevail against a man for any crime or for any wrong in connection with any offense that he has committed; only on the evidence of two witnesses, or of three witnesses, shall a charge be sustained"* (Deuteronomy 19:15). Daniel rescued the righteous woman Susanna, by skillfully separating, and publicly questioning two false witnesses (Daniel 13:44–64).

For the most part, Jesus remains silent, while being falsely accused, fulfilling the prophecy of Isaiah: *He was oppressed, and he was afflicted, yet he opened not his mouth* (Isaiah 53:7). Ultimately, Caiaphas, the high priest asks Jesus directly, *"Are you the Christ, the Son of the Blessed?" And Jesus said, "I am; and you will see the Son of man sitting at the right hand of Power, and coming with the clouds of heaven"* (Mark 14:61–62). None of the liars or false witnesses could convict Jesus. Jesus is condemned to death only when He speaks the truth about Himself. Jesus was sentenced to death because He claimed to be—and He is—the Messiah, the holy One of God.

Jesus has not broken Mosaic Law, but Caiaphas has broken a commandment. *"The priest who is chief among his brethren . . . who has been consecrated to wear the garments, shall not let the hair of his head hang loose, nor tear his clothes"* (Leviticus 21:10). Caiaphas condemns Jesus for telling the truth, and then Caiaphas breaks Mosaic Law by tearing his clothes, *and the high priest tore his clothes* (Mark 14:63). Jesus is innocent. But those who accuse Jesus are not!

Peter's denial—Earlier in the evening, Peter said vehemently, *"If I must die with you, I will not deny you"* (Mark 14:31). While Jesus suffers false accusations, mockery, spitting, and beating in the house of Caiaphas, Peter is warming himself in the courtyard. Peter denies Jesus three times. *"Certainly you are one of them, for you are a Galilean." But he began to invoke a curse on himself and to swear, "I do not know this man of whom you speak"* (Mark 14:71). But, Peter, you *do* know this man. Peter, you said, *"You are the Christ, the Son of the living God"* (Matthew 16:16). God the Father revealed it to you.

After Peter's denial, the cock crows, just as Jesus had foretold. Jesus knows the heart of man. He knew Peter would fall. His denial was a dreadful failure. Peter's tears show true repentance. Mark recounts this failure of Peter to show that there is no sin too big for God to forgive, if one repents, and shows genuine contrition. Because of his own weakness, Peter can empathize with other weak sinners.

Jesus appears before Pilate—The Sanhedrin condemns Jesus to die, but they lack the authority to enforce the death penalty. Mosaic Law specifies that the crime of blasphemy would be punishable by stoning (Leviticus 24:16), not crucifixion. Nothing in Mosiac Law warrants crucifixion. Pontius Pilate, the Roman procurator of Judea from AD 26–36, authorizes the death sentence, demonstrating that both Jews and Gentiles alike share culpability in the death of Christ. The day of infamy unfolds.

Sunrise	Mark 15:1	*As soon as it was morning . . . they bound Jesus and . . . delivered him to Pilate.*
9:00 am	Mark 15:25	*It was the third hour, when they crucified him.*
Noon	Mark 15:33	*And when the sixth hour had come, there was darkness over the whole land*
3:00 pm	Mark 15:33	*. . . until the ninth hour.*
Evening	Mark 15:42	*Joseph of Arimathea entombed Jesus' body.*

And Pilate asked him, "Are you the King of the Jews?" And he answered him, "You have said so" (Mark 15:2). Jesus offers a somewhat ambiguous response. Even though Jesus *is* the King of the Jews, He does not overtly admit it. Jesus simply accepts Pilate's statement. In so doing, Jesus allows Himself to be perceived as guilty of treason, since "there could be no king but Caesar." Pilate was an arrogant, corrupt, and brutal prefect.

Pilate knows that Jesus is innocent. *Pilate again asked him, "Have you no answer to make?"* (Mark 15:4). Jesus' refusal to defend Himself again fulfills the prophecy of Isaiah. *He was afflicted, yet he opened not his mouth* (Isaiah 53:7). Allowing an innocent Man to be crucified, Pilate shows grave cowardice, for which he will always be remembered.

Pilate delivers Jesus to be crucified—In deciding to release a prisoner, he offers the people a choice. Barabbas, whose name *bar'-abbā'* means "son of the father," was a murderer and insurrectionist. In contrast, the innocent Jesus really *is* the "Son of the Father." Pilate knows that Jesus is guiltless and that the chief priests act from envy. Nonetheless, Pilate plays the politician pandering to the crowd, without regard for truth or justice. The chief priests control the mob, and stir them up to request the release of Barabbas. By rejecting Jesus the Son, they also reject God the Father. Pilate acquiesces to the demands of the angry mob to crucify Jesus.

Jesus is scourged and mocked—Pontius Pilate ordered Jesus to be scourged and then crucified. Jesus was stripped and bound to a pillar. Soldiers took leather whips fastened with pieces of bone, nails, or scraps of metal to beat the victim. The scraps of metal tore the flesh and caused excruciating pain and copious bleeding. A victim could die from exsanguination from the flogging alone. A particularly vivid and realistic portrayal of Jesus' scourging at the pillar is depicted in the movie, *The Passion of the Christ*. Flogging caused profuse bleeding prior to the crucifixion. Scourging could also be the sole means of execution of a criminal.

A whole battalion, up to six hundred soldiers, was summoned to punish this one unarmed Man. They taunt Jesus, spit at Him, strip Him, clothe Him in purple, and place a crown of thorns on His head. These cruelties fulfill many Old Testament prophecies. *All who see me mock at me, they make mouths at me, they wag their heads* (Psalm 22:7). *"I gave my back to those who struck me, and my cheeks to those who pulled out the beard; I hid not my face from shame and spitting"* (Isaiah 50:6). The humiliation, indignity, and cruelty are unimaginable. Atheists and agnostics continue to mock Jesus and taunt people of faith today.

Simon of Cyrene, a Jew from North Africa (present day Libya), helps Jesus carry the Cross. Weakened from blood loss at the scourging, Jesus accepts help, and presses on. Meeting Jesus evidently transforms Simon's life. Paul refers to Simon's son Rufus, and his mother, in Romans 16:13, suggesting that Simon's family became part of the early Christian community. Simon carried the Cross for Jesus, sharing in His Passion. However, Jesus died on the Cross for Simon and all of sinful humanity. The Church uses Simon's example to explain redemptive suffering. Christians can unite their sufferings with Christ's suffering.

When Jesus arrives at Golgotha, they offer Him wine mixed with myrrh, but He does not take it. At the Last Supper, the preceding night, Jesus said, *"Truly, I say to you, I shall not drink again of the fruit of the vine until that day when I drink it new in the kingdom of God"* (Mark 14:25). The wine may have been offered as a narcotic. *Give strong drink to him who is perishing, and wine to those in bitter distress* (Proverb 31:6). But Jesus honors His word and declines. The blood loss, torture, and heat of the day would have caused severe dehydration.

Jesus is crucified—Mark relates the crucifixion in stark and concise terms. The horrors of this type of execution are obvious and require no elaboration. They crucify Jesus at the third hour, nine in the morning, and divide his garments among them. *They divide my garments among them, and for my clothing they cast lots* (Psalm 22:18). Ironically, Pilate, who asks, *"What is truth?"* (John 18:38), inadvertently proclaims the truth in an inscription above the Cross of Christ, for the whole world to see. *Pilate also wrote a title and put it on the cross; it read, "Jesus of Nazareth, the King of the Jews"* (John 19:19). This inscription was rendered in Hebrew, Latin, and Greek, for the whole world to read.

Two robbers were crucified on the right and left of Jesus. In truth, sinners are all rebels against God, and deserve death. Mark does not provide the names of the criminals. However, tradition names the good thief Dismas, and the taunting thief, Gestas. In Russian art and iconography, the foot piece on the cross of Dismas points up toward heaven, while the foot rest of the reviling thief points downward to hell. Along with Mary and the other women at the foot of the Cross, there may have been mothers, wives, sisters or loved ones of the thieves as well.

Darkness covers the earth. Good Friday represents the darkest day in all of human history, when human beings crucify Jesus, the Son of God, the Savior of the world. When meditating on the suffering of Jesus, also contemplate the anguish of God the Father on this dreadful day. God did not intend death, nor does He take pleasure in in it. *God did not make death, and he does not delight in the death of the living. For he created all things that they might exist . . . God created man for incorruption, and made him in the image of his own eternity, but through the devil's envy death entered the world* (Wisdom 1:13–14; 2:23–24).

Darkness represents evil, judgment, and death itself. *"And on that day,"* says the Lord GOD, *"I will make the sun go down at noon, and darken the earth in broad daylight. I will turn your feasts into mourning, and all your songs into lamentation . . . I will make it like the mourning for an only son, and the end of it like a bitter day"* (Amos 8:9–10). Following the taunts of the chief priests and scribes, and the reviling of bystanders, gloom descends on the land. *The earth quakes before them, the heavens tremble. The sun and moon are darkened, and the stars withdraw their shining* (Joel 2:10).

At the climax of intense agony, Jesus cries out, or does He pray? *And at the ninth hour Jesus cried with a loud voice, "E'lo-i, Elo-i, la'ma sabach-tha'ni" which means, "My God, my God, why have you forsaken me?"* (Mark 15:34). Jesus prays a Davidic psalm for deliverance and victory over evil. At the moment of death, Jesus is too weak to finish the psalm. If a dying person's last words were "Hail Mary," you would know how to finish the prayer. The continuation of Psalm 22 recounts the mockery and suffering of Jesus, and also proclaims the victory over evil that Jesus wins. *For he has not despised or abhorred the affliction of the afflicted; and he has not hidden his face from him, but has heard, when he cried to him . . . All the ends of the earth shall remember and turn to the* LORD; *and all the families of the nations shall worship before him. For dominion belongs to the* LORD, *and he rules over the nations . . . Posterity shall serve him; men shall tell of the* LORD *to the coming generation, and proclaim his deliverance to a people yet unborn, that he has wrought it* (Psalm 22:24, 27–28, 30–31).

And Jesus uttered a loud cry, and breathed his last. And the curtain of the temple was torn in two, from top to bottom (Mark 15:37–38). The death of any human being evokes deep sadness. The death of Jesus Christ, true God and true man, plumbs the depths of sorrow. The realization that human sin caused the death of God's only begotten Son should elicit deep remorse. That Jesus died to redeem humanity inspires profound gratitude. The Jerusalem temple had two thick curtains separating the Holy of Holies from the people. One curtain was decorated with scenes of the universe. The ripping of the temple curtain signals the end of the old covenant. Just as the heavens were torn open at the Baptism of the Lord (Mark 1:10), now the heavens are torn open at Christ's death. Jesus, our High Priest opened the curtain, giving humanity access to God the Father, which was lost in the Garden of Eden, once more (Hebrews 10:19–22).

Questions have been asked throughout Mark's Gospel. *"Who then is this, that even wind and sea obey him?"* (Mark 4:41). Often, the disciples are spiritually blind, unable to see and to recognize who Jesus really is. Now, a non-Jew, who was not a disciple, who may never have seen any of the miracles, but only witnesses this horrible crucifixion, proclaims the truth. *And when the centurion, who stood facing him, saw that he breathed his last, he said, "Truly this man was the Son of God"* (Mark 15:39). The centurion, a Gentile, well accustomed to death, sees Jesus die on the Cross and believes in Him. He proclaims the truth aloud—Jesus is God.

Joseph of Arimathea buries Jesus—Normally, family members of the deceased bury their loved one. Where are the brothers and sisters of the Lord (Mark 6:3)? A well-respected, wealthy Jew, Joseph from the town of Ramathaim-Zophim, twenty miles north of Jerusalem courageously asks for the body of Jesus. Pilate is surprised that Jesus succumbs so quickly. The centurion testifies to Pilate that Jesus is indeed dead. Joseph takes the dead body of Jesus, wraps it in a linen shroud, and buries Jesus in his own tomb. Pilate, the centurion, and Joseph of Arimathea all confirm that Jesus is really dead. He was not in a coma or swooning, as some contemporary writers suggest. Jesus really died for the sins of the world. Normally, bodies of crucified criminals were left on the cross after death, as a further disgrace. Joseph was looking for the kingdom of God. And Joseph provided Our Lord with a reverent burial, fulfilling Isaiah's prophecy: *they made his grave with the wicked and with a rich man in his death* (Isaiah 53:9).

1. Where did Jesus go to pray? Who did He take with Him? Mark 14:32–33

2. How did Jesus face His impending death?

Mark 14:33–35
Hebrews 5:7–9
CCC 1009

3. What did Jesus know?

Mark 14:36
CCC 473

4. What can you learn about prayer?

Mark 1:35
Mark 6:46
Mark 14:38
CCC 2701
CCC 2849

5. What did Jesus ask of the apostles?

Mark 14: 32–34
Mark 14:37–38
CCC 2612

* When do you pray daily? Prayer includes—*adoration, confession, thanksgiving, and intercession*. How do you include each of these in your daily prayer time? Ask the Holy Spirit if you should pray more or in different ways.

6. How did the disciples respond to Jesus request?

Mark 14:37
Mark 14:40
Mark 14:41

7. How do you know that Jesus is in control? Mark 14:41–42

8. Who betrayed Jesus? In what way did he betray Him?

Psalm 41:9
Mark 14:43–45

9. How was Caiaphas' prophecy *(one man should die for the people)* fulfilled?

John 11:49–52
1 Peter 2:24
Romans 5:6–11

* Reflect on the truth that Jesus died for your sins. What can you say to Him?

10. How did the false witnesses distort Jesus' words?

Mark 14:55–58
CCC 585

11. How do you know that this trial is rigged?

Mark 14:55
Deuteronomy 19:15
Mark 14:59

12. What question does Caiaphas ask Jesus? Is the answer true? Mark 14:61–62

13. How does Peter deal with his sin? Mark 14:72

* What practical application of Peter's response can you make in your life?

14. Find some questions from Pontius Pilate in the scriptures?

Mark 15:2
Mark 15:4
Mark 15:14
John 18:35, 37
John 18:38

** How would you defend "objective truth?"

15. Who is culpable in Jesus' death?

Mark 15:3
Mark 15:8–14
CCC 597–598

16. What can you learn about Simon of Cyrene?

Mark 15:21–22
Romans 16:13

17. What was Jesus offered and why?

Proverbs 31:6
Mark 15:23

* What could you offer to Jesus?

18. What can you glean from the Old Testament passages below?

Psalm 22:1–11
Psalm 22:12–21
Psalm 22:22–31
Isaiah 53:1–6
Isaiah 53:7–12

** Find some examples of people mocking Jesus in Mark 15 and today.

19. What is the significance of darkness?

| Isaiah 13:9–11 |
| Amos 8:9 |
| Mark 15:33 |

20. Meditate on the seven last words of Christ. CCC 2605

| Luke 23:34 |
| Luke 23:43 |
| John 19:26–27 |
| John 19:28 |
| Mark 15:34 |
| John 19:30 |
| Luke 23:46 |

* How do you know that Jesus really died? Give evidence.

** Each Friday, commemorating the day Jesus died, Catholics embrace special penitential practices. What do you do to observe each Friday as a day of self-denial and mortification in prayerful remembrance of the Passion of Our Lord?

Monthly Social Activity

This month, your small group will meet for coffee, tea, or a simple breakfast, lunch, or dessert in someone's home. Pray for this social event and for the host or hostess. Try, if at all possible, to attend.

After a short prayer and some time for small talk, write a few sentences about personal prayer and penance. How and when do you pray? What types of penance do you offer to God in atonement to sin?

Examples

◆ *My prayer life is sporadic. Whenever I am in trouble, my favorite prayer is "God, help!"*

◆ *I go to Mass every Sunday and I try to pray the rosary every day on my way to work or with my family*

◆ *I set aside a quiet time every day to pray. On Fridays, I obstain from meat in remembrance of Our Lord's Passion and Death.*

CHAPTER 18

Jesus Lives!
Mark 16:1–20

"Do not be amazed;
you seek Jesus of Nazareth, who was crucified.
He has risen, he is not here;
see the place where they laid him."
Mark 16:6

Jesus' tomb is empty—The most spectacular event in all of human history takes place, and Mark reports it as concisely as he tells of the crucifixion and death of Our Lord. No one could have imagined the Resurrection of Jesus, which radically transforms all of human history. The God, who tore open the heavens at Jesus' Baptism in the Jordan River (Mark 1:10), and tore through the temple curtain at Jesus' death (Mark 15:38), now tears through the final human boundary between death and eternal life. *Do not be amazed; you seek Jesus of Nazareth, who was crucified. He has risen, he is not here; see the place where they laid him* (Mark 16:6). How could anyone *not* be astonished? Resurrection is totally amazing!

The question Jesus voiced on the Cross, *"My God, my God, why have you forsaken me?"* (Mark 15:34) is now clearly and decisively answered. God has not forsaken His only begotten Son. *"Death is swallowed up in victory." "O death, where is your victory? O death, where is your sting?" The sting of death is sin . . . But thanks be to God, who gives us the victory through our Lord Jesus Christ* (1 Corinthians 15:54–57). God did not abandon His Son. Peter explains, *"This Jesus, delivered up according to the definite plan and foreknowledge of God, you crucified and killed by the hands of lawless men. But God raised him up, having loosed the pangs of death, because it was not possible for him to be held by it"* (Acts 2:23–24).

The empty tomb does not prove the Resurrection of Jesus, but it does provide tangible evidence that something extraordinary has happened. Mary Magdalene knew Jesus well and loved Him. She witnessed the crucifixion. She saw Jesus die (Mark 15:40). She saw where they laid Him in the tomb (Mark 15:47). The sabbath ends at sunset on Saturday evening. On Sunday, the first day of the week, Mary Magdalene takes spices to anoint Jesus' dead body. Heedless of the stench of death and decay, she wants to perform one last act of kindness for Jesus.

Three times, Jesus had predicted that He would be killed, *and after three days rise again* (Mark 8:31; 9:31; 10:34). According to the Jewish calendar, Good Friday was the fifteenth day of Nisan, Saturday was a hidden, silent day of sabbath rest, and the third day would be Sunday, the seventeenth day of Nisan. Therefore, on the third day (Mark 16:2), Jesus' promise to rise again comes true. *But for you who fear my name the sun of righteousness shall rise, with healing in its wings* (Malachi 4:2). On Easter Sunday, *when the sun had risen* (Mark 16:2), Jesus conquers death and triumphantly breaks forth from the tomb, bringing hope to all of humanity.

The two women worry about who will roll away the stone from the tomb for them. Did this obstacle not occur to them earlier? Or did love compel them to ignore any barriers to their mission? Despite inherent spiritual blindness, the women "look up and see." *And looking up, they saw that the stone was rolled back; for it was very large. And entering the tomb, they saw a young man sitting on the right side, dressed in a white robe; and they were amazed* (Mark 16:4–5).

All people are God-seekers, hoping and longing to find meaning and purpose in life. *Hear, O LORD, when I cry aloud, be gracious to me and answer me! You have said, "Seek my face." My heart says to you, "Your face, LORD, do I seek." Hide not your face from me* (Psalm 27:7–9). Mary Magdalene had seen the face of the Lord. Meeting Jesus transformed her life. Jesus delivered her from demonic possession and gave her peace and love. Now, she seeks Him once more. *"I will rise now and go about the city, in the streets and in the squares; I will seek him whom my soul loves"* (Song of Solomon 3:2).

Mary Magdalene does not find Jesus. Rather, she finds a young man, recalling the young man who witnessed the betrayal and arrest of Jesus (Mark 14:51). The previous young man had followed Jesus in a linen cloth. When he saw the armed men seize Jesus, he was terrified, and ran away naked, leaving the linen cloth behind. Joseph of Arimathea had wrapped Jesus' dead body in a linen shroud (Mark 15:46), but Jesus left the linen cloth behind, as well (John 20:6–7). Now, if someone were to steal a dead body, would they leave the shroud behind?

And entering the tomb, they saw a young man sitting on the right side, dressed in a white robe; and they were amazed (Mark 16:5). At the close of the Gospel, Mark is describing the clothes of someone at the tomb announcing the triumph of Jesus. At the beginning of the Gospel, Mark described the clothes of the messenger of the Lord, John the Baptist who prepared the way for Jesus. *Now John was clothed with camel's hair, and had a leather belt around his waist* (Mark 1:6).

The women receive a commission—*"Do not be amazed; you seek Jesus of Nazareth, who was crucified. He has risen, he is not here; see the place where they laid him. But go, tell his disciples and Peter that he is going before you to Galilee; there you will see him, as he told you"* (Mark 16:6–7). During Jesus' public ministry, He would heal people and command them to remain silent (Mark 1:44; 5:43). When Peter proclaimed that Jesus is the Christ, he was also charged to tell no one (Mark 8:30). Similarly, after the Transfiguration, Jesus charged Peter, James, and John *to tell no one what they had seen, until the Son of man should have risen from the dead* (Mark 9:9). Jesus has now risen from the dead. The good news can be proclaimed. The women are sent to spread the good news, first to Peter and the apostles. What will they do? Will they hesitate? Will they remain silent? Will they obey? Who will proclaim the good news? Jesus is risen!

After the Last Supper, Jesus had given clear warnings and instructions to the apostles. *"You will all fall away . . . But after I am raised up, I will go before you to Galilee"* (Mark 14:27–28). The apostles now receive a wake-up call. The man at the tomb tells Mary to remind the apostles that they must go to Galilee, where Jesus will meet them. Of course, Jesus had already told this to the Peter and the apostles directly. So the directive from the women would only be a reminder.

Fear impedes action—Even though Jesus repeatedly admonishes people to relinquish fear, people continue to worry. *"Do not fear, only believe"* (Mark 5:36). *"Have no fear"* (Mark 6:50). Rather than obeying the command and reminding the apostles, the women give in to fear. Fear is useless. They need faith. They look up and see something extraordinary that they cannot understand. But they keep their discovery to themselves. *And they went out and fled from the tomb; for trembling and astonishment had come upon them; and they said nothing to any one, for they were afraid* (Mark 16:8).

Many ancient manuscripts end here at Mark 16:8. Perhaps pages of the original manuscript were lost or destroyed. Perhaps Mark was interrupted in his writing. Or perhaps Mark intends the reader to accept the commission of the women. Once a seeker finds Jesus and experiences life-giving faith, will you go and tell others? Or will you keep the good news to yourself out of fear? Will you remain silent, or will you share the good news with someone else?

Jesus appears to Mary Magdalene and the disciples—We are all God-seekers. Sometimes, God in His mercy seeks out even those who are not looking for Him. *I was ready to be found by those who did not seek me . . . before they call I will answer* (Isaiah 65:1, 24). At some point on Easter Sunday, Jesus appears to Mary Magdalene. Ultimately, she obeys and tells the others, "Jesus is alive." But in their grief and mourning, *they would not believe it* (Mark 16:11). Women were not seen as credible witnesses in antiquity, so the response is not too surprising.

However, Jesus also appears to two disciples walking in the country. *And they went back and told the rest, but they did not believe them* (Mark 16:13) either. The crucifixion proves to be a faith-shattering experience. Unbelief prevails. The disciples are simply too shocked to imagine what is unimaginable. Fear, trembling, astonishment and disbelief are probably normal reactions to the most remarkable event in all of human history. Who would have thought that Jesus would conquer sin and death? Who knew that Jesus would appear to the disciples in a glorified, resurrected body, different from anything that anyone had ever seen before?

The disciples fail to show up in Galilee. Have they lost faith? Are they discouraged? Have they forgotten? While they are at table, Jesus appears to the Eleven. Mark does not mention the death of Judas. How does Jesus react to the apostles' disobedience? *He upbraided them for their unbelief and hardness of heart, because they had not believed those who saw him after he had risen* (Mark 16:14b). To upbraid means "to reproach or to correct in a harsh manner." The apostles deserve to be chastised. Any believer deserves correction for abandoning the mission and commission of the Lord. Jesus called the apostles to follow Him, and He never rescinded His call. Jesus needs followers who will remain faithful in the good times, and also in the confusing, difficult, challenging times.

Jesus commissions the apostles—*And he said to them, "Go into all the world and preach the gospel to the whole creation. He who believes and is baptized will be saved; but he who does not believe will be condemned"* (Mark 16:15–16). The stakes are very high. The apostles must preach the Gospel to all of the peoples of the world, Jew and Gentile alike. Faith requires action. Baptism follows the profession of faith. Saint Peter will take Christ's words to heart, and proclaim boldly on Pentecost, *"Repent, and be baptized every one of you in the name of Jesus Christ for the forgiveness of your sins; and you shall receive the gift of the Holy Spirit"* (Acts 2:38). Peter does not always get it right the first time, but he perseveres, and ultimately he accomplishes what God asks of him. He proclaims the great hope that every Christian has in Christ. *Blessed be the God and Father of our Lord Jesus Christ! By his great mercy we have been born anew to a living hope through the resurrection of Jesus Christ from the dead* (1 Peter 1:3).

Jesus explains four signs that will mark the believers, and demonstrate His continuing presence in the Church (Mark 16:17–18). The apostles will witness to all of these, and prove the truth and power of Christianity.

---

1) Demons will be cast out in Jesus' name—*"I charge you in the name of Jesus Christ to come out of her." And it came out that very hour* (Acts 16:18).

2) Believers will speak in new tongues—*And they were all filled with the Holy Spirit and began to speak in other tongues, as the Spirit gave them utterance* (Acts 2:4).

3) Deadly things will not harm them—On the island of Malta, a deadly viper latched onto Paul's hand, but it did not hurt him (Acts 28:3–6).

4) Disciples lay hands on the sick, and they recover—*Peter said, "I have no silver or gold, but I give you what I have; in the name of Jesus Christ of Nazareth, rise and walk"* (Acts 3:6). And the lame man rose up and walked.

Jesus ascends to the right hand of the Father—When Jesus was led before the chief priests, scribes, and elders, He made a startling admission to the high priest, who asked: *"Are you the Christ, the Son of the Blessed?" And Jesus said, "I am; and you will see the Son of man sitting at the right hand of Power, and coming with the clouds of heaven"* (Mark 14:61–62). The statement of Jesus is partially fulfilled here. *So then the Lord Jesus, after he had spoken to them, was taken up into heaven, and sat down at the right hand of God* (Mark 16:19). The apostles know that despite Jesus' return to heaven, He remains also on earth, working signs and wonders through them.

The apostles also proclaim that Jesus Christ will come again in glory to completely fulfill His word to the chief priest. *For the Lord himself will descend from heaven with a cry of command, with the archangel's call, and with the sound of the trumpet of God. And the dead in Christ will rise first, then we who are alive, who are left, shall be caught up together with them in the clouds to meet the Lord in the air; and so we shall always be with the Lord* (1 Thessalonians 4:16–17). When Jesus comes again, will you be ready and eager to meet Him?

What is the Resurrection of Jesus?

If Christ has not been raised, then our preaching is in vain and your faith is in vain. We are even found to be misrepresenting God, because we testified of God that he raised Christ (1 Corinthians 15:14–15). With these words Saint Paul explains quite drastically what faith in the Resurrection of Jesus Christ means for the Christian message over all: it is its very foundation. The Christian faith stands of falls with the truth of the testimony that Christ is risen from the dead . . .

Only if Jesus is risen has anything really new occurred that changes the world and the situation of mankind. Then he becomes the criterion on which we can rely. For then God has truly revealed himself. To this extent, in our quest for the figure of Jesus, the Resurrection is the crucial point. Whether Jesus merely *was* or whether he also *is*—this depends on the Resurrection . . .

What actually happened? Clearly, for the witnesses who encountered the risen Lord, it was not easy to say. They were confronted with what for them was an entirely new reality, far beyond the limits of their experience. Much as the reality of the event overwhelmed them and impelled them to bear witness, it was still utterly unlike anything they had previously known. Saint Mark tells us that the disciples on their way down from the mountain of the Transfiguration were puzzled by the saying of Jesus that the Son of man would "rise from the dead." And they asked one another what "rising from the dead" could mean (Mark 9:9–10) . . .

Jesus' Resurrection was about breaking out into an entirely new form of life, into a life that is no longer subject to the law of dying and becoming, but lies beyond it—a life that opens up a new dimension of human existence . . . In Jesus' Resurrection a new possibility of human existence is attained that affects everyone and that opens up a future, a new kind of future for mankind . . .

Jesus has not returned to a normal human life in this world like Lazarus and the others whom Jesus raised from the dead. He has entered upon a different life, a new life—he has entered the vast breadth of God himself, and it is from there that he reveals himself to his followers . . . New life was linked to the inbreaking of a new world and thus made complete sense. If there is a new world, then there is also a new mode of life there . . .

For the disciples the Resurrection was just as real as the Cross. It presupposes that they were simply overwhelmed by the reality, that, after their initial hesitation and astonishment, they could no longer ignore that reality. It is truly he. He is alive; he has spoken to us; he has allowed us to touch him, even if he no longer belongs to the realm of the tangible in the normal way . . .

Jesus did not simply return to normal biological life as one who, by the laws of biology, would eventually have to die again . . . It is a historical event that nevertheless bursts open the dimensions of history and transcends it . . . It is part of the mystery of God that he acts so gently, that he only gradually builds up *his* history within the great history of mankind . . . that he suffers and dies and that, having risen again, he chooses to come to mankind only through the faith of the disciples to whom he reveals himself; that he continues to knock gently at the doors of our hearts and slowly opens our eyes if we open our doors to him . . .

He comes to us, in order to raise us up above ourselves and to open up the world to God . . . In faith we know that Jesus holds his hands stretched out in blessing over us. That is the lasting motive of Christian joy.

Pope Benedict XVI, *Jesus of Nazareth, Part Two*, 241–293.

* * * * *

1. Who were the first people to encounter the Risen Christ?

Mark 16:1–6
CCC 641

* Who were the first in your family to come to vibrant faith in Jesus?

2. What can you learn about Mary Magdalene?

Luke 8:2
Mark 15:40
Mark 15:47
John 20:1–18

3. What did the young man say to Mary? Mark 16:6–7

4. Where should the apostles have been?

Mark 14:28
Mark 16:7

5. How did the two women respond to the young man's direction? Mark 16:8

* How would you respond to a miraculous story about Jesus today?

6. Explain as much as you can about the Resurrection.

Mark 16:6
CCC 434
CCC 642–643
CCC 646–647
CCC 648–649
CCC 653–655

* What does the Resurrection of Jesus mean for you? CCC 655

7. Who and what secured the tomb of Jesus? Matthew 27:62–66

8. What tangible evidence for the Resurrection can you cite?

Luke 24:1–3
John 20:6–7

9. What else did the chief priests do? Matthew 28:11–15

10. How did the apostles respond to Mary Magdalene's news? Mark 16:9–11

11. How did the apostles respond to the two disciples' report? Mark 16:12–13

* Explain different types of response to the Resurrection today.

12. Explain the importance of the Resurrection to believers.

Acts 2:22–24	
1 Peter 1:3	
1 Corinthians 15:3–8	
1 Corinthians 15:17	

13. What did Jesus do when the disciples failed to appear in Galilee? Mark 16:14

14. Why did Jesus chastise the apostles? Mark 16:14

* Have you ever been corrected, as an adult, for a good reason? Did it help?

15. What did Jesus commission the apostles to do? Mark 16:15

** Share with your group a three-minute testimony of how God saved you.

*** Do have zeal for evangelization? Share some ways to share the good news.

16. What must one do to be saved?

Mark 16:16
Acts 2:38
CCC 977

17. What are four signs of Christ's presence in believers? Mark 16:17–18

18. Find some examples of Christ's power in the early Church.

Acts 2:4
Acts 3:6–7
Acts 16:18
Acts 28:3–6

19. What happened after Jesus commissioned the disciples?

Mark 16:19
CCC 659

20. What happened after the Ascension? Mark 16:20

Write some key points in your three-minute testimony here.

Brainstorm ways to share the good news with unbelievers and the un-churched.

List three people to pray for and invite to church or the next Bible Study.

Catholic Bible Study

About our Authors

Bishop Jan Liesen, SSD—studied Sacred Scripture at the Pontifical Biblical Institute in Rome (The Biblicum), where he wrote his dissertation on the book of Sirach. He is a distinguished member of the Papal Theological Commission and the Bishop of Breda in the Netherlands. Bishop Liesen is the primary author of *Wisdom*, and *The Gospel of Mark*.

Father Joseph Ponessa, SSD—studied under Cardinal Albert Vanhoye, SJ at the The Biblicum, earning a doctorate in Sacred Scripture. He pastors parishes in eastern Montana and is the primary author of *The Gospel of John, Genesis, Moses and the Torah, Acts and Letters, David and the Psalms, Prophets and Apostles, Return from Exile,* and *The Rise and Fall of Ancient Israel*.

Monsignor Charles Kosanke, STD—studied Sacred Scripture at the Pontifical Gregorian University in Rome. He taught Scripture at Sacred Heart Major Seminary in Detroit and was the rector of Saints Cyril and Methodius Seminary in Orchard Lake, Michigan. Monsignor Kosanke is the primary author of *Isaiah*.

Father Ponessa, Bishop Liesen, Monsignor Kosanke

Monsignor Jan Majernik, STD—a native of Slovakia, earned a doctorate in Sacred Scripture from the Franciscan School of Biblical Studies in Jerusalem. He studied biblical archeology and biblical languages at the Hebrew University in Israel and at the Biblicum in Rome. He is the primary author of *The Synoptics*.

Father Andreas Hoeck, SSD—born in Cologne, Germany, earned his doctorate at the Pontifical Biblical Institute in Rome, where he wrote his dissertation on the book of Revelation. He is the academic dean at Saint John Vianney Seminary in Denver and author of *Ezekiel, Hebrews, Revelation*.

Laurie Watson Manhardt, PhD—earned a doctorate in education from the University of Michigan. She writes all of the home study questions, and the children's books. Laurie wrote the commentaries on *Leviticus, Numbers, Psalms, Proverbs, Ecclesiastes, Wisdom, Judith, Esther, Romans, Philippians, Galatians, 1 and 2 Timothy, Titus,* and *1 and 2 Peter*.

Basic, Foundational Books

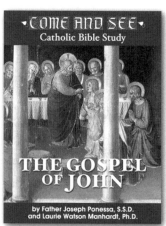

The Gospel of John
This excellent natural starting place for Bible Study covers the life of Jesus and the institution of the sacraments of Baptism, Reconciliation, Eucharist, Holy Orders, and Matrimony in 21 lessons.

202 pages, paperback,
Item #926...$19.95
DVD, Item #954...$49.95

Genesis
The first book of the Bible covers the lives of Adam and Eve, Noah, Abraham, Isaac, Jacob, Esau, Joseph and his brothers. Father Ponessa looks at creation through the lens of science in this 22 chapter study.

216 pages, paperback,
Item #819...$19.95
DVD, Item #994...$49.95

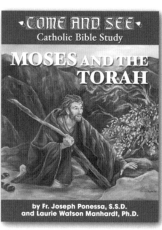

Moses and the Torah
Complete your study of the Pentateuch with the books of *Exodus, Leviticus, Numbers,* and *Deuteronomy* in this 22 week study. See the chosen people receive the law from God through Moses.

220 pages, paperback,
Item #807...$19.95
DVD, Item #808...$69.95

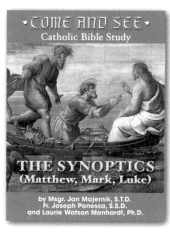

The Synoptics
Compare *Matthew, Mark,* and *Luke's* accounts of the life of Jesus as you journey through the Holy Land in this 22 week study of the Gospels.

204 pages, paperback,
Item #945...$19.95
DVD, Item #947...$69.95

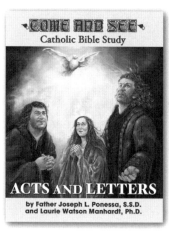

Acts and Letters
Explore the early Church through the *Acts of the Apostles* and the letters of Saint Paul in this 22 week New Testament study.

220 pages, paperback,
Item #814...$19.95
DVD, Item #815...$69.95

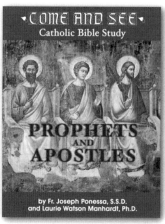

Prophets and Apostles
Discover how the prophets looked forward to God's promised Messiah while the apostles see the fulfillment of those prophecies in the life of Jesus.

206 pages. paperback,
Item #928...$19.95
DVD, Item #998...$49.95

Advanced, Challenging Books

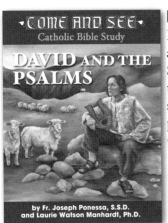

David and the Psalms

In this 22 week study, examine the lives of Ruth, Samuel, and David, and the psalms and canticles associated with them. These prayers emerge in the life of Christ and His Church.

208 pages, paperback,
Item #983...$19.95
DVD, Item #996...$69.95

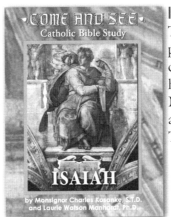

Isaiah

This major Old Testament prophet's writings have been called the fifth Gospel because his prophecies point to Jesus of Nazareth, the Suffering Servant and Redeemer of the world. This is a 22 chapter study.

214 pages, paperback,
Item #855...$19.54
DVD, Item #856...$69.95

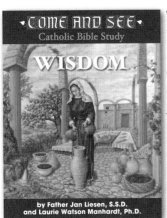

Wisdom

In this 22 chapter study, Bishop Liesen provides commentary on the Wisdom literature of the Bible: *Job, Proverbs, Ecclesiastes, Song of Solomon, Wisdom,* and *Sirach.*

220 pages, Softcover Book,
Item #820...$19.95
DVD, Item #821...$69.95

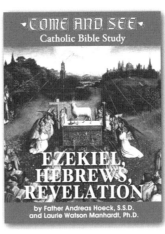

Ezekiel, Hebrews, Revelation

The prophet Ezekiel has some visions similar to those encountered by Saint John on the Island of Patmos and revealed in the *Book of Revelation. The Letter to the Hebrews* reveals Jesus the High Priest in this 22 lesson study.

220 pages, paperback,
Item #834...$19.95
DVD, Item #835...$69.95

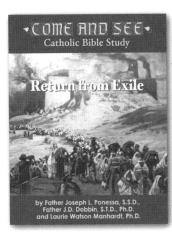

Return from Exile

In this 22 week study, *Tobit, Judith, Esther, Ezra, Nehemiah,* and *1 and 2 Maccabees* tell us about the ways in which God worked in the lives of the Jewish people as they returned from their exile in Babylon.

220 pages, paperback, $19.95
DVD

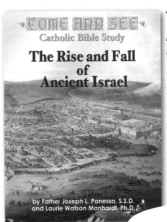

The Rise and Fall of Ancient Israel

Complete the "Come and See ~ Catholic Bible Study" series, covering all 73 books of the Catholic canon, with this study of *Joshua, Judges, 1 and 2 Kings, 1 and 2 Chronicles, Amos, Hosea,* and *Jeremiah.*

220 pages, paperback, $19.95
DVD

Come and See KIDS Books

Come and See KIDS *is a Bible Study series written for pre-school to early elementary school age children. These companion books to the adult series could also be used alone. Each book contains the following features:*

- Bible memory verses and a Bible story
- Coloring pages illustrating the Bible story
- Craft activities for the child to make with a little bit of help
- Traditional Catholic prayers

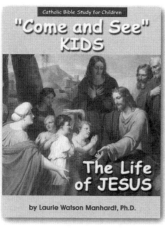

The Life of Jesus
can accompany *The Gospel of John* or *The Synoptics,* and teaches about the life of Jesus with stories, memory verses, prayers, coloring pages and crafts. 23 lessons cover the Annunciation to the Resurrection.

128 perforated pages, Item #941...$9.95

In the Beginning
goes with *Genesis* and teaches children about God's creation and the first book of the Bible. 23 lessons include stories, prayers, coloring pages and crafts, from creation through the story of Joseph and his brothers in Egypt.

112 perforated pages, Item #812...$9.95

Friends of God can accompany any adult book. The 22 lessons cover heroes of the Bible from Moses to Saint Paul. Some children and young people from the Bible are also included: Samuel, David, Daniel, Mary the Mother of God, and the little boy who shared his lunch with Jesus.

128 perforated pages, Item #801...$9.95

Come and See ~ Catholic Bible Study
www.CatholicBibleStudy.net
(772) 321-4034

Emmaus Road Publishing
827 North Fourth Street
Steubenville, OH 43952

www.EmmausRoad.org   (800) 398–5470   (740) 283-2880